LIFE WITH LUKE

AND OTHER EXCITING RACING ADVENTURES

Jimmy Sills
(AKA LUKE WARMWATER)
WITH DAVE ARGABRIGHT
FOREWORD BY JEFF GORDON

LIFE WITH LUKE

By Jimmy Sills
with Dave Argabright

© 2019 American Scene Press

ISBN 13: 978-0-9899426-6-9

Published by:
American Scene Press, LLC
P.O. Box 34
Noblesville, IN 46061
(317) 598-1263
www.daveargabright.com

Proudly written, produced and printed in the USA

No part of this book may be used or reproduced in any manner whatsoever without prior written permission from the copyright holder, except in the case of brief quotations in reviews.

Acknowledgements

Racing friends are the best. As this project got underway a number of our longtime friends and associates stepped forward to help make this book possible.

Jeff Gordon took time from his busy broadcast schedule to contribute our Foreword, which rekindled good memories all around. Jeff and Jimmy's friendship dates back many years, and their mutual affection and respect quickly became obvious. Jeff's associate Jon Edwards was also helpful in the process.

Kevin Eckert provided statistical information from his historical database that greatly helped with tracks and dates. Richie Murray of USAC also provided helpful detailed information on Jimmy's USAC Silver Crown career. Gary Gerould and Bobby Gerould also helped track down some data related to the CalExpo State Fairgrounds.

Photographers John Mahoney and Bill Taylor went the extra mile to provide a number of images that helped illustrate Jimmy's career and exploits. All other photos are from the Sills collection and credit is given when possible.

During the creative process a number of people offered ideas, insight, guidance, and just plain encouragement. Joyce Standridge; Bones Bourcier; Doug Auld of *SprintCar & Midget Magazine*; Bobby Gerould; and Cary Stratton and Lew Boyd of Coastal 181; to all of you, please know that your ongoing help is always appreciated.

Background information and research data was gained from several publications, including *National Speed Sport News*; *SprintCar & Midget Magazine*; *OPEN WHEEL Magazine;* and the *National Sprint Car Annual*.

Several books were also a great resource, including *Dirt Road to a Silver Crown*, published by Witness Productions and authored by Bob Gates, Pat Sullivan, Ed Watson, and John Mahoney; *All-Star Circuit of Champions* by Bill Holder; and *Knoxville Nationals* by Eric Arnold and Bob Wilson. The annual *USAC Media Guide*, expertly written and produced through the years by Dick Jordan, was also helpful.

Promotional help is greatly appreciated from Doug Auld of *SprintCar & Midget Magazine* as well as Mike Kerchner and crew at *Speed Sport Magazine*.

Most of all, thanks to the many readers who continue to support our book projects. Your interest—and intentional support—is what makes racing books like this possible.

Contents

Acknowledgements - 3
Foreword by Jeff Gordon - 7
Introduction by Dave Argabright - 11

1. The racing thing. *Bad.* 17
2. Touched by tragedy 22
3. Life-changing move 29
4. Tuition money 37
5. Hitting the road. 45
6. The Midwest 57
7. On our own 66
8. Birth of the Outlaws 73
9. First RV 80
10. Hurt, win, fired 91
11. Sam and Fred 103
12. Chasing the Outlaws 115
13. Traveling with Lenard 122
14. My friend is hurting. 135
15. Luke Warmwater 144
16. A slice of Americana 154
17. Stanton and me 163
18. A second title 174
19. Title number three. 183
20. Ziggy 197
21. Mayhem. No, really. 203
22. A new direction 214
23. The Professor 223
24. The ride of a lifetime 229
25. Students 239
26. An amazing new world. 247
27. Tormenting Trostle 259
28. The Preacher 264
29. Down Under, again 270
30. The greatest thing 281
31. Reflections 288

Index - 297
Ordering info - 311

Foreword

It's easy to remember those early times, and the memories still generate a lot of excitement. I was a young kid then, sitting in the stands with my family at places like West Capital Raceway or Baylands Raceway Park in California. Sprint cars were the featured attraction, and that was good because I was a huge sprint car fan. As I watched them race there was always the same thought running through my mind.

Man, I hope I get a chance to do that someday.

One of the guys I watched was Jimmy Sills. Jimmy was really fast in a race car, and he won a lot of races—especially at Baylands. He was a friend of my step-father, John Bickford, and after the races we would stop by Jimmy's pit and visit.

Jimmy was the type of guy any young person would admire, and want to emulate. He was a winner, and the way he carried himself…he was confident, he was good with people, and he always had a smile. On the track he was on the gas, and he always ran up front.

When I reached my teen years, I got the chance to make my dreams come true. When I was 13 years old I had a chance to get into a sprint car for the first time. Sprint cars are badass race cars, and in 1985 the idea of a 13-year-old kid in a sprint car was pretty radical. My family was confident that I was ready, but it wasn't that simple. There wasn't a precedent for someone my age to race a sprint car. After some discussions, the promoter at Hanford Speedway in California finally agreed to let me take some hot laps. I was not allowed to race; I was only permitted to participate in a hot lap session with the other cars.

Not everybody was on board with this idea. There were definitely guys who were not supportive of me being in a sprint car. They were uncomfortable with someone that young driving such a badass race car. And I understand, believe me. Today, I might think the idea was crazy, too.

But here is what made it work: Many of the established racers that day were supportive. And one of those guys, I distinctly remember, was Jimmy Sills. In fact, I remember telling him of my idea of getting into a sprint car. Jimmy was very supportive, and thought it was cool. He encouraged me and told me it would all work out just fine.

Hearing that from someone like Jimmy was huge. I can't fully explain how much it means for a young guy to get words of support from someone he admires. It's impossible to measure.

I vividly remember that day at Hanford. I felt so much pressure; it's hard to put into words. This was my opportunity to show that I had the ability to drive a sprint car, and if I screwed it up I was in trouble. I wouldn't get another chance. I wanted to make good lap times but most of all I didn't want to do anything stupid.

We got up to speed pretty quick—sprint cars don't take long to get going—and everything felt all right. I didn't know this at the time, but Jimmy was following me, watching me, getting a feel for things. Was this kid ready to drive a sprint car? We're finding out, right now.

I felt good in the car, but I was obviously very inexperienced. On an open track I was fine, but when I came up on a slower car I balked a little bit. I hadn't developed the instincts you need to deal with traffic. When I let up, Jimmy raced right past me.

The next time around I saw a big crash. It was Jimmy! Something had apparently broken on his car and he crashed pretty hard. Everything was happening fast, and I had to take evasive action to miss him. Here was my opportunity flashing by, right before my eyes, and I was going to run over Jimmy Sills! I could envision my sprint car career being over before it had even started.

But I missed him okay, and everything worked out. He wasn't hurt, and we convinced the right people that I had the ability to drive a sprint car. My family moved to Indiana to allow me to pursue my career, and everything played out just like Jimmy had assured me: things will work out just fine.

A couple of years after that Hanford hot lap session I had an opportunity to spend some time racing in Australia. What a trip for a 15-year-old kid! This was, I think, the first time I was truly allowed to hang out with the grownups. Jimmy was one of the other drivers with us, and I can honestly say that Jimmy taught me how to be a real race driver on that trip.

It was definitely a bonding experience. We spent some time racing around Perth, on the western coast of Australia. The cool thing about racing in Australia is that you have a lot of downtime to hang out with people. We raced a lot, but there was still plenty of idle time.

It was a great chance to develop bonds and friendships. I immediately gravitated toward Jimmy, partly because I knew him. But mostly I wanted to hang around with him because he's such a cool guy. He wasn't flamboyant, he was just…*Jimmy*. I admired that then, and I still do today. Jimmy was very comfortable with being himself. People wanted to be around him.

The Australians are known for their hospitality, and there were a couple of good parties in Perth. One in particular was set in someone's back yard, and I remember the experience well. I definitely needed some adult supervision on that trip. However, it was hard to have adult supervision from a guy—Jimmy—who was having just as much fun as I was! If you know Jimmy you'll probably smile at that statement, because this is a guy who really knows how to have fun.

We became good friends on that trip. The things that made such an impression on me then, I still think of those things when I see Jimmy today. He's such a fun-loving guy, and he always has a smile on his face. This is a man who enjoys life!

So I've told you about Jimmy Sills the person, but I want to make sure and talk about Jimmy Sills the racer. Because they are two different people, trust me! Jimmy is one of those rare easy-going people who can somehow flip a switch to become an intense competitor. Jimmy might laugh and smile, but when he puts on a helmet and fires up the race car, he instantly becomes this fierce competitor. He's your friend but in the race car he wants to beat you as badly as anybody possibly could.

I remember one race in particular in 1991, at Eldora Speedway at the 4-Crown Nationals. I was driving Rollie Helmling's midget, and Jimmy was in Gary Zarounian's car. We had a great race, battling for every inch. I passed him in the late going and went on to win, and Jimmy finished second. That was my last USAC victory, and it's all the more memorable because I raced Jimmy for the win.

Jimmy is a racer's racer, because he could run good in anything. He was a smart race car driver, one of those guys who didn't make many mistakes. I think that's why he did so well in USAC Silver Crown cars. Those cars, you have to be smart and patient and let the track and the car come to you.

You have this big, giant fuel cell in the back and it's a long race. Jimmy was always thinking and that's why he was so successful.

There were so many great moments through the years. In 1990 I finished third to Jimmy at the USAC Silver Crown race at Sacramento. There's a picture of Jimmy standing atop the podium with this dazzling girl, and I'm staring up at them with this "look." Kind of like a star-struck kid. Well, Jimmy, if you think I'm looking up at you…no way. I'm quite certain I was looking at that fantastic girl! In fact, I was jealous of Jimmy at that moment, because I wanted to be standing where he was!

In 2015 my driving career was winding down and that season was all about reconnecting with people. People I drove for, people I raced against, people I looked up to. One of the highlight moments of the year came in July, when we invited several of the guys I raced with in earlier years to be our guest at the Brickyard 400. Those years in the Midwest were a crucial period in my life, and Indianapolis was a great location to bring everybody back together.

These were people I consider heroes. When I started racing I looked up to all of them, and their support was huge. Jack Hewitt, Kenny Jacobs, Steve Kinser, a bunch of guys joined me that day. It was really cool. I was surprised that so many people accepted the invitation and showed up. I definitely appreciated the opportunity to say thank you and let those guys know how much they mean to me.

Jimmy Sills was right there among the group, as it should be. In Jimmy's case, he was especially helpful in my earliest years. What I'm most grateful for is that, all these years later, Jimmy is still my good friend.

I am so excited that Jimmy decided to write a book! When he asked if I'd write the foreword, I was truly honored. Plus, I can't wait to read the book. He's had a great career, a great life, and it's only fitting that he shares all his stories with us.

Jimmy Sills is a real American racer. He is funny, competitive, outgoing, and above all, very interesting. This is his story. I'm sure you'll enjoy it.

***Jeff* Gordon**
Charlotte, North Carolina
March, 2019

Introduction

From the beginning, there was an element that made Hall of Fame racer Jimmy Sills different from all the rest: *humor*.

Throughout his long and successful racing career, nobody had more fun than Sills. Somehow, amid the force and fury of modern motorsports, Jimmy had the gift of being able to see the humor amid the insanity, and that included making fun of himself.

But don't be confused: Sills was intensely serious when the visor was down. When a race was on the line he was focused and determined and intense. Sills won races and championships at the top levels of the sport, and only a skilled, tough racer could accomplish that.

That's why talking about the humor of Jimmy Sills is rather tricky. He was not a "class clown" type of guy who was merely silly. Instead, he had a unique ability to observe the racing life that swirled around him, and a knack for relating the crazy, unlikely, and ironic things he experienced.

He logged a million miles as he chased his destiny, and around every corner it seemed that a good story awaited.

Deep inside Jimmy Sills is a happy, carefree young boy. He wakes up smiling and doesn't mope too long if he skins his knee. Moving quickly to the next adventure, the boy will laugh that evening as he points to the scrape, relating the funny circumstances of his spill.

The years came and went, but the spirit of the young boy remains within Sills.

Certainly, he had his dark moments; you'll find those moments in these pages. But the positive spirit of Sills was indomitable, and he always found a way to (eventually) smile through the disappointment.

That's what has defined Jimmy, and made him a beloved member of the racing community. He was a ray of sunshine on a sometimes stormy scene, and his humor and spirit steadily lifted those around him.

If you're strolling through the pit area at a race track, you might look up and see that familiar shock of curly hair. You make eye contact, and you both smile. You're glad to see Jimmy Sills, because you know it's going to be a humorous, enjoyable encounter. You're going to discuss some topic—past or present—and Sills will give you a take on the issue that is going to inspire a lighthearted laughter.

Sills took his work—driving a race car—very seriously. At the same time, he didn't take himself seriously at all. Maybe that's why he was admired by nearly everyone in the racing community; he never lost sight of his humble roots, and his ego remained in check.

To this day, that's one of the things the world loved about Sills.

Respect. It's easy to use that word when discussing Sills, because he inspired plenty of it.

He was a winner from the beginning, tasting victory within weeks of his first outing as a racer. His ability was obvious, and it wasn't long before car owners began to seek him out. In due course Sills ascended to national prominence and his name was inevitably mentioned when the top drivers of the day were discussed.

But it wasn't an easy ride.

Jimmy's story includes lots of struggles and setbacks. Lots of endless miles on the highway as he chased his dream. Moments of personal disappointment and disillusionment. Painful and lingering injuries. Episodes of tragedy and heartbreak.

But Sills stuck with it, and when he was finished he had plenty to be proud of: National Sprint Car Hall of Fame, first three-time USAC Silver Crown champion, USAC Hall of Fame. Ohio Sprint Speedweek champion, five-time Dirt Cup winner, twice winner of the Hoosier Hundred, and the first American winner of the Grand Annual Classic in Australia.

Here's an added caveat that truly puts a unique light on things: Sills is one of the most successful teachers of open wheel racing in history. His Jimmy Sills School of Open Wheel Racing instilled and improved the skills of hundreds of young racers from 2000 to 2015.

His brief moment of doubt—when he "retired" for a few weeks in late 1989—remains one of the most enduring and humorous episodes in sprint car history. That wonderful, wacky, absolutely *perfect* racing alias—"Luke Warmwater from Hot Springs, Arkansas"—used in his return to competition remains indelible in our collective memory.

When he looks back at his career, Sills smiles at the good memories and gently shrugs away the heartache. He is gracious and truly grateful that his dream came true: he successfully made his living as a professional racing driver.

Many times along the way, after a night of a beer or three and a steady flow of great racing stories—he was told, "Hey Jimmy…you should write a book!"

Well, here it is. The Jimmy Sills story as only Jimmy Sills could tell it: Funny and poignant and honest and tragic. He is careful not to boast—although he earned that right—while poking fun at the crazy characters that surrounded him. Of course, that cast of crazy characters included Sills himself.

Sills, we can honestly say: you are one of a kind. For that—and for your friendship, of course—we are truly grateful.

Dave Argabright
Noblesville, Indiana
March, 2019

To all the ladies—including my mom and Cheryl—who brought me joy, love, and life's lessons;

To all the car owners who trusted me with their equipment and then treated me like family, no matter what;

And to the fans who spent their hard-earned money to watch me do what I loved;

This book is for you.

1

The racing thing. *Bad.*

The countryside is beautiful up around Elverta, California, a rural area north of Sacramento. That's where I grew up, the third arrival in my family behind my older sisters Valerie and Carleen. My parents—Marilyn and Jimmy Sills Sr.—were trying for a boy when I came along in 1953. They tried their luck again and my sister Peggy arrived a little over two years later.

There weren't many neighbors around, so I spent a lot of time playing on my own and I also hung out a lot with my grandpa, Raleigh Sills. As far back as I can remember the subject at hand was racing. Even our house layout was in the shape of the Indianapolis Motor Speedway. If you came in the front door, that was the exit of turn four. A right turn through the living and dining room brought you to the front straightaway. As you entered the kitchen area that was turn one, and you progressed through the kitchen (short chute). Turn two led you into the den and progressed down the hall to where my bedroom was located (back straightaway). Turn three passed by the main bathroom and my sister's room, and one more short chute brought you past the master bedroom. The front door finished up at turn four.

It was impossible for me to walk around the house without thinking about the Speedway. I was sideways through the corners, as all race cars should be. I don't know if Dad planned it this way, but you couldn't grow up with a more exciting house layout. I have yet to see a layout that was better.

I was a kid in constant motion and at the center of constant noise. I made racing noises when I ran, and always rode my bicycle at top speed with engine noises provided by rubbing playing cards against the spokes, attached via clothes pins.

At an early age I had the racing thing. *Bad.*

My dad's life still holds a lot of mystery, because he passed away when I was three years old. I've always felt like I knew very little about my dad, and that sparked a lifelong curiosity. Luckily several of his friends have provided me with details of his life, and Jimmy Montgomery—a historian with BCRA—helped me learn a lot about Jimmy Sills, Sr. My friends Larry "Captain" Burton and Wally "Crazy Wheels" Baker have also shared lots of insight into my dad's life. Wally and Dad were good friends and they spent a lot of time together.

Dad was really into racing, and that's where I got the original infection. He raced on Friday nights in Auburn, a little foothill town where my sister Peggy lives today. According to Wally, Dad had 'em pretty well covered there on Friday nights.

Each Saturday morning Dad and Wally would head for Pacheco Speedway. That was a long haul, with most race cars being "flat towed." This involved a tow bar attached to the front nerf bar of the race car. However, Dad owned a trailer and a fast pickup, so even if he didn't win the Saturday night feature he definitely won the race home.

Dad may have had an impatient side, and Mom recalls the time when a car in front of him didn't see a green light at an intersection. Dad waited about a quarter of a second before he gassed it up and shoved the guy through the intersection. I absolutely inherited the impatient trait. No doubt about it.

Cal Stock was the main stock car organization in our region, and Dad raced with them on occasion. Jack McCoy and Ray Elder were prominent racers with the organization, and a few years ago I had the honor of meeting both gentlemen at a Motor Sports Press Assn. banquet. Jack wrote a beautiful book about his career, and in the book he mentioned Dad running in the Mexican road race back in the day. I have seen old home movies of this race but I've never been able to locate many details.

In 1955 Dad ran a NASCAR Grand National race at Willow Springs, a road course near Rosamond, California. He finished 11th against drivers such as Chuck Stevenson, Marvin Panch, Johnny Mantz, Scotty Cain, and northern California driver Sherman Clark.

Dad would race almost anything with wheels, and not long after I was born he began to run a lot of midget races, particularly the winter indoor season at Oakland.

Dad was quite the adventurer, and I inherited that gene as well. When he was younger one of his favorite swimming holes was down by Rio Linda, but the place was hard to get to. Rather than making the long walk, Dad would let the air out of his tires just enough that his wheels would straddle the rails along a train line that went near the pond. He'd just wheel up on the tracks, and away he'd go. However, the rail line was still active, leading to some exciting encounters where Dad had to take evasive action.

Childbirth seemed to bring good luck to my dad's racing endeavors. On May 26, 1953, Jimmy Sills Sr. was off racing his hardtop at Pacheco Speedway, winning the race on the day when Jimmy Sills Jr. made his debut back in Sacramento. I am very much okay with those circumstances, especially since he won.

In February 1956, on a cold winter's night, he was battling the effects of cancer but still had enough strength to win his final midget race at the Oakland Exposition Building. Later that same night my sister Peggy was born.

I've heard the story of my dad coming to watch a race at Pacheco a couple of weeks before he died. He was very weak from the treatments—and the disease itself—but another driver saw him in the pit area and offered his car for my dad to take some hot laps during intermission.

According to Larry Burton, dad took about 10 laps, laying down a time as fast as any laps ran that night. Everyone in the place knew it was probably the last time they would see Jimmy Sills where he loved to be, behind the wheel of a race car and blasting around the track. Larry recalled that when Dad finished his hot lap session there wasn't a dry eye in the house, including his own.

My father only raced for six years, but he made a lasting impression. In 1999 he was inducted into the Bay Cities Racing Assn. (BCRA) Hall of Fame in the hardtop division, and he was later inducted into the West Capital Raceway Hall of Fame as well.

The West Capital induction was especially cool, because dad actually helped build the track. He was a farmer, and brought his bulldozer over to move the dirt that would eventually host the track and the grandstands.

Each year I enjoy attending the Calistoga Classic, and a couple of years ago I had the honor of sitting next to Johnny Franklin. Johnny is in his 90s but he is as sharp as a whip. (His real name is Bob Johnson but he changed his name for some legal reasons, and the name Johnny Franklin sounds racier.) Johnny owned several muffler shops around Santa Rosa and he was one of the top racers of his day, particularly in the hardtops. It was great listening as Johnny told me stories about my dad. He explained that my parents would spend the weekend with Johnny and his wife. That was cool, and it made me think that maybe the racing family used to hang out together a little more in a previous generation.

In spite of what you might imagine, I was not always the easiest kid for a mom to take care of. I needed the flyswatter across my ass on many occasions, and Mom provided assistance in that area.

We had a '46 Mercury parked in the driveway, minus engine and transmission. The steering was unhooked, so the wheel turned free. It was a great place for a young boy to pretend to be a racing driver. One day when I was supposed to be doing chores I was behind the wheel, having myself a terrific race. Suddenly the door jerked open and the thrash was on. Mom was yelling about me playing around while I was supposed to be doing chores, and she was definitely not happy.

She was hitting me while giving me the lecture and I felt like it was time for her to stop hitting me so I pushed her away. I immediately discovered that it was *not* time for the hitting to stop and in fact it was growing more intense. That was by far the maddest she ever got at me.

If you walk through the pit area at any race track in America, you'll find a pattern: Most racers grew up with another racer as a role model. A father, an uncle, maybe even a neighbor. But most of the time there was somebody who influenced that person at a young age and steered them toward racing.

I had a double-dose, you might say. I was young when my dad died, but even as a small child I had racing on my brain. For as long as I can remember everything around me was *racing*.

When I was six years old my mom remarried, and Dick Johnson came into my life. Dick raced supermodifieds at Roseville and Capital speedways in Northern California, and he signed on for a big job when he married my mother. Mom had tried hard to raise her kids properly but the truth is, my sisters and I were rough around the edges. When Dick joined our family we got a much-needed dose of discipline that would follow us through the rest of our life. Dick and Mom also had a child together, my sister Marcy.

Dick was capable of winning every week at Roseville and Capital. I also remember him winning a big race on the dirt at Champion Speedway, a half-mile track near San Francisco. He beat some major racers that day, including Bill Vukovich Jr., George Snider, Al Pombo, and Marshall Sargent.

In 1963 Dick and Ed Watson built a lightweight race car in our shop. Most of the hardtops (the forerunners to supermodifieds) of the day were very heavy; that was important because this was full-contact auto racing. A lightweight car could have a huge advantage at that time but you'd have to avoid a lot of contact.

Capital Speedway hosted the Gold Cup Race of Champions as their season finale. This race is still the biggest race in Northern California, and it takes place at Silver Dollar Speedway in Chico. Back then it was a 200-lap race held in the daytime. The track announcer at Capital, Jim Hadlock, used to call it "A grueling test of man and machine!" I think Jim was right.

Unfortunately, the 1963 race came right in the middle of harvest season. Dick made his living farming—he learned how to farm rice and was good at it—and the only steering wheel he would be holding that day was our John Deere harvester. So Dick called upon LeRoy Giving to drive their car at the Gold Cup (LeRoy's granddaughter Alissa Giving is a fine sprint car driver these days).

Well, that wasn't a good day in 1963 for LeRoy or Dick. The car was destroyed in a huge flip into the second turn fence. This car ended up sitting on a trailer in front of our house for months before Dick finally cut the car up for scrap.

Harvest season was very busy for us. When I was a little bigger I drove a bank-out kart, a huge four-wheel-drive vehicle which hauled the rice from the harvester to the grain transports. The Bank Out Kart had six-foot tires and four-wheel steering.

If the fields were especially muddy we used karts that had tracks instead of tires. These were very uncomfortable to operate because you sat on the same side as the engine exhaust, and you were blasted with heat.

Rice dust is a lot like fiberglass dust; it itches like hell. I always wore a hoodie with a handkerchief tied across my face and goggles to protect my eyes. The typical work day was between 12 to 15 hours. Today the karts have cabs which make for much better working conditions.

2

Touched by tragedy

Although I've traveled a million miles, life began not far from where I am today. From my current home I can look out and see the house where I lived until I was 15. Here I am, all these years later. And I'm good with it.

It's kind of cool to look at the exact spot where things happened, and relive the memories. For example, I can still find the places where I rode my first motorcycle, a '64 Honda c200 touring 90cc.

That Honda served an important purpose, as it was used as a tool to make a young Jimmy Sills behave himself. Mixed results with that one, I'll admit.

There were four qualifications to be allowed to ride. One, keep my grades up. Two, do my chores. Three, be nice to my four sisters. Four, if my parents were not home. Number four was not one of the official qualifiers but I adopted it myself—with limited success.

Things backfired one afternoon when I took a leisurely ride while my parents were away. It had rained and the fields were soggy, and I got the bike buried in the mud within sight of our back door. Of course my parents came home as I was scrambling back and forth with boards and shovels, trying to dig it out. Busted!

I was back to bicycles for a while. However, just because I was now self-propelled didn't mean I couldn't manage to hurt myself. When I was six years old Santa decided I was ready for a bigger bicycle. It was a three-speed, which meant greater speed. It was also my introduction to front brakes, and head injuries.

On my very first outing I noticed that the chain was rubbing. Back to the garage for quick repairs, and then a speed run down the highway to the Riego Inn, maybe a quarter-mile away. That's the last thing I remember until my head began to clear about two hours later.

I was brought back home by a woman from the Inn who had watched me trying to stand up, only to fall down again. She came outside to check on me, saw the bike in the ditch, and put two-and-two together.

A few weeks later we were towing each other around on a skateboard, using a rope and a motorcycle. My front wheel hit a small rock and came to an abrupt stop, and I did not. Head first into the concrete, and concussion number two was in the books.

For a while after that Mom required me to wear a helmet if I was leaving the house.

You might envision California as urban and hip and glitzy, but we actually lived in a rural area. In fact, we lived far enough out in the country that we didn't have trash pickup. Our disposal system was to dig a hole out back with a D7 Caterpillar bulldozer, where we'd burn the trash and eventually bury the residue. California would frown on this practice today.

My job was to haul the trash out to the hole and burn it. Setting the fire was kinda fun, but transporting was a lot of work because it was a couple hundred yards out there. After using a wheelbarrow for a while, Dick allowed me to begin using his '62 Ford pickup to haul the trash cans to the pit.

It didn't take long for a race track to form up around the pit. Every day after the dump, it was time for hot laps. One day I was on my third lap around the pit when out of the corner of my eye I could see Dick standing by the edge of the shop, watching my laps. It wasn't the kind of watching where he was timing my laps and encouraging my style; it was the "I'm going to bust this kid's ass" kind of watching. My foot immediately lifted off the throttle but it was too late.

Back to using the wheelbarrow for a while.

A little later Dick put wider wheels and glass pack mufflers on the truck, which made it all the more appealing. One rainy day when the folks were gone I noticed that the keys were hanging in the ignition. It was obviously time for another hot lap session.

It was easy to get the truck sideways on the slick track. At the front of our shop there was a patch of gravel, and I figured I could get a good run off the gravel. Yes, the gravel improved my traction, but with the increased speed I immediately experienced what racers would call a "severe push." I went flying off the track, dropping my front wheels into a muddy rut at the edge of the plowed field.

Throwing safety to the wind—there was a lot of safety being thrown to the wind in my earlier years—I left the truck in reverse (it was an automatic) and as I stepped outside to push with all my might, I used an umbrella to reach down and work the throttle. It's not difficult to see that this could have had a really bad outcome but luckily I was able to rock the truck onto level ground without running over myself.

However at this point the truck looked like it had been driven hard around a muddy track, and every inch of the painted surface was covered with mud. I hurried to do a thorough cleanup, but my parents returned home shortly after that and I was busted. Back to the wheelbarrows once again.

We changed schools when I was in sixth grade, and fitting into the social system at the new school was kind of like you see in movies that are set in a prison. Everybody seemed to want to fight the new kid to see where he fell in the pecking order.

On my second day of school I had to simultaneously fight two brothers on the bus, and once I got to school I had to fight another kid at recess.

But eventually things settled down and I made lots of new friends.

Two years later I was starting eighth grade at Rio Linda Junior High, where some inter-district paperwork hadn't been filed and that left me in limbo. The vice principal told me to wait in the office until they figured out the paperwork. He called my house to let them know that I was being kept in the office because of the paperwork snafu.

While I was waiting we experienced an earthquake that really had the building rolling. It was like everything was on rollers, going back and forth. I've experienced several earthquakes in my lifetime but none rolled like that one.

Just as everything settled down my step-father—Dick Johnson—arrived at the school. Dick found the vice principal and proceeded to tell him what a fucked-up job he was doing and that he was an idiot. It was kind of fun to hear the vice principal get his ass chewed by a professional, but at the same time I was embarrassed.

After my father's death in 1956 our house seemed to be filled with girls. They didn't have the same idea of a good time that I did. At night they wanted to watch their shows on TV, they played with different toys, and they talked about things I had no interest in.

Luckily I could turn to Grandpa Raleigh Sills for friendship. Grandpa didn't want to ride bikes or play war, but at least we spoke the same language and enjoyed the same TV shows. We mostly watched westerns such as *Gunsmoke, The Rifleman, Maverick, Sugarfoot,* and later on, *Bonanza. Bonanza* was very cool because it was in color.

My mom ruled that I had to eat dinner with her and my sisters, but as soon as we finished I hurried out to the little mobile home where Grandpa lived. We'd fire up the TV and begin sharing some quality time, man-to-man. Most of the time I'd spend the night at Grandpa's.

Life had been hard for my grandpa. He had experienced more than his share of heartache and tragedy. *MORE* than his share. In 1956 he lost his son to cancer, and that same year he lost his wife in a house fire. He and grandma had divorced, and they were living apart. She had left grandpa and married another man, but a couple of years later realized she still loved Grandpa.

They were in the process of getting back together when the fire occurred. Apparently the fire started with her gas stove, and she made it out alive but realized her beloved parakeet was still inside. She went back in and was overcome by smoke and didn't make it back out.

Grandpa found joy in different things, especially fishing. That was his major source of enjoyment. A day with Grandpa almost always meant at least a few minutes of fishing. We'd often go to Joe's Place on the river in Verona, where everybody knew Grandpa. We'd have breakfast and then head out on the boat.

I loved spending time with Grandpa but I didn't like fishing. I didn't have the patience. My friend Jack Hewitt would rather fish than, well, almost anything, but to me fishing is just boring. Too much sitting around, waiting for something to happen.

We'd sit in the boat, and I'd get restless. Grandpa would say, "Be still!" Then I'd say, "Hey Grandpa, can I drive the boat?" This would repeat about every 10 minutes.

Sometimes the fishing was more spontaneous. We'd be driving around the fields checking water levels, and Grandpa would look at me and say, "Guess what? It's fishing time!"

Grandpa's fishing program had a couple of options. There was the conventional fishing with a pole and line, but there was also the .22 pistol. Either way, it was my job to keep an eye out for the green truck the game warden drove.

When I started school I had to sleep at home because Mom needed to wake me and get me ready for school. Plus I was gone during the daytime, and Grandpa was now on his own. Things were changing...Mom married Dick Johnson, and we all changed our name to his last name. He came in and started running the farm, and everything was different. He was a father figure and he took over most of the discipline.

Don't get me wrong, this was not a bad thing. We needed more structure, and more discipline. Mom did the best she could, and obviously Grandpa was also there to help, but it wasn't the same as having the father presence in the house.

Still, this was surely hard for Grandpa. He had to stand by and watch as another man took over his late son's entire life. Dick took over his son's farm, Dick was husband to Marilyn, Dick was father to his grandkids, and Dick started working on his own race car in the same shop where Grandpa's son had worked on a race car just a few years earlier. I was too young to understand any of this, but today it's all very obvious.

I remember Grandpa and Dick having a huge argument one day that nearly came to blows. I loved them both and I couldn't understand why they would be mad at each other. But I understand it now, very clearly. It was an extremely difficult situation, especially for Grandpa.

Then came the morning when my mom woke me up and I thought it was time for school. Instead, she gently told me that Grandpa had died sometime through the night. I immediately felt guilty, because I knew that Grandpa and I had disconnected somewhat once Dick came to live with us. I felt conflicted and I felt partly responsible for his death. I guess that's for some shrink to figure out someday.

Grandpa was only 63, but I think life just wore him out. Losing his son, his wife, his farm, and in a sense, his family…it was all too much and it just broke his heart.

Every kid growing up around Sacramento in the 1960s remembers Jack Gordon. He was a very successful Ford dealer in Roseville, and Jack Gordon Ford ran lots of commercials on TV and radio.

Jack also owned several race cars, including three of the top supermodifieds at the local race track. My step-father, Dick Johnson, worked for Jack at the Ford dealership and also drove one of his race cars.

Jack's son, Jimmy Gordon, was on the cusp of becoming one of the biggest racing names Northern California had ever seen. In no time at all I came to idolize Jimmy.

When I was in sixth grade, Dick Johnson and the Gordon's opened up a slot car track. Slot car racing was a sensation in the 1960s, and it seemed like every kid in America was interested. I got a job sweeping and cleaning up the place on Saturday mornings.

Jimmy and Jack had so much fun at those Friday night slot car races. There was laughter, some big crashes, and just lots of fun. Everybody was having a great time.

Jimmy and Dick were teammates, and they were sponsored by local radio station KXOA. They were touted as the "KXOA Batman and Robin" team and it was really cool. Dick, the older veteran, was Batman, and Jimmy was Robin, the Boy Wonder.

Obviously, this was major stuff for a young kid like me.

One day they were working on the race cars out at our house, and Jimmy came driving up in a pristine '56 Corvette. I already knew this was the coolest guy on the planet, plus he always had pretty girls hanging around. This racing deal was looking really good to me!

Big things were happening for Jimmy Gordon. He caught the attention of noted car owner J.C. Agajanian, who set him up for an Indy car test at Phoenix. This kid was on the way to the top, it was plain to see.

On October 25, 1970 they held an open-competition race at the California State Fairgrounds one-mile dirt track in Sacramento. Looking back, you can easily see that the event was a little bit shaky. The track was rough that day, especially for short-wheelbase cars and guys who didn't have a lot of experience on such a big track.

Three well-known Northern California people lost their life that day. For a lot of us, this day would forever be known as "Black Sunday."

Ernie Purssell, an up-and-coming driver from Grass Valley, flipped down the front straightaway in a horrible accident that took his life. The field was bearing down on him as his car came to rest on the track, and Walt Reiff ran out onto the track to try and warn the oncoming cars to slow down. Walt was hit by a car and was also killed. All of this took place right in front of the crowded grandstands.

A few laps later Jimmy Gordon tangled with another car and began flipping on the backstretch. Jimmy was driving a car owned by Leonard Faas and was trying to make up time after pitting for a flat tire. Jimmy went for a terrible series of flips and then was struck by another car at almost full speed. There was a bad fire and Jimmy was pronounced dead-on-arrival at a nearby hospital.

Man, that was an awful day. Jack Gordon lost his son, and I still have memories of the two of them, laughing and having fun at the slot car track.

I also have vivid memories of Walt Reiff. Walt was a great driver and car builder from Sacramento, and I'd tag along when Dick went to Walt's shop. As they talked I'd sit in the cockpit of a rear-engine midget Walt had built.

We were living in North Carolina at the time of the accident, and Dick traveled back home to Sacramento for the funeral services.

It wasn't the end of the heartache for Jack Gordon. In 1983 Gary Patterson—a highly successful and beloved Northern California driver—was killed in Jack's car while racing at Calistoga. I think that was just too much for Jack to bear and he got out of the sport altogether after that.

Racing has a dark side, a side nobody talks about much. It's always there, every day, every lap, and you know it can strike. But if you spent all your time worrying about death, you wouldn't live.

I've always been a guy who laughs and clowns around and I can have fun in almost any situation, even when things are tough. That's my way of dealing with life, I guess. Or maybe just my personality.

But there weren't any smiles when we got the news about Jimmy, and Walt. We were some 2,000 miles away when it happened and it was like a black wind that reached all the way across the country and sucked the air out of the room in an instant.

I will never forget Jimmy Gordon, and the day we got the terrible news. All these years later…those memories are as vivid as ever.

3

Life-changing move

In 1967 my world had a huge change when Dick Johnson decided to try NASCAR stock car racing. He and Ed Watson traveled to watch a race in Darlington, South Carolina, where Ned Jarrett was in a '66 Ford Fairlane, and after the race they bought the car Ned had driven. They purchased a trailer in Chattanooga, Tennessee, loaded the Ford, and they were officially stock car racers.

They spent all winter going through the car, learning about independent suspension. Their first race would be on the road course at Riverside, California, so they had to make a lot of changes, including moving the fueling inlet to the other side of the car.

The NASCAR inspectors went over the car closely and found lots of issues including an oversized gas tank. Dick didn't get much practice time, and he was hobbled in qualifying when he lost third gear. But he made the show!

While we were in Riverside some of my sister's shadier Rio Linda friends decided to come out to see the race. Most of these guys were thieves just for the sport of it, although some of them eventually made it a profession. Their later claim to fame was building an operation that stole scores of Honda motorcycles, just for fun. The police later said it was one of the biggest theft rings they had ever busted.

We found a restaurant for some dinner, and some obnoxious and loud cowboys had left their hats on the stand by the door. When they finished eating and started to leave they noticed that someone had taken their cowboy hats. Man, there were some mad cowboys that night.

On race day we found a spot at the esses to watch the race. We ran into an old friend who used to help with Dick's supermodified, and he was complaining that some asshole had stolen his cooler.

As the race went on we started walking to different parts of the track. We ran into the Rio Linda boys, and they were wearing cowboy hats and drinking beer from a cooler they "found." We did the righteous thing and took the cooler back to its owner, minus a few beers. We figured it wasn't possible to return the cowboy hats so the Rio Linda boys were on their own on that front.

Soon after the Riverside adventure we packed up everything and made a cross-country move to Arden, North Carolina, a small town not far from Asheville.

My sister Carleen had recently gotten married and she and her husband Tom stayed in California. Later they moved east for a while and Tom worked on the race team. There were two problems with that arrangement: Tom was not mechanically inclined, and he was a little on the lazy side. So that was not a long-lasting employment.

We were a low-budget team; our team consisted of Dick and one or two helpers. Yes, it's kinda hard to pit with two guys on the crew. Lots of smaller "independent" teams were in this predicament so they pooled their help to make pit stops. They separated the tires and fuel for each car and tried not to pit at the same time.

NASCAR is a little different today, don't you think?

The fast guys of the day were David Pearson, Cale Yarborough, Lee Roy Yarbrough, Bobby Isaac, Buddy Baker, Bobby and Donnie Allison, Tiny Lund, Bobby Johns, and James Hylton. Some of the independent racers included Big John Sears, Clyde Lynn, Henley Gray, and J.C. Spencer.

We shared a small workshop located under a grocery store and Pure Oil gas station. Bill Siefert and Don Beiderman were also operating out of the shop. Don was a French Canadian that everyone called "Frog."

I was 14 years old and felt like I had died and gone to heaven. We were going to races at Daytona, Atlanta, Darlington, and Charlotte. Later we went on a northern tour that included Trenton, New Jersey; Islip and Fonda in New York; and Oxford, Maine.

At Oxford the promoter put on a lobster feed after qualifying had finished. Apparently none of these southern boys had eaten lobster and they weren't excited about the idea. Luckily they also offered Holly Farms chicken. Eating dinner around all those NASCAR stars was pretty special for this young kid.

Race track travel meant my parents and my sisters piled into our Ford Country Squire station wagon and hit the road. Yes, it was the "woody" model with faux wood strips on the side.

I took special pride in pissing off my sisters on those rides. We were jammed in the back which didn't much improve their disposition. I would lightly touch them and yell that there was a bug on them; I would stare at them for no reason without looking away; I would give them wet willies. All the things a brother should do to make his sister miserable.

We were riding on the New Jersey turnpike one night when Dick showed us his driving skills. Our car was loaded with people and had a bunch of luggage tied to the roof. We blew a rear tire at speed and despite all that weight and our high center of gravity Dick managed to save it. That burned-up tire sure smelled nice, lying in the back with us while we rode to a tire shop the next morning.

Years later when I watched "National Lampoon's Vacation" I recognized our family—only we had been renamed "Griswold." That movie perfectly described our experience on the NASCAR tour.

Joe "Shane" Warren was our crew chief, and he was cool southern gentleman bachelor who had plenty of action.

I wasn't old enough to get into the pits but I figured out how to sneak in with the passing crowd. That worked well until NASCAR official Bill Gazaway began to recognize my face and he always ran me out.

Asheville is one of the most beautiful places in the world, nestled in the Blue Ridge Mountains with four distinct seasons, each more spectacular than the last. It is the home of poet Thomas Wolff, the Biltmore Mansion, and is also known as the land of the sky.

When we settled into our new home I was hoping I wouldn't get the same tough "new kid" treatment I received when I changed schools in sixth grade. I figured if I tried out for the football team, maybe the kids would accept me. Plus if you got into a fight at least you'd have a helmet on.

T.C. Roberson High School football camp started one week before the fall school term began. That was good, because I would at least know some kids when I got to class.

I was never in the military, but from my understanding it's a lot like football camp under the supervision of Coach Jones. The entire team—including coaches—slept in the gymnasium on cots (or on the floor if you didn't bring a cot). We were awakened at 6 a.m. for an all-you-can-eat breakfast that included watery scrambled eggs, pancakes, greasy bacon, sausage, toast, orange juice, and coffee.

All football players want to be *BIG*, especially high school kids. So we stuffed ourselves, at least at our first breakfast. Then we suited up in full gear for an intense physical workout under the blazing Carolina sun.

I think the coaches were trying to weed out any kids who weren't serious about playing football; at least three guys tossed their breakfast that first day, and the rest of us were real close.

Despite the hard work, I enjoyed playing football. I learned a lot, and proved to be a decent player. I made all-conference my senior year, an offensive lineman (guard) at 165 pounds. I was not a big lineman but we weren't a very big school. Still, we were 7-3 for my senior season.

During my senior year the school decided to field a wrestling team for the first time. This proved to be hilarious. None of us had ever wrestled, and we had no training or education on things like technique or strategy. We figured out that the best way to start a match was to lower our head and charge the other guy.

We learned that one of three things would happen with this strategy. One, the shock and surprise of the charge might throw the guy off guard and you'd win a takedown. The second scenario—and this happened only once, to my friend Bob Butler—is that you hit the guy so hard head-to-head that it actually knocks him out, and that's the end of the match. The third scenario—and this happened to me—is that you'd hit the guy and piss him off so badly that you get into a fight. That also ends the match immediately, as I discovered.

The bus ride to the wrestling meets was also very different. The bus ride to a football game was very serious, and nobody said a word. You sat quietly and focused on the game you were about to play. Coach Jones taught us a lot about mental preparation and that really came in handy throughout my life. If we lost the football game we all stayed very quiet on the ride home, thinking about what you might have done to play better. This approach was something I also adopted throughout my racing career, always thinking on the ride home about what I might have done differently to win the race.

But the wrestling team bus rides were "party on," win or lose. There was always a shoe fight, dirty jokes, checking out girl's legs from the bus window (and sometimes shouting our approval), and various mayhem.

I even drove the team bus for one meet but that wasn't as much fun, so I insisted they get a different driver next time.

One day I noticed that the school had established a designated smoking area for the students. This is obviously another reminder that times have definitely changed! But the smoking section was very interesting. It was this huge social gathering between classes, attracting kids from every socio-economic group. There were scholars, rich kids, poor kids, the class president, gearheads, hot chicks, and football players.

I will admit: I took up smoking to try and fit in, and maybe chat up one of those hot chicks. This was a decision I would later regret, as smoking is a crummy habit with no redeeming qualities, at least none that I'm aware of.

Learning to smoke wasn't easy, and I remember going to class feeling sick to my stomach, with cold sweats. My body was definitely trying to tell me that these hot chicks were not worth what I was doing to myself.

My official racing debut came in North Carolina. A schoolmate, Mike Moffett, had a beautiful 1956 Chevy and he later built a street stock. Mike asked if I would like to drive the car next weekend at New Asheville Speedway.

My answer to that question—"Would you like to drive my race car?"—has been very consistent throughout my life. "Oh, hell yes!" is how the response came, a fraction of a second after the question was presented.

Mike was a real craftsman, and even his street stock was pristine. It was a '56 Chevy with a six-cylinder engine.

The car had only one problem, but it was kinda significant. You couldn't turn that thing in a 40-acre field. Mike had welded the spider gears in the rear end—the poor-man's locker—and to say that it pushed is a major understatement.

The lousy handling made it tough to pass anybody, so while we were under caution I got the idea that I would rev it up and dump the clutch to get a jump when the race restarted. But that broke the welds in the rear end and I was fired from my first ride on opening night.

When people think about how the government works they often laugh because everybody knows that nothing makes less sense than how the government operates.

I am proud to say that I am "Exhibit A" as a perfect example of that. When I was still a high school student the State of North Carolina officially thought it would be a good idea to hire me to drive a school bus.

When I look back at that reality today I can only say this: "What were they thinking?"

But the process was simple. If you had no moving violations and could pass all the tests, you could be approved as a bus driver. So I signed up and pretty soon I was assigned as the driver of bus No. 33. I had two routes each day, one long and one short.

We had a snowstorm one morning and after I had made a few stops some of the kids came out to the bus stop to tell me that school had been cancelled because of the storm. So I turned around and dropped off my riders before heading home.

I learned a couple of interesting things that day. One, if you get a school bus hung out sideways on a country road, you have your hands full. Two, a sideways school bus takes up a lot of road.

The speed limit for a school bus was 35 mph, and most of the buses had a governor to limit their speed. I am happy to report that bus No. 33 had no such governor. One day my friend Rudy Hipshire was riding with me when we dropped off my first load of kids.

We headed down a road with a series of "S" curves followed by a long downhill run of about a mile. I told Rudy we were going for the record today, and he might want to hold on. We exited the last turn with max speed and began our descent down the hill, one eye on the speedometer.

Just as we hit 75 mph the front wheels went into a serious high-speed wobble. The bus was shaking so violently I honestly thought the fenders and doors were going to fall off. I knew at that exact moment what Chuck Yeager must have experienced when he first hit the speed of sound.

Of course there were no kids on the bus—except for Rudy, who was hanging on for dear life—which was best, because the extra weight would have probably kept me from setting a new record.

I was popular with my riders, mainly because we didn't have many rules. No fighting, and no throwing stuff out the window. Aside from that, anything goes.

We were riding to school one morning with a very full bus when we had a fire. It was nothing serious, just a wiring fire under the dashboard. However it had all the ingredients of a major burn and for a moment I was concerned for the safety of the kids. However they weren't at all alarmed and they were actually cheering for the fire; it seems they wanted to watch the bus burn to the ground.

The bus driving gig was actually pretty cool, and it paid better than any other job I had at the time. You kept the bus at your house, and with a siphon hose I always had a backup supply of gasoline for my personal car.

One cold morning I was letting the bus engine warm up, as I had done lots of times. The brake was set and there was a rock for a wheel chock, so what could go wrong? After breakfast I came outside to discover that the bus was gone. It had apparently rolled down my side street and across Royal Pines Drive. After crossing an easement it hit a small berm and stopped just short of a steep dropoff. Luckily bus No. 33 was none the worse for wear and life went on.

Here's an ironic thing: After I graduated from high school the principal took me aside and asked if I would consider staying on as a bus driver. He said my driving record was good and they'd love to have me back.

Like I said: What were they thinking?

Another cool job in those early years was hiking rental cars. My friend Ernest Taylor worked for National Car Rental at the Asheville airport, and sometimes the agency sent a group of drivers to Greenville or Charlotte to shuttle cars back and forth to Asheville.

Ernest hooked us up to help shuttle cars, and we immediately realized that this presented a wonderful opportunity to race each other to the destination. Our route included freeway miles for high-speed drafting and lots of two-lane mountain roads for road racing.

There were times when we arrived at the Asheville airport with radiators steaming because we had been drafting so closely, with the sidewalls worn off the bias-ply tires.

On one trip I encountered a hitchhiker coming back from Charlotte. I picked him up right at the start of the Salida Road section of our drive, which was the road-racing section. After a few miles he thanked me very politely and let me know that he had decided that he'd rather walk the rest of the way if I didn't mind stopping to let him out.

On another trip from Charlotte we were traveling through Spartanburg. Sam Bishop was leading, and I was drafting him very closely as we were running in the 100-mph range. Ernest Taylor was drafting me in third when out of the corner of his eye he spotted a South Carolina trooper running the other way on the Interstate. Ernest prudently backed off and slowed.

If you have an idea that you can outrun a South Carolina trooper, let me tell you: You can't. This guy made a quick U-turn and ran us down in no time flat. At first he was pissed about the obvious danger we were causing on a public highway, but as we explained that we were shuttling rental cars he seemed to lighten up and enjoy the situation. He informed us that the North Carolina state line was just another mile over the hill, and once we got there we could go as fast as we wanted. However, he insisted that as long as we were in South Carolina we had better, "Slow your ass down."

He wrote us a ticket for 100 mph in a 70 zone, and our fine was $20 each, payable on the spot. (Cotton Taylor—older brother of Ernest—once had to surrender his spare tire as bail after being stopped for speeding in one of the rentals.) We paid our fine and when we crossed into North Carolina the green flag waved once again.

The state of South Carolina was pretty lenient when it came to speeding. Maybe that's how they produced badass race drivers like David Pearson and Cale Yarborough.

We had lots of wonderful races in those rentals. Greenville had a good road course section that offered very few passing opportunities, and one day Sam was once again leading when we came into a half-mile straight section. This was my chance to pass, and I had a run on him coming off the corner.

We were each driving a Chevy Impala and my run gave out with only a fender lead on Sam as we approached the curve, a long right-hand radius. I didn't feel like lifting was a good option, and my plan was to let Sam back off first and let me in. However I suddenly realized there was some traffic coming the other way but they were quite cooperative as they pulled off the road so that our race could continue.

Sam finally let me in but we were cutting it close, requiring me to turn in harder than I wanted to. This caused a loose condition in my Impala. After a couple of major tank-slappers I straightened out and held the lead.

That race didn't pay a thing, but could have cost big. Like, totally big. The concept of risk-versus-reward was something new to me, however, and luckily the traffic gods chose to spare Sam and me from anything bad happening. But when I think back now to some of those close calls it sure does give me pause.

4

Tuition money

We moved back to California in early 1973 and returned to the world I had known much of my life. Our old farmhouse had been sold, so we eventually lived at a couple different places in Sacramento.

By now I had graduated from high school, and it was fairly obvious that the great universities of the nation were not aware of my tremendous academic achievements. I was okay with that oversight, because I wasn't interested in any further schooling anyways.

From my very earliest memories, I wanted to race. It seemed like my mom embraced the idea, and took some solace in the fact that I was sincere. Seriously, that's a good thing for a kid, because it gives him some direction.

Mom agreed that in lieu of paying my college tuition she would pay Ed Watson approximately $3,000 to help finish a second supermodified for his driver, Larry Burton. The deal called for me to work in Ed's shop at night and on the weekends, and when the second car was finished I would get to drive Ed's old car.

The general understanding was this: If I showed no talent for driving, then I would agree to move on to something else. Of course, I had no intention of following those terms; even if I sucked, I would have kept trying. But like any young kid I didn't even consider that possibility. I figured the world was about to discover this incredible racing superstar who would win races the moment he cinched his belts up tight.

Larry didn't like Ed's old car because it was a short-wheelbase car and a little twitchy. At that time most of the cars were cross-spring suspension front and rear, which gave a little stability—but not a smooth ride—on rough surfaces. We were three weeks into the 1973 season and Larry was getting impatient to drive Ed's new car, which wasn't yet finished. Plus, I think Larry wanted me to get the chance to race.

One Friday afternoon I was hanging around the shop and Ed was on the phone with Larry. The conversation got a little heated and Ed finally slammed the phone down and called out to me, "Get ready, kid…you start your driving career tomorrow."

I couldn't have been more thrilled if he told me I had just hit the lottery. In a way, I *did* hit the lottery. I had just been given the opportunity that every aspiring young racer so desperately wants.

At the same time, I was scared to death. Not scared that I might crash and get hurt; I was scared that I would suck. That would be devastating, because it would ruin the dreams I'd spent all my young life nurturing. My life's ambition was now laid right out in front of me, and it's a scary thing to realize you might blow it.

I had watched people race all my life. I had seen countless races, countless laps, countless situations on the race track. I had driven my bicycle like a racer would, I had ran lap after lap in my go kart…I had even walked around my house processing everything like it was a lap in a race.

Many years later at my driving school I would counsel people as they climbed into the race car for the first time: this is more difficult than it looks, and it's more difficult than you think it's going to be. Of course, as a kid I didn't know this…yet. I was about to find out.

My idea of just hammering the throttle down and merely pitching it into the corner immediately turned into a huge series of tank-slappers and throttle jacking, continuing the entire length of the front straightaway at West Capital Raceway. It was an embarrassing, humiliating, and hugely disappointing moment.

West Capital drew 60 to 70 race cars every Saturday night, and if you weren't in the top 40 qualifiers you went to the C-main with no transfer to a B-main. I started mid-pack in the C, with the idea of following some good advice to just be smooth and stay out of trouble.

The middle of the C-main is where trouble lives. We didn't even get to the starting line before I was dead center of somebody's big wreck. So my first race resulted in a bent front end and zero experience. The next week was a little better, with better racers around me and a few more laps in the B-main.

Jack Hunter had helped Ed with his supermodified for many years and was pretty knowledgeable. Jack was also my advocate and he lobbied Ed to get me more track time. Jack talked Ed into taking me to Vallejo Speedway on Friday night; Vallejo had longer radius corners and less grip, which made it much easier to rotate the car than I had experienced on Capital's sticky black gumbo. It also gave me more time in the corner to figure things out.

After five weeks I was starting to get the hang of it and I won my heat race, which got me into a heat winner's trophy dash. I won the dash, and that's what they call a "transformative moment." I climbed out of the car after the race and people were actually cheering for me, and people were congratulating me. And the best part: I got my picture taken with a pretty girl, and I got to kiss that total stranger right on the lips in front of everybody.

It was exciting, a little bit embarrassing, and a turn-on, all at the same time. Oh, how could life get any better than *this??!!*

We went on to win the B-main but in those days you didn't transfer to the A. The downside to all this progress was that Ed decided we didn't need to go back to Vallejo.

Obviously I still had a lot to learn but I was getting better at making laps. The following week I (barely) qualified for the A-main, and I was on the pole because of the total inversion. Don Hicks—an old altered drag racer—built Ed's motors and that's all I needed to win the race to the first turn. I was leading the race, making good laps, when I came up on LeRoy Van Conett in Leo Vucannon's No. 80. Leroy was and is a hero of mine and a tremendous champion—National Sprint Car Hall of Fame, eight-time NARC champion—but tonight he was fighting Leo's car and I managed to lap him right before a caution came out.

We did double-file restarts and the leader could choose the inside or outside lane. I had been running the top so I chose the outside. Coming around for the start I realized that this is my race to lose so I'd better be on the gas when the time comes. The time came and that's what I did: I dropped the hammer and spun the tires. This resulted in me spinning the car in the wrong direction. Luckily the third-place car straightened me out, but it stacked the rest of the field in a big pile. It was a long caution period while they cleaned up the mess so I was talking to myself about how to properly start a race.

The next start I pulled it off and was leading by turn one. There were just a few laps left, which kept me out of traffic. So I proceeded to win my very first race in my sixth start, and it happened to fall on my 20th birthday: May 26, 1973.

This gave me some press and accolades and the feeling that I should now win every week. Uh, *NOT SO.*

I did fairly well in the weeks following that first win, but I had a tendency to over-drive the car. This led to my education via repairing crash damage. We weren't allowed to run a live-axle rear end, so we used a shortened '48 Ford housing. I had a bad habit of allowing the right rear wheel to contact the fence, which almost always resulted in breaking the weld or bending the housing. My friend Leroy Nicholson had a jig and welder to repair the housing, and I got to be a regular visitor to Leroy's shop: just about every Monday night.

Late that season I was working in the rice harvest, driving a bank-out kart. I was released from work which enabled me to race at the Gold Cup Race of Champions, the biggest and most important race in our area. It was a daytime race with a 100-lap feature; in previous years it had been a 200-lap race, and a lot of guys—including race leader Jimmy Boyd—ran out of fuel at the end, and Larry Burton won the race in the car that I was now driving.

This was truly a new age for racing in our area, because Jimmy showed up with a four-bar sprint car that changed our world. It was built in Pennsylvania by Charlie and Mike Lloyd and was a great race car. The wing was six feet long with big sideboards, and the car even had a weight-jacker on the side.

If you qualified in the mid-13-second range you were probably in the trophy dash; Boyd was in the low 12's. Not only did Jimmy have the fastest car, but he was a good-looking guy and he had the hottest wife in the pits. Even her name—Betty—seemed perfect. Jimmy wore an open-face helmet with a Norm Rapp leather mask which was just cool as hell. He sat with his head upright in the car and he made everything look effortless. After that I tried to sit that same way when I raced.

If all that wasn't enough, Jimmy went out at the Gold Cup and put a lap on everyone except Gary Patterson in Duke McMillen's car. The track was very slick that day and I was in the B-main where I spun out. I just didn't have the experience to deal with those slick conditions.

Overall, my first year was not bad. I didn't make rookie of the year for a couple of reasons. One, I missed the first three races of the year. Two, Rendy Boldrini ran all the races—including some pre-season runs—and had done pretty well. Rendy was a very good driver who stopped racing much too early in his career. Later, when we moved up to start racing with NARC, Rendy won rookie of the year there too, when we took some time away from NARC to race in Pennsylvania.

The cars in our area were changing pretty quickly in 1974, with many cars going to live axles and torsion bar suspension. Our car, however, still had a cross spring on the front. We also acquired a power steering unit, but it wasn't like the specialty-built units everybody runs today. The early units were from a fork lift and they were bolted to our existing steering box. This made the car steer too easily on the straightaway, but it was still hard to turn in the corners. We were running big tires, and combined with the sticky surface at West Capital, any steering assistance was welcomed. We were also in the process of lightening our cars, but they were still heavy enough that power steering was pretty much needed.

My sophomore season started out with high hopes. We built a new supermodified from the ground up, and I do mean *built*. There were no kits to buy and assemble, there was no bolting together store-bought items. It was a very basic process which meant we had to fabricate many of our own pieces and parts.

The new car netted an early feature win, so the 1974 season was shaping up pretty well.

I really wanted to travel and race outside our northern California circle. In early June there was a series of races in northern Washington built around the Dirt Cup, a big event at Skagit Speedway. Skagit is just a few miles from the Canadian border, and it's a long haul from northern California. But we were itching to get up there and give it a try.

Hey, mom! Time for more tuition! Actually, I later learned that mom had already put up a little money to allow us to travel up there. Good ol' mom.

Ed assigned me the job of finding somebody to weld our aluminum fuel tank. I immediately ran into two problems. One, finding somebody who can weld aluminum. Second, finding somebody crazy enough to weld an aluminum fuel tank. Duke McMillen was the answer to both of those challenges. I called Duke at his muffler shop and he told me to bring the tank over to his house and meet him after work.

I was working for Ed Watson and Max Rankin at their muffler shop, and they let me off early so I could take care of getting the tank welded. My only set of wheels at the time was a 750 Honda motorcycle, so I strapped the tank to the back and away I went. It was very bulky so I had to hold the tank with my left hand while steering the bike with my right hand. When I reached a stop sign or traffic light that got kind of interesting as I had to let go of the tank at the last moment and grab the clutch.

Duke carefully looked the tank over. Then he ran a hose into the washed-out tank to fill it with Argon gas, and welded it up with no problem. No leaks, it was perfect. I got the tank back to Ed's race shop where Ed, Chuck, and John Wright (our Bowes Seal Fast sponsor) were loading the truck.

Ed informed me there wasn't room for me in the truck, so they were going to fly me up to Seattle. Man, I'm moving up! Now they're flying their driver to the races! Pretty cool, I figured.

The first race up there was at Sky Valley, and I was in awe of the cars in the pit area. I studied the cars and saw names I'd read in the *National Speed*

Sport News and *Racing Wheels* newspapers. Ross Fontes, Dick Wilskey, Don McCloud…it was cool. A lot of the Skagit regulars were there, and a lot of cars from our area. It made for a stout field of cars.

The fastest guy there, by far, was Wayne Sue of Live Oak, California. Wayne had the Lloyd car in which Jimmy Boyd had won the Gold Cup the previous year. Wayne was bullet-fast and won that first night at Sky Valley. Wayne was leading the West Capital points driving for Bill Shadle and Duke McMillen, so Wayne had to drive back to Sacramento for that week's race. This caused him to miss Skagit on Saturday night.

I did well enough to give me the overall points lead going into the final race at Elma on Sunday. Wayne hustled back to Elma, and despite missing Saturday night's race he was in the hunt for the overall points. Don McCloud was driving for Rebel Jackson, and he blew up in hot laps. Don then jumped into an older spring-front car and won the race. Rebel liked the older car so much he brought it for a spare, and I later purchased the car from him for my first trip to Australia.

Wayne would have had enough points to win the overall series, but he was informed that he had forfeited the points from Friday night because he didn't run all three races. That made me the overall points champ for the series.

Yes, I had a little help, but I was over the moon with excitement. Hey, I was a second-year driver going against some very tough veteran racers, so I was proud to even be in the hunt. It's hard to describe how much something like that helps a young racer with his confidence.

I first met Mike Andreetta at Walt Ross's Carmichael Auto Service. Mike is also known as "the Rat," a nickname that came about through his friendship with Gary Patterson. Mike went over to Patterson's house one day to help weld on a race car, and the garage wasn't wired for 220. They sent Gary's son Jimmy up into the attic to find a wiring connection. Jimmy was getting hot and claustrophobic, and he was starting to voice his complaints. Mike kept telling Jimmy, "Crawl through there like a worm!" Jimmy finally got mad enough that he yelled, "Shut the fuck up, you Fat Rat!" And from that moment on, Jimmy was "the Worm" and Mike was "the Fat Rat." Mike later lost a lot of weight and the name was shortened to just "the Rat."

Mike is one of those guys who can do just about anything mechanical. He was working for Walt at that time, and on the weekends was driving Walt's supermodified on the pavement at Roseville on Friday and on dirt at West Capital on Saturday night. Plus he would pick up a sprint car ride as well. I looked up to Mike because I wanted to drive a different race car at a different track every day, too.

The Rat would eventually become an official for NARC, USAC, and the Golden State series, as well as local races at Chico and Placerville.

I drove a local car at Chico on Friday nights, and it wasn't a great car but if you drove the hell out of it and had a few things go your way you had a shot at getting to victory lane. Skip Jones owned the car and he was a fun guy. Every Friday night when the heat races started and it got dark, a skunk would show up outside the pit fence. At least it smelled like a skunk. Every Friday I would say, "What's up with that damned skunk? He shows up at the same time every week!" The crew would just laugh and tell me, don't worry, just drive the race car. Of course today I realize that the smell was them going outside the fence to "burn a rod."

One hot summer night I flipped down the back straightaway, and Mike was watching from turn four. He was concerned for me and he ran right over to the car. He yelled, "You all right? That looked like a nasty one!"

I gave him a blank sort of stare and a confused look and said, "Hey mom, what's for dinner tonight?"

Mike turned around to call for an ambulance and I started laughing. I suppose I shouldn't be a smart-ass like that but I can't help it.

On my 21st birthday—May 26, 1974—I received a $5,000 inheritance from my late grandfather's estate. I was working at a muffler shop in Carmichael owned by my car owner Ed Watson and his partner Max Rankin. They found a muffler shop in Vacaville that was for sale, and asked if I wanted to go in with them as a partner at the new shop.

I always figured I could make it as a racer, but in the back of my mind I also figured it would be smart to have something to fall back on.

However, my first priority was getting a vehicle to drive. I was riding a 750 Honda at the time, and that got a little rough in the winter. I remember sitting at a stoplight looking at people sitting in their car with the heater running and listening to the radio, and thinking that would be a nice luxury. Plus it was hard on my dating life because girls apparently didn't want to ride on a motorcycle when it was raining.

So I bought a Mazda rotary-engine pickup, and used the last of my money—about $3,000—to join Ed and Max in the muffler shop business.

I needed to learn the business, so Ed drove to Vacaville for a couple of months to get the shop going. When I took it over we stayed busy for a while and then it seemed like everyone in Vacaville had their muffler needs taken care of. It got so slow there were days when I literally had no business come through the door. I dreaded those calls to Ed to report our sales for the day.

One night I called and Ed had some news. He had returned to his house after work to be greeted by the echoing sound of an empty house; his wife had cleaned it out and departed, destination unknown. This was the second divorce I saw Ed endure. In the first episode his wife and three daughters showed up at our house to lay low until the dust cleared. Ed would go through one more divorce before finding Shirley, who was with him until the end.

One day an old man in a Ford pickup needed his rusty tail pipe welded. The guy told me he was a professional gold miner. Judging by the old truck he was driving, it hadn't been a lucrative career. He explained that his method was to search the bottom of rivers. He had an old bronze diver's helmet that was heavy enough to hold him under water, and his air supply was a gas-powered air pump floating on an inner tube.

He told the story of when he was approximately 15 feet underwater when two kids with a .22 rifle decided to shoot his inner tube. The miner was barely able to free himself from the helmet and make it to the top; he nearly drowned. The kids had stuck around to see if he came to the surface, and he managed to chase them down and haul them to their parents. The next day their father made the kids pull the air pump and diving helmet to the surface and he was back in business.

The old man paid for his tailpipe repair with cash, a few gold nuggets and a good story.

The downhill trend in the muffler shop was still going when it was time for me to leave for Australia in late 1974 to go racing. Ed and Max felt like my loyalties should be to mufflers, not race cars. They bought me out at a reduced price but I certainly had no regrets. They kept the shop open for a couple of months but things had ran their course. They sold off the lifts, bender, and other equipment, and closed the doors.

5

Hitting the road

Ed Watson and I were a little strained as the 1974 season went on, and he decided to put Gary Patterson in his car for the Jimmy Gordon Memorial race. This was a big race in honor of a man I idolized and I really wanted to win that race.

Larry Burton was driving for Dwayne Starr, but was thinking about spending more time promoting his pavement track in Roseville. So I immediately called Dwayne and he agreed to let me drive his car at a race a week before the Gordon race, kind of a tune-up. It felt good that I could get a ride on talent alone.

I was faster than Ed's car in qualifying, which felt pretty good. We were in the same heat race with GP (Gary Patterson) starting second and me starting fourth. The green came out for the start and GP appeared to hit the brakes. We got another start, and the same thing happened. On the third start I was certain that GP was jacking with me so I gassed it up and ran right over his wheel and nearly took out the flagger.

Dwayne was pissed at GP for the continued bad starts but he was okay with me, so I was still in the seat for the Gordon Memorial race. We got the car repaired and were ready to go.

Dwayne was an innovator, and his cars always had some forward-thinking devices. Back when we had to run springs, he had a coil spring car with Jerry Miller driving. All supermodifieds had to be self-starting, so Dwayne invented the "Torque Multiplier Transmission" and it was referred to as the "T.M.T." Don Tognotti sold these at his speed shop and Don joked that T.M.T. stood for "This Mother's a Thou(sand)."

Don was a cool guy. When Mike Andreetta was driving his race car they made a few thou, that's for sure. I learned a lot from both Dwayne and Don and I loved to talk racing with both of them. Many years later I did a sprint car seminar and Don and Dwayne helped me pull it off. Dwayne's car had the engine laid over to the left side, like a pavement roadster. On the sticky West Capital track the car felt like you could drive a ton into the corner without the car wanting to tip over. I set a goal to get a perfect lap during qualifying without lifting the throttle.

In the six weeks I ultimately raced the car, we never missed the trophy dash and had several fast times. They inverted the field, and at the Gordon race we came from the back to run fifth. (I had to wait another year to win this race, by the way.)

On my final night in the car we had fast time, and turn one had a hole right where your right rear tire needed to be during qualifying. After time trials the track crew bladed the track before the trophy dash. After doing the driver introductions we were always given a couple of hot laps before the dash.

The track was perfect, and I was thinking that this might be the night for my wide-open lap. I took off at turn two and didn't lift the gas in three. Dwayne's car was gripping the track like never before; this was going to be *the* lap. As I entered the turn I quickly discovered that the track crew had only slightly covered up that hole. As the right rear tire connected with the hole the car bicycled big-time.

I don't know if it was saveable, but I do know that when my foot sent the big Moon-foot gas pedal to the floor, it wasn't happening. We plowed wide open on two wheels straight into the fence. The car went up in the air and twirled around and landed flat on its wheels, sending the torque tube up into the seat and compressing the seat and my back. That was my first trip to the crash house but was I released later that night, sore as hell.

Dwayne's poor car was j-u-n-k and that ended my tenure with him, although we later raced together and won a sprint car race. Dwayne went on to win the Gold Cup with Johnny Anderson and at least one NARC championship with Rick Hirst.

After I killed Dwayne's supermodified, Bob Davis asked if I was interested in driving his car. I must say, I lived in a great era; car owners were willing to put a kid in their car without asking him to bring money.

Bob had just sold his business, the Bent Dime Saloon. So we called him Bent Dime Bob.

Bob started the season with Jimmy Boyd in his car but Jimmy headed east when the Pennsylvania sprint car season got underway. Bob was a little spoiled, because after having Jimmy in his car nobody else could live up to those expectations.

Bob and I shared a vision: we both wanted to go racing at faraway places we had read about in the racing newspapers. After we finished the season at West Capital we traveled to Clovis, a big half-mile near Fresno. Then we won a race at Marysville, which was special because we beat Jimmy Boyd in Gil Stroppini's car.

Later that winter I purchased the cross spring sprint car and went to Australia. We worked on the car in Bob's shop on El Sutton Lane, but we referred to the street as Gasoline Alley. It was amidst a bunch of interesting people and there was always something going on.

Gil Stroppini was right next door, and Gil owned a supermodified and did metal fabrication. He was known far and wide for his engine stands, which could be found in just about every race and engine shop in the country.

Next to Gil were Larry and Sid, the hippy painters at Free Form Art Studio. These guys were striping cars for all the local car dealers as well as painting hot rods and lettering race cars. Larry and Sid also built just about the coolest car on the planet…although the car had one significant feature that proved difficult. It was a show car that featured a front end that looked like a top fuel dragster and a body encased in tinted glass. It was powered by a 750 Honda engine with chrome spaghetti headers coming out of the top. Behind the Honda sat an 18-inch drag slick, making it the most awesome trike in the world.

It sounded great but they couldn't run it much because it blued up the headers and that messed up the showpiece.

However…when Larry and Sid mounted the rack-and-pinion steering box they didn't realize they were installing it upside-down. It fit perfectly, but you can imagine their surprise when during the test run they immediately discovered that when you steered right, it went left! That was the significant feature I mentioned earlier.

Next door to Free Form was an import car repair shop, and the proprietor had a Triumph Spitfire road racing car. He was also the manager—we called him the godfather—of the shop complex, and he mentioned that he was looking for someone to paint the shop. I found a legitimate painter to put in a quote, and I submitted a slightly lower quote and got the job.

Bob's neighbor, John Lorman, helped us on the race car and he also helped me paint half the buildings. The other half I sub-contracted to Mel Baker. I actually considered going into the painting business, because I could see the potential for making good money.

In the back part of Gasoline Alley was a Super Modified team belonging to Roy Wilhite and the Budget Motors team. Ron Simmons was their driver, and he had recently moved in from Redding, California. I can still recall the day he showed up with his supermodified with pavement tires on it. I asked Bob, "Hey, who is that guy?" Bob explained that Ron had just moved in and was going to go to work for Duke McMillen at his muffler shop next door. A few weeks later Ron put dirt tires on the car and won at West Capital, which was impressive.

Ron was good friends with Jimmy Boyd who was still living in Redding, and during the off season they rode dirt bikes together. This was right down my alley so I went to the Suzuki dealer—located just around the corner from Gasoline Alley—and bought a used CZ400 Dirt bike.

We connected with Carl Bedford and headed for Redding to meet up with Bob Guthrie, Jimmy and Betty Boyd, and Jimmy's brother Johnny. Along with being the heartthrob of the pit area, Betty was a very good dirt bike rider. She rode a 360 Yamaha and could out-ride some of the guys.

(A funny story about Betty: many years later we went out to Hollister to ride, and Betty and her sister-in-law Sherry were each riding a 175 Yamaha. One of the riders that day was a guy with a 490 Yamaha and all new riding gear. We got to the top of a fairly tough hill and were waiting for the rest of our party to get up the hill. The guy on the 490 would start up the hill and fall over, then cuss his bike and throw it down. He did this several times and was getting madder each time. Here comes Betty and Sherry on their little 175's and they went right up the hill. The guy on the 490 loaded up and went home.)

Ron Simmons and I became good friends and rode together quite a bit. One night after the races at West Capital, Ron was standing with Bill Medlock, a writer from the *Sacramento Bee* newspaper. Bill's girlfriend Cheryl was a beautiful girl who had just moved in from Minnesota. Bill asked Ron to sit with Cheryl while he called in his story to the newspaper. This was a big mistake as Ron and Cheryl had an immediate connection, which led to a mutual attraction, which led to no more Bill. Ron and Cheryl later married and had two great kids, a girl and a boy.

We were all good friends and Ron and Cheryl were a part of my first wedding a few years later. We would lead shared lives with birthday parties for our kids, Christmas, Super Bowl parties, and so forth. Eventually our lives changed; I went racing out of town more and more, was eventually divorced, and Ron quit racing. We lost touch for nearly 30 years, and one day in 2007 I got a call from Cheryl with the sad news that Ron had died from mesothelioma. I went to the funeral and their children both gave a beautiful eulogy to Ron, and the love and respect they felt for their father was obvious.

You will hear more about Cheryl later in this book, I assure you.

Wendell "Andy" Anderson owned a used car lot called Broadway

Andy's in Sacramento. Andy and his wife owned race cars and supported Capital Speedway, and all four of their sons were ultimately involved in the sport. Johnny, Billy, and Wendell Jr. drove race cars, and Bob built race cars and did engine work.

Johnny was a very successful driver, and I admired his driving ability. He won a couple of championships at West Capital, and he had driven champ cars, midgets, and sprint cars before they had a roll cage.

I was leading a race at West Capital in Bob Davis's sprint car with a few laps to go when Johnny passed me. I was pissed at myself; this was my race and he was taking it away from me. Johnny was running the bottom and I'm up top when we got the white flag and entered turn one. I don't believe in taking anybody out to win a race (although I see it in NASCAR all the time), but Johnny missed the bottom and was drifting across a slick shiny part of the track right towards my front bumper.

Yes, I had a brake pedal. But I just couldn't make myself use it. So I tagged him at his most vulnerable time and he spun into the infield. I drove around to the checkered flag.

Johnny was mad, his folks were mad, and we didn't speak to each other for a few years. Then one day I had a ride for a race at Ascot and was boarding a plane for LAX. As I located my seat I looked over and I'm sitting right next to Johnny Anderson. We talked it out right then and have been friends ever since.

After winning the Gold Cup (and beating the World of Outlaws guys) in September 1980, Johnny was seriously hurt that November at Corona. We raced the Pacific Coast Championship at Ascot, and everything in Southern California was run without a wing. Bruce Flanders—a very cool announcer at Ascot—wanted to see a winged race in southern California so he promoted a race at Corona the day after the Pacific Coast Championship.

Corona was a half-mile that featured an elevated back straightaway and a downhill slope into turn three. It was a daytime race and it was very dusty down the backstretch. I was driving Don Snow's car, and Johnny was right in front of me as we rode around the track under caution. I could see that Johnny's left rear tire was flat, and I pulled alongside and pointed to the tire. Johnny gassed up the car to get a feel for it, and continued on.

We restarted and strangely enough his tire wasn't that bad until he got beside Bobby Davis Jr. That's when the tire might have finally come apart; it was too dusty to see for sure but I could see a car pop up through the dust. I turned away from him and found myself heading for the infield. There were motorcycle jumps with people standing everywhere and I was headed right toward them. As I got turned back towards the track after catching a little berm, I could see Johnny still flipping through the dust and hear his engine racing as it was free winding in the air. I stopped on the front straightaway and looked up at the back straight to see all the cars piled into the wreck.

Johnny was badly hurt, and word began to spread that he had lost all vital signs. There were rumors that he had lost an arm, which was not true. There was a trauma center across the freeway from the track, and that fact saved Johnny's life.

The accident ended Johnny's driving career and that was a very sad day for the fans of Northern California. The good news is that I see Johnny all the time these days and he's doing well. He's had a happy life and that's ultimately what matters.

At the beginning of the 1975 season I had a sprint car ride but nothing in a supermodified at West Capital. Early in the season I was sitting in the grandstand and having a beer with a pretty girl, Vicky, watching the races. Gary Patterson found me in the stands and said, "Hey Sills, get your helmet! Gary Coster just climbed out of Tommy Boltinghouse's car and they need a driver!"

So, like any good redneck I looked at Vicky and said, "Hold my beer and watch this!"

I had never drank beer on the day of a race so I wasn't sure how this would turn out. The track was very sticky and they were running 23 inches of stagger on the car, which made it easier to turn in the corner but also made it want to turn on the straightaway. It took a few laps in the B-main to sober up and get used to the car. We went to the front but there was no transfer to the A, so I went back up into the grandstand to watch the final race with my girl—and finish that beer.

Tommy was happy, so I now had a supermodified ride if I wasn't racing the sprint car.

Two weeks later we ran Tommy's car again, and a friend of mine brought a girl named Karen that he wanted me to meet. It was her first time at a race. The top four cars in time trials ran a four-lap trophy dash, and we won it. The girl said, "Oh, that's nice, he won his race. Let's go."

She was sufficiently impressed that we were introduced later that night at the Yolo Club, where everybody hung out after the races. We made out in the parking lot and she was further impressed enough that she agreed to go out on a date, and I picked her up a few days later on my 750 Honda. I thought it was James Dean romantic, but her dad said, "Doesn't that boy have a car?"

Five years later we were married and in 1982 had a daughter, Stephanie.

When I returned from Australia, Bob Davis was putting the finishing touches on the most beautiful sprint car I had ever seen. Complete with a free form paintjob, the car was actually over-finished. It had all steel braided lines with blue anodized fittings, and was meticulous. Bob had hands the size of a catcher's mitt, and he used those big paws to recheck the tightness of the fittings.

We towed to Ascot for the first race, and when we fired the engine we discovered that every fitting had cracked from being over-tightened. Fuel was running everywhere so we had to go home and replace all the fittings.

We read in *Speed Sport News* about a race at Manzanita Speedway in Phoenix, a 100-lapper. What a great opportunity to get some track time in the new car! However, they had qualified a week earlier and we missed that little detail. When we got to the track Bob and I approached all the other car owners, trying to convince them that we weren't out-of-towners trying to swoop in to take all their money like Rick Ferkel had done. I was just a rookie looking for a race!

They agreed to let us race if we started in the back. About 40 laps into the race I was coming off turn two when I heard something go, "Cha-ching!" At the same instant I spotted something approximately one foot in length flying over the fence. I was thinking, "That might be something important to the safe operation of this race car!" Actually, the abbreviated way to say that is, "Oh, shit!" I felt the car do down on the right front so I pulled into the infield. It was indeed the right front torsion arm.

They stopped the race at halfway to fuel the cars, so I ran outside to look for our part. Luckily, it wasn't in turn three or four where they had the infamous junkyard dogs. But it was too dark and I couldn't find the damned thing.

When we got home we started winning some local races, and that gave us the fever to get back to southern California to take on the CRA guys. So we went down for a weekend that would begin on Friday night at Chula Vista, a track so far south that you could see the lights of Mexico.

We started the feature and were running second to Jimmy Oskie in the JFK Special. The track was really heavy, and I immediately ran through all my tear-offs. I had to let Oskie get away little bit so I wasn't getting pelted with mud. I drove with my shield up and the next day my eyelids were bruised.

The following night we were at Ascot, one of the most famous tracks in America. One of those tracks where you're proud just to be on it. We ran well, but had some damage from our heat race that would require a trip back to Sacramento for repairs.

We had a choice for Sunday: the half-mile Santa Clara fairgrounds with a wing, or the NARC opener at Calistoga. NARC would not be very excited about us running a race directly against their opener. But Santa Clara won out and we were leading the race until a trick aluminum wing bracket broke and I had to pull in. Bob yanked the wing off with those huge hands and I went back out, but the engine dropped a valve and we were done anyways.

We did indeed get in trouble with NARC, but we did a little sleight-of-hand and sold the car to a crew member, Chuck Lysalt. So we were back in business with NARC.

We were leading the points at the Dirt Cup, running the finale at Elma where Gary Patterson caused a false start that resulted in a big crash. I dove for the infield to avoid the wreck but climbed the infield berm and flipped. Bob saw Patterson as the cause of the crash and was mad enough that he ripped off a two-by-six board from the rodeo chute and flung it toward Patterson. He missed, but nearly took Ron Simmons's head off.

We headed east with Kenny Woodruff, who was towing two cars—his own car and a car driven by the Australian champion Garry Rush. We were all traveling together, going racing, and when I think about it now I'm not sure I realized at the time how special it was.

I was only in my third year, and we were already racing on the road. We were competitive and I'm proud to say that I won some races. When you're young, however, you don't usually understand that this special time will not last forever, and will not be repeated. Even if you travel and race for the next 30 years, nothing will compare to the first time of going out on the road.

We went to a track in Sioux Falls, South Dakota that was the biggest and fastest track I had ever seen. Roger Larson was driving Bob Trostle's car, and Roger made it a full lap without lifting. I was racing for the win in the heat race, but couldn't do anything with the leader and moved up the track and bicycled on the cushion. I saved it okay but after the heat race a guy approached our pit and said, "I wouldn't do that again!" I asked why not, and he explained that there was a rock quarry just outside of turn three and there was no catch fence to keep you in the track. That would be a helluva drop, I imagine.

I didn't go look to see if he was telling the truth, but years later I drove past the track to see that yes indeed, there was the quarry. They didn't race very often at that track, and maybe that's the reason why.

A week later we were at Knoxville, but were parked because our big engine had an issue. I was a spectator and watched Larry Kirkpatrick flip Dave Van Patton's car during qualifying, a really spectacular crash that got my attention. Unfortunately, Larry later lost his life at West Memphis.

We headed east to Pennsylvania to race with KARS, an organization ran mainly by Williams Grove Speedway promoter Jack Gunn. They were trying to cut costs and make racing more competitive by implementing a 317-ci engine limit and running a 16-sf wing. We kept our car at the Lloyd shop where it was originally built. We installed our small engine but broke the rear end at Lloyd's shop before we could get to the track. We didn't have a spare, and with no time to repair the car we were done.

Bob Davis decided he was ready for a drink so we cleaned up and went to a neighborhood bar in Highspire. Like many times before, drinking at a Bob Davis pace can mean trouble.

The very next thing I remember was Bob waking me up and asking me, "How do you feel?"

"I have a headache, I must have drunk too much last night."

He explained that no, I crashed the car at Hagerstown last night.

"You're crazy," I told him. "I distinctly remember talking to those girls at the bar last night, and I've never been to Hagerstown!"

So I got dressed and we went to the shop. There, sitting on our open trailer, was our race car. It was totally wrecked and the roll cage was nearly torn off.

I guess I *had* been to Hagerstown, after all. How about that.

The next few days were spent repairing the car and welding on a new cage. My job was to hold the pieces together while Mike Lloyd welded. That night I woke up in the middle of the night and thought I had somehow got sand in my eyes. I was in the bathroom splashing water in my eyes when Bob shouted from the next room, "What the hell's wrong with you?"

"I got sand in my eyes!"

"You got a welding flash! Go back to sleep, it will go away by tomorrow."

He was right…it went away. But it sure was a weird feeling.

We got the car fixed in time to run the Summernationals at Williams Grove on Friday night. This was known as Pennsylvania Speed Week, and we raced at the Grove, Penn National, Selinsgrove, and Hagerstown.

At Hagerstown I was third-fast in time trials, and somebody mentioned that I wasn't intimidated by my big wreck there a week earlier. I told the guy, "As far as my brain knows, this is the first time I've been here!" We qualified well and ran top-10 most nights, but we were still a ways from winning there.

Pennsylvania has always been one of the toughest areas to go racing. Lynn Paxton, Smokey Snellbaker, and Kramer Williamson were mainstays, along with California racer Jimmy Boyd. Keith Kauffman was just getting started, and he would become another great driver. A driver couldn't help but get sharper when he ran against that kind of competition every weekend, and racing there helped us. Before we left I led much of a feature race at Williams Grove until Smokey moved me to second. It felt pretty good to be leading against that level of competition.

When we returned to California it felt like everybody there had slowed down. This is by no means an insult to anybody, but that's what it felt like. The Pennsylvania guys—as well as the Midwestern racers—were really good and they forced us to up our game.

We returned to Clovis for the 100-lap race where we had struggled the year before in the supermodified. We had fast time and were leading the 100-lapper when at about 80 laps I noticed we were losing oil pressure. I could see that the pressure was dropping on entrance to the corner. The car was running a wet sump system and the oil was hot, and I kept an eye on it.

When I came off turn two I saw that the pressure wasn't coming back up. I was in a tough position; if I pull in I'm definitely not going to win the race. However, if I decide that it's just the gauge and we blow up, I will miss much more than just winning this race. So I decided to pull in.

Bob came running over and demanded to know why I pulled in. I told him, and he was pissed. "Don't you know the oil gets hot and the pressure goes down?"

Gary Patterson was on my ass, too. "What the hell are you doing looking at the gauges, anyway?"

What a relief the next day when we pulled the pan off and the oil pump was laying there in the bottom.

Erie, Colorado had a two-day wingless race, and Bob and I went out there along with Australian racer Steve Brazier riding along with us. It was kind of a meeting of the Midwest and Southwest racers, and we were the only ones there from Northern California.

We didn't run well, and Bob and I had a rather heated disagreement about chassis theory, so it was a quiet ride home. Quiet, that is, until we came upon a couple of carloads of kids goofing around and running side-by-side in the road. They finally let us pass, but by then Bob is plenty pissed. I was thinking that this is a good thing because instead of being mad at me, Bob is now mad at the kids.

Bob comes upon a car doing about 45 mph and decides it's time for a payback. He runs alongside the guy at about 45, with one of the carloads of kids impatiently following behind us.

It didn't take long for the kids to try to pass on the shoulder, and Bob made a quick swerve to the left to run the kid down into the medium. They were sliding sideways down the slope of the medium, not hitting anything, finally coming back up alongside Bob.

One of the kids threw a full beer can and it hit the front fender of Bob's new crew cab dually pickup. Bob instantly reached into the glove box and retrieved a .38 pistol and waved it out the window, cussing at the kids.

I don't know if he was actually going to shoot at the car…and neither did the kids. At the appearance of that pistol their heads dropped out of sight and they sped off.

Bob and I used to go to a nearby bar after work and have a beer. When I was growing up I always wished I was big because I figured that if you're big nobody wants to fight with you. Not so! Bob was a big man, and it seemed like everybody constantly wanted to call him out.

One night I was sitting at the table with Bob, and he had his arms up on the table, folded. A drunk of big stature came over slobbering, wanting to fight. Bob warned him twice that he didn't want to fight, but the guy wouldn't go away. Finally as the guy was leaning over Bob's left shoulder, Bob took his right fist directly from the table to the guy's jaw. The big guy flew straight over backwards and landed on his back, out cold.

BOOM! Out go the lights.

Bob Davis was a huge influence in my career, and I owe him a lot. There was no way anyone else would have taken a chance on such a young driver and provide the opportunity to travel to all the tracks we went to. I didn't get paid for driving Bob's car, and I was okay with that. We just lived off what the car made and got ourselves to the next race.

Clyde Lamar, a longtime car owner and businessman from West Sacramento, took Bob and Gary Patterson under his wing and created Side Bite racing and together they won the Gold Cup in 1977. But the Side Bite chassis didn't catch on, and Clyde eventually closed the doors. However, Bob Davis was an important part of racing in our area.

Bob and his wife Donna went through parental hell in 1984 when their lovely daughter Marcy was abducted and murdered in a city park just down the street from their house. A predator lured Marcy to a hidden place where she was raped and murdered. It was a horrific day and it changed a lot of lives.

Each day Bob went to the guy's trial, listening to graphic testimony on what was done to his daughter. The guy got the death penalty, but the experience—and hearing all that testimony—was more than anyone could be asked to endure. Bob was never the same after that.

He drove a truck for a few years, but the pain never stopped eating at him. Bob and Donna tried hard to keep it together but they eventually divorced. Donna later had a boyfriend and one day Bob saw the guy driving down Watt Avenue. Bob pulled the guy over to confront him, and a wrecker driver who was passing by stopped to see about the commotion.

The wrecker driver pulled a gun on Bob, and Bob told him, "If you're going to pull a gun on me, you'd better use it." The guy did, putting several bullets into Bob's midsection. Bob staggered back to his truck and died on his front seat.

I think about that day a lot, and it makes me really sad. I suspect that Bob just wanted the pain to go away. At that moment he found what looked like the only way to finally make it stop. It was a very sad ending for a good guy.

6

The Midwest

When Bob Davis and I ended our tenure in 1975 I joined the team of Bill Shadle and Duke McMillen. The bonus of that move was that it allowed me to work with Duke. From that day a couple of years earlier when Duke welded my aluminum fuel tank, he and I had a special bond that would last until his last breath on earth. Duke was a special man to me, and some of that was inherent. Duke's father was a Presbyterian minister, and his mother was a saint. When Duke was a young boy his family served as missionaries in South America, and when they returned to the U.S. Duke could barely speak English.

One of the Commandments that Duke seemed to struggle with was the one about telling a lie. Man, he had that skill down to a science. He would tell me a race was paying twice what it really was in order to convince me to go race it. Which wasn't necessary, because I just wanted to race. I didn't care what it paid anyway.

When people asked Duke what setup we were running he could bullshit with the best of 'em. It was comical to listen to what he told people.

One day we were cleaning out some stuff from the shop and I cut my hand with a rusty nail. I needed a tetanus shot, so Duke gave me his Kaiser medical card and sent me to the clinic. As I was leaving he said, "Oh, by the way…your name isn't Duke."

"Okay, what's my name?"

He pointed to the card. "It's Pyron Galloway McMillen."

Let me tell you, when they call out that name in the waiting room everybody stares.

The McMillen family is quite an assortment of various individuals. Their oldest son Scott is a craftsman who has built many race cars. He now operates Hanson Machine, a business he and his father founded. Scott's brother Jason was a sprint car driver with a NARC title on his resume, and their sister Samantha moved to southern California where she launched a clothing business that provides apparel to many movie stars. Duke's wife Carol is one of the nicest people I've ever known and she has looked out for all of us at one time or another.

Our team got off to a good start, winning several races around home. We were ready to hit the road, so we headed north to Washington. On the way up we stopped to see Jerry Day at his house, and we were to stay there while we raced at Sky Valley. That was cool because Jerry was the owner and builder of Ram Race Cars, and Jan Opperman was driving his car that weekend and was also staying at Jerry's.

That gave me the chance to hang around with Jan, one of the biggest heroes in the history of sprint car racing. He was a major star and when I watched him drive I immediately saw why. One thing I believe all great drivers have in common is the ability to be smooth; Jan was so smooth everything looked effortless. He was also a smooth person with a warm smile and a good philosophy for life. It was easy to see why he had so many fans and followers, and a great many people listened when Jan spoke of the Lord.

Another great memory from that weekend was winning a thousand dollars for breaking the track record. I think that was the highest pay-per-lap of my career.

Duke was like a lot of racers in California with the way he transported the car to the track. He had a hauler that was basically like a flatbed truck, with the car loaded on a bed with compartments underneath and a tire rack on the front. Vehicles with a trailer were limited to 55 mph but a transport like ours could run 65 mph.

We continued our racing journey, heading east. The cab of the truck was a little crowded, and John Boy Sullivan showed me how you could lay down on the bed of the truck and sleep while we traveled down the road. If you crawled alongside the race car and lay down between the left-side wheels, the ramps that were bolted to the side of the truck kept you from rolling out onto the highway.

This worked well and on my first ride we went over the Cascade mountain range. It got a little cold as we rolled into Coeur d'Alene, Idaho, and I could feel a little vibration under my bed. I looked out over the ramps and could see some lug nuts missing from our rear wheel, and the remaining nuts were loose and the wheel was wobbling. Of course the guys couldn't hear me yell, especially with their windows up. We finally got to red light and I jumped off and yelled loud enough to get their attention.

Our first destination was the Lincoln, Nebraska shop of our car builder, Don Maxwell. Don was a cool guy, and very smart. He built some of the best cars of the day. Our first Midwestern race was at Oskaloosa, Iowa, and there was a parade of great racers from Lincoln there that day. Gary Dunkle, Dick Morris, Lonnie Jenson, and Don Maxwell, among others.

Osky was a good introduction to Midwest sprint car racing; it was big and fast, with long flat corners where you could run almost wide open. Two of the new guys I met that day—Bill Robinson and Greg Helms—had deep red eyes from a flip the previous weekend. It was a vivid reminder that this was some serious racing. Jimmy Boyd won at Oskaloosa in Kenny Woodruff's car and we were third. Man, I loved Oskaloosa.

The next day my first laps around Knoxville Raceway were memorable. I was amazed and impressed that a track could be that fast. One good part of racing during this era was the fact that everyone knew the dangers and respected each other a lot more than today. You didn't see fathers spending a lot of money to put their young kid in a car, because back then there was a fairly good chance the kid might not be coming home with them that night.

Maybe that's one reason it was easier to get rides back then.

I knew immediately that Knoxville was a place I wanted to come back and race again. Later, I would twice move to the Midwest to do just that, the same way so many other people have done, people from all over the U.S. and Australia.

Knoxville looked very different at this time. Outside turn four was a grandstand that was very old but strong and held probably 800 people. The remainder of the grandstands along the front straightaway were newer, but seemed shorter. There was an old barn behind where the office is now that was called the Arizona barn. This is where the famous shady card games took place. Each August, every barn was full of race cars for the Nationals.

The track seemed to be banked a little more at that time, and it felt stickier. There were two metal guardrails around the outside, and it was easy to flip out of the place. In fact, many cars did. Lenard McCarl once flipped out of turn three and landed out near one of the barns. The tires of the day were four-ply sidewall tires with a very square edge on the outside and were 96 inches around. They were called Diamonds and when you slid into the cushion these tires would really grip. They also gripped when you hit a rut or a hole and it was a treacherous situation.

In an effort to loosen the grip and reduce the number of flips the track mandated at least 20 pounds of air in the right rear tire. Earl Wagner—who was a great racer in his day—was the lead official and his word was the law.

Knoxville! What a track and what a town. I would grow to love this place more and more as the years went on.

Another track we visited on this trip was Belleville, Kansas. Known as the Belleville Highbanks, this is without a doubt the fastest and most treacherous track I have ever raced. It is bigger than Eldora, and the progressive banking makes the fast groove right up next to the (short) guardrail. From the track you can see bushes lining the outside of the back straightaway…except those are tree-tops, not bushes. So it could be a long drop if you went over the fence there. That was my guess; luckily I never tried it.

The weather had been very wet in the days leading up to the race, and the track was rough. At most tracks a rough surface would cause the car to hook and bounce up; but at Belleville your car is planted with too much force for the car to bounce. It sort of jumps around and with each bump it feels like the steering wheel is being wrenched from your hands.

It was hot and humid that night, and we won our heat race. When I drove back to our pit I realized I had sweated through both layers of my uniform, and I knew this was going to be a tough night.

During one of the heat races a driver from South Dakota barrel-rolled the length of the back straightaway and landed with the car on fire. He was killed outright.

He had towed his car there with a station wagon, and his wife and kids were looking on. This was the first time I had experienced a fatal accident at a race where I was competing. (Many years later I would see another fatality at Belleville in a midget.)

They hauled the poor guy from South Dakota off and we went back to racing. We were running in the top four in the feature, and about 20 laps into the race my motor started running really crappy. For the first—and last—time in my career I was glad to have a motor lay down. Thank you very much; I'll just drive this thing to the pits.

Later that night, when we were all at the pay window, the man's wife was standing there in hysterics, pleading with the promoter and asking him what she should do. It was one of the saddest things I've ever experienced.

The top three cars that night all had power steering. They weren't necessarily the fastest cars but they were the only guys who could hold on to the steering wheel for the entire race.

Our next stop was Mason City, Iowa where our engine was really shaking in hot laps. I pulled into the pits and told Duke what was going on. "We have to qualify, does it bother your vision?"

"No, I can see okay."

So off we go to qualify and it held together for one lap. I should have been satisfied with that but I figured I could improve my time so I kept going for my second lap. That's when whatever was shaking broke, and that was that.

Our spare engine didn't have a set of injectors installed, so our motor change took a little longer than normal. We went out for our heat race and the ignition timing was off pretty bad and we were shooting ducks all the way around the track. The racing gods smiled upon us and there was a caution; I pulled to the inside of the track with the engine running.

Duke and Gary Patterson hurried over and yanked the hood off the car. Duke loosened the magneto hold-down and GP turned the mag while Duke revved the engine. Patterson yelled, "Lock 'er down!" and we were back in business. We didn't have time to put the hood back on and off we go. I realized two things during that heat race: one, a tremendous amount of air blows through the car at 100 mph; two, the front wheels of a sprint car flop around a lot.

Later we returned to Mason City for a daytime race and the promoter had the idea that if he didn't prepare the inside groove nobody would run down there. When the feature started, of course that's where the pole car went as quickly as he could. Nobody behind his rear wheels could see a thing. Doug Wolfgang drove off into a cornfield, and I remember bumping into something on the backstretch. I quickly discovered it was Shane Carson in the Nance car. The promoter realized his mistake and he paid the race as you qualified.

One night we left Knoxville and headed for a race at North Star Speedway in St. Paul, Minnesota. That's a pretty good haul and we had to hustle to get there. I was leading in Duke's hauler and Gary Patterson was following in Walt Ross's truck. We had CB radios, and Gary came on to tell me he just saw a set of headlights pull out and he was going to slow down to check it out.

A few minutes later I heard, "Buckwheat, you've definitely got a bear on your ass!"

Sure enough the cop pulled me over, and he waved GP over as well. I explained that we had just raced at Knoxville and would have to change our engine before racing tomorrow at St. Paul, and we had to hurry. He took my license and walked back to GP.

"Going a little fast, weren't you?" the cop says. GP explained that we blew up tonight and we're trying to get to Minnesota. As GP handed over his license the cop says, "Yeah, I've heard that one before!"

The cop wrote us both a ticket and we went on down the road. At that time the states didn't share information like they do today, so we didn't bother to check on paying the fine. We just drove carefully in Iowa for several years after that, thinking that those old tickets sometimes accumulate interest as the years go by.

We blew out a lot of tires on Duke's hauler, and we wondered if we were a little overloaded. Kinda curious, you might say. One day an Iowa Highway Patrolman was curious as well and he made us follow him to the nearest grain terminal where we were weighed. He let us continue on our way…after Duke paid a little fine, of course.

Another minor problem on the hauler was the fact that our power steering pump had a pretty bad leak, and fluid seemed to run right through it. It took a lot of strength to turn the wheel, which was pretty good training for running Belleville.

We won a case of STP at an IMCA race and we had the idea of pouring a can of STP into the pump. I mean, thicker oil will leak more slowly out of the seals, right? It didn't run out as fast, but when it did it made a helluva mess.

Eventually the bushing on the top of the steering column wore out from too much load, and if you were turning hard left something in the column would grab the shifter and throw it toward Park or Reverse. So a left turn became a two-man operation; one guy would turn the wheel and the other guy grabbed the shifter to keep it from slamming into Park. One time Duke was asleep in the truck and I woke him up.

"What's wrong?" he said.

"Left turn."

Without a moment's thought he grabbed the shifter. Now that's an efficient operation right there.

After running the 1975 Knoxville Nationals we started to work our way back west. Me, Duke and John Boy first headed to Don Maxwell's shop because Randy Hunt and Don had a nitrous oxide system he wanted Duke to take home and work with. As we exited I-80 the hauler's fuel pump started going out.

Duke had an unconventional solution. He put his mouth on the opening on the tank and blew air into it, pushing the gas up into the carburetor enough that we were able to get going again. Duke must have had some great lungs because he blew us the remaining eight miles into Lincoln.

The next day we replaced the fuel pump and got everything loaded up to head for Sedalia, Missouri. Don gave us some Goodyear rain tires to try at Sedalia, and our tire rack was already so full we used a rope to tie the three mounted tires on the rack. It was an early example of a philosophy I would see repeated dozens of times in racing through the years: "What could possibly go wrong?"

It was getting dark and Duke was tired—still worn out from blowing us into Lincoln, I suspect—and he decided that sleeping on the side of the truck ramp wasn't such a bad idea after all. It was a cool night in early autumn, and John Boy and I were tooling along in the cab of the truck, heater on and listening to rock & roll on the radio. We were running about 70 mph when all of a sudden somebody was banging on the passenger window of the truck. It scared the hell out of us; how could we be receiving visitors this time of night? Good thing it was only Duke, but he had a look of panic on his face. Well, maybe not "panic" but let's just say that he looked very concerned.

Somehow the tires had come untied and fell right on top of him, with the mounted right front wheel trailing us on the Interstate with the rope still through it. (Okay, well, *that's* what could go wrong.) Duke managed to reel it in as he was screaming at us to stop the truck before he fell off and died on Interstate 29. After he retrieved the wheel he had nowhere else to lay down, and at this point he really didn't have sleeping on his mind. Duke climbed over the race car and shimmied along the outside of the tire racks at 70 mph to finally knock on our window.

However, the rain tires worked pretty well at Sedalia and we won the daytime show. They followed it up with a nighttime program, where we ran third.

Our next stop was Dewey, Oklahoma, a sticky short track that allowed you to run any fuel you wanted. Duke dumped in a little nitromethane and we were off to the races, so to speak. Bobby Marshall won it, Rick Ferkel was second, and we were third until the nitro caused a small explosion in the engine.

We hooked up with Patterson and Hans Paulson to travel together the rest of the way back to California. Going through Colorado I rode with GP and Hans rode with Duke and John Boy. Coming west out of Denver you encounter a 10,000-foot summit that is steep and long. GP and I got over the top all right and we pulled over to wait for Duke. It must have been 30 minutes later when they came rolling to the summit, barely moving, steam belching from the radiator. A hundred yards short of the summit Duke's throttle foot was flat on the floor and John Boy and Hans had to get out and help push the final hundred yards to the peak.

We waited a little while to allow the truck to cool down, then away we went again. A few miles down the road we encountered a good-looking girl hitchhiking. Of course we immediately pulled over to give her a lift.

It was a downhill grade, and after a few miles Duke built up enough momentum to get a run on us. When he swung out to pass we asked our passenger if she would mind ducking down out of sight for just a moment, and as Duke and the guys went past we looked at them and grinned.

To this day their warped minds have the idea that our passenger was pleasuring us. Heathens with dirty minds!

We got home just in time to catch a NARC race and as soon as I went out for hot laps I smelled the nitro we had used in Oklahoma. I drove back to our pit and told Duke, and we diluted the fuel as much as we could. We still had enough in the tank to set fast time!

Somewhere along the way during our Midwestern tour Duke called John Sullivan "John Boy" and the nickname stuck throughout the trip—and beyond. John embraced the name, and later when he went into business— he made the first swedged aluminum radius rods and steering links for sprint cars—he called his business "JB Enterprises." John later expanded his business to build complete sprint cars.

I've always thought nicknames were cool…for other people. One day while driving Dwayne Starr's car I walked into Tognotti Speed Shop and Jay Bolton, who worked at Tognotti's, saw me come in.

I had curly hair that was really long—like an Afro—and Jay hollered, "Hey, Buckwheat!"

I just lowered my head and thought, "Oh shit, I hope that doesn't stick."

It stuck.

Halfway around the world in Australia, people called me Buckwheat. All the way on the east coast, people called me Buckwheat. In Indiana and Kansas and Florida, people called me Buckwheat. In Canada and in New Zealand, people called me Buckwheat.

I didn't mind the name too much and, in a way, got used to it. After a while it was just something I didn't pay much attention to. Then one day I was picking up my daughter Stephanie from school, and another first-grade kid yelled out, "Hey, Buckwheat!"

My immediate thought was that I didn't want my daughter to grow up with a dad named Buckwheat. I was an adult, and I had never heard any adult referred to as "Buckwheat."

But what could I do? The name had really stuck by that point.

In 1991 Bruce Richardson wrote a very nice profile story about me in *OPEN WHEEL Magazine*. During the interview Bruce asked if there was anything I wanted to say. I explained that I really don't like the name

"Buckwheat." Bruce was nice enough to print that comment.

Unfortunately, it had exactly the opposite effect as intended. The very next race after the issue was published, all I heard was, "Hey, Buckwheat!" "Hello, Buckwheat!" "What's up, Buckwheat?" I couldn't take two steps without hearing Buckwheat.

It has mostly passed at this point—maybe it's because I don't wear my hair in an Afro—but every once in a while I hear it.

"Hey, Buckwheat!" I still hate that nickname.

7

On our own

In preparation for our trip to Australia in late 1976, we loaded our stuff into a container and shipped it Down Under. After we finished I was just hanging out, waiting to fly out with the other American racers making the trip. That's when Bill Shadle invited me to join him on a trip to Death Valley. Bill and Duke McMillen had sold a welder to a guy down there, and it had to be delivered. Bill also had a cousin in the area and the plan was to visit him as well.

Bill had a short-wheelbase Chevy pickup and we piled in for the ride south.

During this era, any trip—with anyone—called for a couple of beers along the way. Somebody had given Bill a bag of radishes—yeah I know, that's kind of random—and we were eating the radishes and knocking back a few beers as we rode south.

We were smoking down Hwy. 395 when we spotted two girls who were hitchhiking. We gave them a ride, but they were not overly impressed with two guys who smelled like beer and radishes. We dropped them off a short distance down the highway.

We delivered the welder, then went to visit Bill's cousin, who owned a ranch and a campground. It was nightfall and I noticed that the lights were very dim in the house. The cousin explained that the home's electricity was generated by the water running off the mountain behind the ranch. If you've ever been to Death Valley one of the first things you notice is that there isn't much water; that's why the lights were dim.

After we went to bed it got really dark. There was absolutely no light pollution, and it was a moonless night. Man, it was dark as a cave.

The next day we had breakfast and went outside. There were a bunch of pet burros wandering around, and we went over to pet them. We immediately discovered that their hides were full of burrs, and petting them was hard on the hands.

We decided to go four-wheeling out in the nearby desert, and we went up through the canyon to the Barker Ranch. This is where Charles Manson and his followers used to hang out, and where he was arrested following the Tate and La Bianca murders. It was easy to see why the police had a hard time catching him because Manson had lookouts posted who could warn him and he could hide. When he was arrested they found him hiding in a cabinet under the bathroom sink.

The Barker ranch is quite large, and it sits right on the state line. We exited the ranch into Nevada and found an old Victorian house that was a bar, casino, and brothel. We stopped in for a drink, and I won $200 on the dice table. Let's see, I covered the bar and the casino, what was that third thing they offered? Hmmm…

So I went for a clean sweep.

By the time we got back on the road it was dark and we were intoxicated, so they insisted that I drive. Looking back, that definitely was not the best choice.

I was doing what I do best, driving fast. That may have led to an over-rev, causing the fan belt to depart our vehicle somewhere out in the desert. This resulted in overheating; it's always a cause-and-effect.

We realized the truck was overheating and we shut it off before we hurt anything. We spent the rest of the night driving until the truck got hot, then sleeping while it cooled down, then driving again. Lather, rinse, repeat.

The sun was just peeking over the horizon when we got back home. Just another episode of the fabulous adventures of hanging out with my friends.

I mentioned the Mazda pickup earlier, and I should say a few words of homage about the vehicle. This truck had a very hard life.

You know how, when you get a new vehicle, you have that period of newness where you treat it very carefully? No eating or drinking, keep it washed, and driving it very gently? Well, the Mazda had no such grace period. From the first time it came off the lot it was driven hard, and it was all downhill from there.

When it was brand new Mike Andreetta and I drove it to a Christmas party held by Wayne Sue and his wife Beverly. On the way up to Live Oak we bought a twelve pack of beer for the party.

Mike carried in the beer and after a greeting at the door and two steps into the room the bag tore and the beer hit the floor, producing a large area of foam. Before the first bottle hit the floor Mike was headed for the couch, saying "Sills look what you did!"

I was still a rookie kid, intimidated by all the veteran drivers. Every eye in the place was looking at me, and I was really on the spot. Bev Sue handed me the mop and I was in charge of clean-up.

On the way home I was showing Mike how fast my new truck was. When it got close to 100 mph, a buzzer went off (due to over-revving). I was explaining to Mike that pretty soon the rest of the truck made so much noise that it would drown out the buzzer. Which was true, but the high speed caused a huge pocket of air to infiltrate the roof headliner. Suddenly the entire headliner turned into a roof air bag, literally covering us up to the point of blindness. Luckily we were on a straight road because we couldn't see a thing until I got slowed down.

At the end of the racing season I was driving Mike McCreary's car, which had manual steering. I figured we would be faster at Gold Cup if we installed power steering. Mike found a steering box, and I found a pump in Concord. It was on this trip that I experienced another educational episode with a rotary engine.

Mazda rotary engines use a small amount of oil that is injected into the rotors. This can eventually deplete the engine oil supply, but this isn't a problem if you keep your eye on the oil level. Which, I didn't.

We were almost into the town of Fairfield when I felt the engine begin to seize. I quickly took it out of gear and shut off the engine, coasting into a gas station. I replenished the oil supply, but the damage was done. The primary problem was a burned-out seal at the back of the engine. If you kept power on you were okay, but the moment you let off the throttle the car emitted a blinding smoke screen.

This didn't interrupt our mission to get the pump and the ol' Mazda soldiered on.

When I left for Australia my sister Peggy needed a vehicle to drive so I let her use the truck while I was away. My last words to her were, "Be careful in the rain, because the rear end is very light and it gets loose easily." It was a foretelling of events yet to come.

When I got back a couple of months later the Mazda had a bent right rear wheel and a bent rear end housing. It was raining, Peggy missed her line, too much throttle, got loose, and pounded the right rear into the curb.

Later that spring I was away when my older sister Carleen used the Mazda to go camping. On the trip home she loaded the barbecue grill in the back and took off, and the air flow across the barbecue got things going and the next thing you know she's got a nice little fire. She managed to keep the damage to a minimum, but the paint was charred in the bed.

The next Mazda adventure came when the truck was stolen and was missing in action for a couple of weeks. Then I got a call from the police; they had found it in a field wrapped up in a barbed wire fence. It had several dents and scratches but it still ran okay.

We had the body repaired and my sister Marcy took the wheel. She was working at Tognotti Speed Shop, and became acquainted with some local drag racers. Sacramento Raceway was on Excelsior Road near Mather Air Force Base, and it's fairly remote out there on Jackson Highway or CA 16. People drive pretty fast because it's so remote.

One night Marcy brought the Mazda to a fitting and premature end when she pulled out in front of somebody while exiting the speedway. Marcy was very lucky she wasn't hurt, because it was a hard hit. The Mazda went away to that great salvage yard in the sky but I still have lots of good memories.

But man, that truck endured a lot. For a while after that whenever I walked onto a car lot I could almost hear the vehicles begging and pleading: "Dear God, please don't let him pick me…"

When I arrived home from Australia in February 1977 I didn't have a ride lined up for the upcoming season. So I sat out a few races until Ed Watson came out with a new car, a really good-looking piece.

Ed's car was a Maxwell chassis, and I had run a Maxwell with pretty good success the year before. However, I could never get Ed's new car to work for me, couldn't get it to work like I wanted. After my tenure in the car Ed hired Dub May from Pennsylvania and later Gary Howard of Southern California, but neither of them could do much with the car either.

Several years later I learned the backstory of this car, and it explained a lot. It seems that Ed had put a deposit down with Don Maxwell for a new car, but Maxwell didn't have enough tubing to build a car right away. Ed had a way of insisting on getting what he wanted, and he got a Maxwell car. However, Maxwell used .120-wall tubing, and he built Ed the heaviest and most rigid sprint car ever.

John Boy and I teamed up again to take Ed's car to the Midwest, hoping to find a track it liked. Ed stayed home, and when we blew our only engine Ed told us to come on home.

However, John Boy and I hatched a plan. We decided to go to Butch Bahr's shop in Grand Island, Nebraska and used Butch's machine tools to build a new engine out of spare parts. A plan involving spare parts seldom works out, but the Knoxville Nationals were only a week away and we couldn't bear the thought of missing the Nationals.

Ed gave us his approval and we made it happen. Our next race was Mason City, Iowa, where the new motor immediately blew up. Doug Wolfgang told me that Dave Van Patton had a spare engine sitting at Bob Trostle's shop. I called Dave and he said we could meet with him when we got to Des Moines.

My call to Ed was that we were running ok when something broke on the car. I figured it would be better if I didn't share any explicit details about the motor blowing up because I figured Ed would insist that we come home immediately.

Dave said, "Son, I won't put my motor in your car, but if you want to get my car out of the shed and fix it up, that's fine. You'll need to clean it up and fix the water pump, and it's all yours. But you have to run all the NSCA races while you're here."

That was definitely no problem, because we would have probably raced all those events anyway.

My girlfriend Karen came out to travel with us for a few races. We were towing with a short-wheelbase Chevy step-side pickup and an open trailer. I guess three of us in the cab of that truck got to be a bit much, and I could feel tension between John Boy and Karen.

We qualified for the Saturday night A-feature at Knoxville, and we were drinking beer with Gary Patterson and Walt Ross in one of the barns to celebrate. Karen and John Boy started arguing back and forth until it turned into a major shouting match.

Approximately 90 percent of all fights involve a woman in some way, and this was no exception. JB finally stepped over the line with something he said, and it was on. He and I were rolling around in the sawdust and cow shit, just like you see in a western movie or TV show.

As we were rolling around I got a mouthful of sawdust (and probably some cow shit) and I began coughing and choking. That's when the fight took a turn for the worse. There are no rules in barn fighting, and when my ass whooping was complete I looked like Rocky. I kept wondering when Mickey was going to cut my eye so I could see, and I kept calling Karen, "Adrian!"

That led to a parting of the ways with John Boy. I then recruited my nephews—12 and 10 years old, respectively—and some of Dave's grandkids as my crew. We got as high as fifth in the Saturday feature but dropped out just before the end of the race.

We ran pretty well at some of the NSCA races, finishing in the top five and winning one. We made enough money to get home, and I put Karen on an airplane and started the long drive back to California.

I will never forget that drive. It started on the day Elvis Presley died—August 16, 1977—and the radio stations were playing non-stop Elvis songs. I wasn't a big fan, so I stopped in Wyoming and bought a Jackson Browne 8-track. By the time I got home I knew the lyrics of every song on that tape.

I could never pull this off now, but I was able to race Dave Van Patton's car for six races with Ed believing it was his car. This would be impossible today with social media, etc.

What I did wasn't right, and I know it. If someone did that to me I would be pissed. I would call Ed after the race and give the results, and it just never came up which car I was driving.

However, as I was traveling home, Ed somehow found out what had happened and the party was over. I wheeled into Ed's body shop with the race rig, unaware that Ed knew all about the little charade. Tim Lowery (a great hot rod builder today) was working for Ed, and Tim got to witness my ass chewing. Tim recently told me he never saw Ed that mad, before or after that day.

One good thing that happened after my episode with Ed was that I got a call from Bruce Bromme. Bruce owned a sprint car that raced with CRA, one of the best cars in southern California. Their driver, Dean Thompson, was injured and Bruce needed somebody to fill in at a CRA race at Ascot.

Beating the CRA guys at Ascot was a dream of mine. So I jumped at the chance and told Bruce I'd be honored to drive his car.

However, when I got into the seat there was an obvious problem: my head was sticking way too high in the cage. It was so high, in fact, that I literally had to bend down and crane my neck to look under the front crossbar.

But there was no way I was going to let that stop me from driving this legendary race car. If I got into a crash—especially at a fast track like Ascot—I would very likely suffer a head injury, or worse. It wasn't the smartest decision but I really wanted to drive Bruce's car.

It performed just as well as I imagined it would. We were fast, and in the feature race I found myself chasing down the leader, Tommy Hunt. It was only a matter of time before I passed him and fulfilled my dream of winning against the CRA guys at Ascot. But just as I caught Tommy, our driveline broke.

Winning a CRA race was always special and I later did so at Placerville, Chico, and Petaluma, all in northern California. I also won with CRA at Manzanita and later the Oval Nationals at Perris. None of that would compare to beating them at Ascot.

It's always tough when you feel like you should have won a race but didn't. But some disappointments are bigger than others; that night at Ascot was one of the big ones, and I've never forgotten that sick feeling when I pulled into the infield and climbed from the car.

"If only..." That's a phrase we racers use a lot. If only...

8

Birth of the Outlaws

In early 1978 I got a call from Archie Simpson asking me to drive his car that season. This was a good car, the No. 86 that Steve Kinser had driven in Florida and at the Knoxville Nationals the previous August. Archie and Jerry Smith, the chief mechanic and partner in the car were based in Columbia, Missouri. Larry McCown, another silent partner in the car, lived in Sedalia.

The sprint car world was in the midst of a huge change. Ted Johnson had launched the World of Outlaws, and Jimmy Boyd won their first race in March 1978 at the Devil's Bowl in Texas. Jimmy and his car owner, Kenny Woodruff, were getting $500 show-up money as series point leader for the next race at Eldora.

Woodruff told me I could catch a ride with him to connect with Archie and get my season going. We headed east and our first stop was at Speedway Motors in Lincoln, Nebraska where Doug Wolfgang and Tommy Sanders were prepping the Vice Grip No. 4x for the season.

My first race with Archie was at Lakeside Speedway in Kansas City. Lakeside is a big half-mile, and they had a formula which allowed you to run any engine you wanted and run without a wing, or you could use a 16-sf top wing with an engine limit of 317-ci.

Can you imagine that today? This was an interesting time, when change was in the air in a lot of ways.

It seemed like every badass sprint car racer in America was at Lakeside that night. I was eager to get some seat time, but Archie and the car didn't show up until hot laps had finished. So my first lap at speed would be during qualifying.

We pushed off on the front straightaway and I tried to gain speed to take the green for my first qualifying lap. As I came off turn two I couldn't feel the front end, and the car pushed to the wall, then pushed to the infield wall, then back to the outside wall. And this was all happening very quickly.

All the experience I had gained at this early point in my career told me the next push to the right would result in a big crash. So I spun into the infield. The push truck driver yelled at me to put the car in gear so he could push me off. "Hell no!" I yelled back. At that point I wasn't sure I wanted to drive this car, even with the engine off.

He rolled me back to my pit and I hurried over to grab Kenny Woodruff and ask if he would look at the car before I gave it another try. Kenny looked at the front axle and said in his low voice, "Bud, the king pin is rolled forward."

In a few short words Kenny explained the principle of reverse castor. I'm not sure I got all of what he was saying, but I was definitely sure something had to be fixed or I was going to crash this thing all the way across the Missouri River.

Jerry Smith fixed the front end and we got one lap at the end of the qualifying order. The car was actually pretty good, and we finished third that night with a little help. Fred Linder towed in from Ohio with a Nance car with coil-over springs and the 317-ci package, and he blew up while leading the race. We were running fourth but with Fred's misfortune we made the podium.

The next night was at Paragon, Indiana, where it was so cold that people were building campfires in the grandstands. This night brought one of Steve Kinser's first starts in Karl Kinser's car, and it also put me into a fraternity that would eventually include probably a hundred other racers: we finished second to Steve and Karl Kinser.

We had damaged our car a little bit from a tangle in our heat race, so we towed up to Indianapolis and the shop of Lloyd Shores, one of the leading chassis builders in the region. Danny Smith was working for Lloyd, and Danny welded on the car until around 2 a.m. We then hurried to get to Eldora for the very first World of Outlaws event there. It was April 30, 1978.

I had read about some of the fast race tracks of the Midwest, but Eldora was unlike any track I had seen up to that point. Fast, fast, fast. I felt good about qualifying sixth and I made the transfer from my heat race, putting me on the pole for the feature. This was a day race, and the track was drying out. My guys had also never been to Eldora; they put on the setup they usually ran at a day race on the tracks around home, which was two Firestone Diamond tires on the rear with two inches of stagger.

The green flag waved for the feature and my car drove straight for the fence in turn one. I got the car aimed in the other direction and it did the same thing at the other end. In the interest of self-preservation and public safety I pulled into the infield and figured I'd be a good spectator at this one. I watched Rick Ferkel win the race, driving with one hand while holding his helmet shield with the other, lapping up to fourth place on a rough track with no power steering. I decided right then that Rick Ferkel is a unique specimen.

At the end of the first weekend I had made some money and figured Archie's car was a pretty solid opportunity. I decided to return home and move my girlfriend, Karen, to Columbia for the summer.

Karen was good with the plan so we loaded Herbie the cockatoo and everything we owned into our Chevy van and a 10-foot U-Haul trailer. Columbia is the home of the University of Missouri, so rental properties were kinda scarce. We sub-let an apartment from a couple of Middle Eastern guys who were going home for the summer; once we got used to the curry smell it wasn't a bad setup.

Archie and his guys had a sponsorship deal with Olympia Beer. I don't know if any cash money was involved, but the deal included a case of Oly every Saturday for the trip to Knoxville. The beer would end up in my van and a couple of the crew guys would sip on a few cans on the way to the track. It was always a little embarrassing when we pulled up to the sign-in area and when the sliding door on the van opened a couple of beer cans fell on the ground and rolled way. That is a unique sound that everyone recognizes! And you know, somehow there was never any of the Oly left when the races had finished.

Every race team needs a PR guy, an organizer, and a comedian. Archie's team had all three roles in one guy: Mosely, or just Moze. He was the one responsible for Oly beer, procuring and consuming. Moze was also deathly afraid of snakes and spiders, so whenever a hose or belt was found in the pit area the guys threw it at Moze and he would take off running. One night he was under the rear end changing gears when a spider dropped down onto his face. Of course he freaked and raised straight up, ramming his forehead into the quarter-inch studs on the back of the rear end. Now he's not only screaming and running full speed across the pit area, but his whole face is covered in blood. Quite a sight!

One day at the shop we captured a huge hairy spider that would jump at you. We immediately gave the spider an assignment and put together a plan. We covered the spider with a paper cup and placed it on a race flyer and waited for Moze to show up. When he arrived we began talking about a certain race and the discussion soon centered on the exact date of the race. It was only a matter of time before Moze began looking for that flyer and found it under the cup. When he lifted the cup and reached for the flyer the spider performed his assignment perfectly, jumping right at Moze as if on cue. Moze seemed to be frozen in shock as he tried to suck in enough oxygen to both scream and run at the same time.

Looking back, we probably weren't doing Moze's heart much good.

Archie's main wrench and partner, Jerry Smith, also owned another car in addition to working with us. A couple of other guys were also involved as a partner with Archie to varying degrees. Our car was a Stapp chassis, and Jerry's car was a McCarl car with a 317-ci engine, which allowed him to run a wing at Lakeside. The car also had power steering which was really nice until it started blowing hot oil out of the top seal.

One of the top tracks in the Columbia area was at the Missouri State Fairgrounds at Sedalia, which became one of my favorite tracks. It had plenty of racing room, was flat but fast, and we won a couple of races there.

There were actually two tracks at Sedalia; the half-mile dirt and a one-mile dirt track. They only ran the mile track once each year, and I was eager to get a shot at it.

Unfortunately, as the mile date approached the owners of the No. 86 car decided to park the car and split up the partnership. We had just won the Fair race on the half-mile the previous week with Steve Shultz as our setup man.

I took my helmet bag to the mile in hopes of finding a ride, and I had good luck. It was a nice-looking Nance car that Jay Woodside had been driving, but apparently Jay didn't want to run the mile that day. Jay was a former winner of the Knoxville Nationals and if he was driving this car, it was probably a good car. I didn't know Jay personally, but I knew that he was a big guy.

I jumped in the car to fit the belts, and immediately noticed that the seat was huge and the shoulder harnesses were too long to hold me snug in the seat. They tried to fit it up better, but when we pushed off I was still a little uncomfortable in that big seat.

As I rolled slowly around the track, the corners seemed to go on forever and when you cleared the corner the straightaway was so long it was like you couldn't see clear to the other end. Man, this is the best! I'm finally running on the mile! I couldn't wait for them to throw the green flag and I could run wide open down that long straightaway.

But when I stepped on the throttle the engine ran like crap. But even with the motor running crappy, I was still hauling ass. I mean, this was a whole new definition of "fast."

I didn't feel very secure, sliding around in that enormous seat, and that's when I noticed that the shoulder harnesses were so loose they were flapping in the wind. Well, okay, we've got some work to do with the ol' gal.

There was a small hump along the outside of turn four where the half-mile track merged with the mile track. This caused the car to squat in the rear and pogo a couple of times due to the lack of shock rebound. The ride height of the car was so low that the torque tube would hit the bottom of the seat when I rolled across that hump. This is when I discovered that the bolt holding the back section of the seat was missing. So every time the torque tube hit the seat bottom it threw the top of the seat forward and I would move several inches until I used up the slack in the shoulder harnesses. Because of the pogo effect this would happen two times in quick—very quick—succession every time I crossed that hump.

As much as I really wanted to race that day, the angel of common sense on my shoulder convinced me I might live longer if I just went to the beer tent. So that's what I did, and I watched Shane Carson blow 'em away in Bob Trostle's wedge car.

It was a good season running in the Midwest. Our local schedule took us to Lakeside on Friday night, Knoxville on Saturday night, and Marshall, Missouri on Sunday night. We raced with a lot of great racers: Gary Scott, Doug Wolfgang, Shane Carson, John Stevenson, Mike Brooks, Rick Weld, Bill Utz, Randy Smith, Dick Morris, and several others. I learned a ton during this time, especially at Knoxville when it developed a two-foot cushion right out next to the guardrail.

The summer drew short and Knoxville had one final weekend of racing on Labor Day weekend. I called Fred Aden from Lincoln, Nebraska, and he agreed to bring the No. 4J car over for the weekend. Karen and I drove up with the idea of sleeping in our van each night. I was very excited to drive Fred's car, as I remembered Eddie Leavitt winning the Knoxville Nationals in the car in 1976 with John Singer as the mechanic and engine builder.

We arrived at the track and Karen headed up to the stands to sit with some friends. There would be drinks involved, which would help get Karen through the night of racing.

When the driver's meeting began, every driver in the pit area had a car...except me. In the spirit of good faith I suited up to be ready when Fred and the No. 4J came rolling in. That didn't happen, and as the night progressed the madder I got. I felt that at the very least Fred could have called the track and sent word to me that he couldn't make it.

I was mad enough that when the races had finished I decided to immediately drive back to Columbia and skip the racing the next day.

But when I got to the van Karen had a different idea. She didn't relish the thought of driving four hours home and then me getting over being pissed off and wanting to drive back to Knoxville the next morning.

After much discussion we piled into the van and headed south out of Knoxville. Karen climbed into the back to sleep. We had made just a few miles down the road when Karen snuck up behind me and punched me right in the eye. I hit the brakes and she went flying into the dashboard. I pulled off the road for another round of discussions, which consisted of us screaming at each other.

After a few minutes we got back into the van and continued on. I think I drove for about 30 minutes and was starting to relax when she socked me again. Same eye, same process. Brakes, dashboard, screaming. I finally decided to park and sleep right there, and we called it a night.

The next day I swallowed my pride and drove back to Knoxville, black eye and all. Fred showed up for that one, and we ran second. Things had gone well enough that we decided to head west to Erie, Colorado to race with the Outlaws.

Al Unser Jr. was there, and it was the very beginning of his career. He was driving Walter Judd's car, and I was amazed at how small the seat was. But you could definitely see that Little Al was destined for great things.

It seemed that every time I raced at Erie we had a big thunderstorm, like it was part of the normal racing program. When it quit raining we ironed out the track and started the heat races.

I was in the first heat, and I noticed a big puddle coming off turn four. I had the lead coming out of two and I had a plan: when I get to turn four, I'll just clip the edge of the puddle and throw enough water onto the track to slow the guys behind me. I guess I caught a little too much of the puddle because as I passed the flag stand I could see the starter reaching for the yellow flag. When I got back around under caution I saw almost the entire field in a pile in turn four. I don't think they were very happy with me at that moment.

Charlie Swartz took a big flip off turn one that night in Gary Stanton's car, which almost took Charlie's thumb off.

Later that night we were celebrating a good night of racing and somebody had some pot. I hadn't smoked any weed since high school, and I assumed this stuff would have the same potency as the stuff from way back when. Wrong! Karen and I were so stoned that it took us an hour to find our campground spot.

We ran well enough at Erie—finishing second to Steve Kinser—that we stayed with the car and headed west. Deuce Turrill was turning the wrenches, and I had high hopes. But when we got to the sticky California tracks and put a wing on the car the motor just didn't have enough juice to pull it.

My memory is sketchy, but I recall that Fred had a guy named Arnie from Nebraska building his motors and the one he sent out west was not right. When they adjusted the valves we found Arnie may have had too much to smoke when this thing was put together.

Fred's team had no shortage of stuff to smoke. We kept the car at Duke McMillen's shop, and one day we were heading to West Capital with me in the front passenger seat. The guys in the hauler were smoking weed so I rolled down my window so I wouldn't get high on the second-hand smoke (there may be performance-enhancing drugs for racing, but I don't think weed is one of them.) Deuce was driving the hauler down the street in Sacramento, and naturally we were hauling ass because we were running late. Right about then a car pulled out from the right and stopped in our lane.

Fred's tow rig was a Dodge van with an extended back section where the generator was mounted. It was very heavy because it had to power the roof air conditioning and the huge stereo system. The trailer had huge tongue weight, which tends to lift the front wheels of the van. We were skidding at a high rate of speed toward this parked car and what looked to be certain disaster, especially for the guy behind the door of the parked car. At the very last moment a car to our left saw the impending collision and gave room for Deuce to move into the lane. Thus, a van full of stoners towing a sprint car avoided obliterating the idiot who pulled out in front of us. That near-miss scared all the inhabitants of the van straight.

For a little while.

9

First RV

Jan Flammer operated a speed shop in Carson City, Nevada, and his father owned a Chevrolet dealership right next door. Jan had a history in northern California pavement circles, building sprint cars and supermodifieds that were driven by Tom Silsby, Bill Gadda, and Gary Patterson. In early 1979 Jan decided to go dirt racing, and Duke McMillen built him a copy of a Maxwell sprint car.

A big factor in how any race car works is how well the motor runs. Jan's cars never had a shortage of power, even though they were kinda small in the 355-ci to 372-ci range.

Jan hired me to drive his new dirt car and our first outing was a wingless NARC race at West Capital, an afternoon race. Qualifying order is very important in those circumstances; we timed last in the order, when the track was slick and rough. That put us in the B-main. The heats didn't offer a transfer so we changed the rear suspension and won our heat, won the B-main, and won the feature from 19th.

This car proved to be hard to beat at West Capital and most of the tracks in Northern California. It was equally potent with or without the wing.

However, we didn't win at Calistoga. We led quite a few races, and several times Mike Andreetta ruined our party late in the race. During this period the field was fully inverted, so we often qualified in the top four and started in the back of the A-main. I was getting a lot of criticism for not being able to win at Calistoga; we could win everywhere else but couldn't get it done there.

One night I flipped hard at Calistoga, and the following night we were scheduled to run a $1,000-to-win open competition show at West Capital. We took the car to Duke's shop and assessed the damage. The car had hit on the top left side of the cage at a backward angle, and it pushed the entire cage forward. It also pulled the torsion bars way out of line in the rear.

Duke cut the rear cage brace and heated the rear torsion tubes and pushed them back down to their original height then strengthened the brace with a sleeve. The front cage brace was cracked partway around the dash, and Duke welded that up as well. We bolted the wing on and realized that the cage was so twisted that the wing was tilted way over to the right. So we built a four-inch extension to level out the wing.

Our repairs did the trick, because we won that night at West Capital. Most importantly, I kept the car on four wheels and didn't test our roll cage repair.

We headed east for the Midwestern season, and I drove over to Carson City to connect with Jan Flammer. He had a box van filled with tools, spare parts, a welder, and a parts cleaner. His trailer had dolly wheels on the front and a single axle. There were four people making the trip: myself, Jan, Rick Douglas (a good motor guy), and Bob Tobin, whom we called Bomber.

We laid out some foam mattresses across the top of the toolbox so that we could sleep while rolling down the road. If it got hot we would raise the rear door. This was before the days of toter homes and air conditioning, I might add. But it still beat sitting upright in a pickup truck for 12 to 15 hours at a time.

I had first shift behind the wheel, and after my stint crawled on top of the tool box to rest. I was in deep slumber when my bed/tool box dropped about six inches, and at the same time I heard something distinctly like the sound of a box van crashing. I wasn't sure what was going on until I realized I was floating in the air and out of the corner of my eye could see nothing but sagebrush.

Oh, now I get it! We've run off the road!

Sure enough, Jan had fallen asleep and when he drifted off the highway we clipped the end of a bridge abutment. When we finally got stopped and climbed out to look things over, we were amazed to find that the only damage was a lost mirror that was taken out by the bridge. We pulled some sagebrush out of the grill and we were good to go.

We arrived in Sedalia, Missouri where longtime friend Russell McNish let us stay in his home and utilize his shop. Russell closed his business while we were in town, so we had plenty of room in the shop and Russell was able to hang out with us.

We ran the Missouri Nationals and scored a 5th-place finish and a 3rd-place finish.

From there it was Eagle Raceway near Lincoln, Nebraska, where we ran second to Doug Wolfgang in Bob Trostle's car.

LaVern Nance was there with his famed "house car," and he asked if I would like to hot lap it and give him my assessment of the car. I was very honored to be asked, and I later drove for LaVern in Florida.

Knoxville Raceway had not hosted a winged race for several years, but they scheduled a "wings optional" show for July 21. All across the country the sport was trying to decide what direction to go: winged cars, or traditional cars with no wing. Knoxville was an important track and people from both sides were weighing in with which direction they should go. I think they scheduled the winged race as a way to gauge how the cars would race, and to test the reaction of the fans.

We qualified quick-time with a NEW TRACK RECORD. The old record was held by Kenny Weld, so I felt pretty good about setting a new mark.

I was standing at the concession stand getting something to eat when I heard the crowd yell. I looked up just in time to see a car flipping into the flag stand, completely taking it out.

It was a terrible crash. Dick Stoneking was the driver of the car, and he was killed in the accident. The flagman, Gary Johnson, suffered serious injuries and was unable to walk on his own again. Gary is a good man and was a good starter, and it was just a devastating situation.

The Knoxville community was shocked. Just a couple of weeks earlier—July 2—Darryl Dawley and Roger Larson were killed in a violent crash on the front straightaway.

Dawley and Larson were in wingless cars. Stoneking was not running a wing. Yet, somehow there was the belief that wings were the problem. Knoxville resisted, and said no more winged races. It would be three years later—1982—when Gary Scott's fatal crash at Knoxville finally brought about a move to wings.

We had a similar situation at Calistoga, where the debate about wings also raged. At two consecutive races at Calistoga I was sitting in my car ready for my heat race when someone was killed in a bad crash. Two straight races! Yet the track continued to say no to wings.

It wasn't until Gary Patterson was killed in 1982 that Calistoga finally accepted the inevitable.

Those against the use of wings argued that it cost an additional $800 every time you crash, and wings were more demanding on the motor.

Personally, I was definitely an advocate for wings because I knew they made the car safer. I was just getting going with this driving deal and I didn't want that "oh by the way" possibility—death—to cut short my life and career.

From Knoxville we headed for the Eldora Nationals. I had been to the Big E twice before, but had never crashed there. I made up for that little detail on this trip.

The first night we were starting the feature around mid-pack. Coming off turn four on the opening lap a car came across my right front, and as soon as my car turned left and squatted on the right rear and dug in. I was all set for a big, big ride. It was one of those long crashes where you're almost wishing it would knock you out because every part of your body is getting beat up, and the pain sensors are sending urgent messages to your brain but there isn't a thing you can do about it.

The next day we found a welding shop where we could repair the frame, and replaced almost all the bolt-on stuff. We raced that night with no problem, and I don't have any idea where we finished.

On the third and final night the track was dry and slick, so we softened the torsion bars to get some bite. There was a series of holes in three and four, and I ran through the holes because the grip was good. But with the soft bars the car hopped all over the place, so I moved up to run above the holes.

There was a red and I pulled into the pits. Jan said, "I don't know how you feel about it, but if you're going to go forward you'll have to run through those holes."

"Yeah, but the car didn't like it when I tried it a minute ago."

Jan just kind of looked at me, and I said, "Well, okay, I'll give it a try."

Two laps later there was another red, and yes it was for me. The car *really* didn't like it that time, and I'm here to testify that you don't have any easy crashes at Eldora.

By now we were completely out of spare parts, so we loaded the wrecked stuff into the box van and headed for home. I was the picture of good health: severe red-eye, and black and blue marks from head-to-toe. I rode along in the back of the van, self-medicating myself with beer as we rolled along.

We stopped at Topeka, Kansas to watch the Jayhawk Nationals, where I may have missed the chance of a lifetime. Thad Dosher was a local racer who won the Knoxville Nationals in 1967, and he had recently retired. We all know how that goes; you're doing fine until somebody says, "Hey, ya wanna drive my car?" So Thad stepped out of retirement and he put the car on the pole for the feature race.

Apparently he had a change of heart, and he asked if I was interested in driving the car in the feature. I was really tempted to say, "Here, hold my beer and watch this!" But I had consumed a little too much painkiller at that point, so I had to gracefully decline the opportunity.

When we got home we fixed the car and won three out of the next four races, including the Jimmy Gordon Memorial at West Capital, a race I had wanted to win for a long time. We also won the Tri-Holiday Championship.

But we still couldn't win at Calistoga. We won 11 races that year but my best at Calistoga was a couple of 2nd-place runs and three 3rd-place runs. People were still telling me that I couldn't win at Calistoga.

The fact is, I didn't care for Calistoga at that time. It was dark—the lights were really poor—and rough and full of rocks. The turns were much too tight for those long straightaways, and it was really hard for me to get comfortable there.

One of the problems was the car design of that time. There was much less offset in the rear wheels compared to today, and the cars had rear brakes located out by the birdcage that held the bearing to the axle. The birdcage positioned the torsion arm at the bottom and the radius rod at the top. As brake was applied the radius rod pushed on the frame at an uphill angle, which tried to lift the car. When you combined all this with the normal cornering forces at a high speed, and the fact that you're making a slight downhill run into the corners at Calistoga, it's the perfect recipe for a really hard flip.

And if you managed to get outside the fence—which a number of people did—you were greeted by a line of very stout trees which were placed there to keep cars from traveling farther out into the fairgrounds. However, those trees were an extremely dangerous threat to the driver.

If you needed to slow yourself down and get back to sobering reality, all you had to do was position yourself to stand in turn one and watch. It was almost a sure thing that somebody was going to eat it and it wasn't going to be pleasant.

Seeing something like does have an effect on you. It sounds funny but it's real. For example, a few years later I was standing with Doug Wolfgang watching the C-Main at the Western World Championship at Manzanita Raceway. Cheryl Glass, a very talented and beautiful black woman, was trying to transfer to the feature race. The track was still greasy, and Cheryl knew she needed to really get after it if she wanted to make the transfer.

Her right rear slid over the cushion and tagged the wall. The car began a series of monster flips that brought her all the way to the top of the wall where she flipped a bunch of times, then dropped hard onto the race track for several more flips. It was a terrifying crash and although it really beat her up, she lived to race again.

The moment the car stopped flipping Doug turned to me and said, "Well, that just added about a second-and-a-half to my lap times!"

I mentioned Bob "Bomber" Tobin a moment ago, and I should explain his nickname.

When Gary Patterson was driving for Jan, he and Bob decided to make some acetylene bombs. They placed a balloon at the end of a ten-foot length of tubing, and filled the tube with acetylene gas. They used some sort of electric igniter to fire off the gas, and it made a helluva noise.

They set off a couple and were having a nice time of it when someone called the cops, who soon showed up at the front door. One of the guys—Gary, Bob, Jan, somebody—came walking out of the house and said with a totally straight face, "Gee, officer, I haven't heard a thing!"

Undaunted, the cops launched an investigation and somehow got Bob's name. They did some legwork and found that a Bob Tobin was a former demolitions expert in Vietnam who now lived in Carson City. In due course they arrested the wrong Bob Tobin.

Some years later the group was standing around talking about the night they blew off the acetylene bombs, and a guy standing nearby—the *other* Bob Tobin—walked over and said, "That was you? They tried to put me in jail for that!"

From that point on, Bob's nickname was "Bomber." Forever and ever.

My trips to the Midwest each summer meant I was doing a lot of traveling, and my van was getting awfully crowded. RV's—also known as motorhomes or mini-homes—were just starting to catch on with racers, and I decided I needed one.

Jack Gordon in Sacramento was just the man I needed to see. I went over to his dealership and he sold me a Honey (that was the brand) RV that I just couldn't wait to try out.

Sacramento Raceway was hosting a big drag race the following weekend, and I figured that was the perfect chance for an RV test run. I invited my friend and occasional crew member Terry Grubbs and his wife to ride along with Karen and me. We figured we were in store for a fun, relaxing weekend. I envisioned sitting on the roof of the RV on a cool spring day, drinking beer and having a great time.

As the racing program drew to a close it's fair to speculate that Grubbs and I had consumed too many beers. I climbed behind the wheel and got in line to exit the parking lot. Our exit was backed way up, but another exit looked less crowded. Both exits eventually funneled onto the same two-lane.

We were patiently waiting when I noticed some jerks cheating up the left-hand lane, hoping to crowd in at the head of the line. Ever vigilant of injustice, I took it upon myself to be the monitor of that lane. I pulled into the lane just enough to deter any further traffic from cheating the lane. The car behind left room for me to pull back over when we got to the head of the line.

Everything was going just fine until an asshole in a primer-gray '67 Camaro decided to force the issue. I crowded him and he ripped around me, but he ran out of room and clipped the front bumper of my brand new RV, peeling it clear off the vehicle.

At that instant I floored the throttle and it made that familiar "buuuhhhhlllll" sound of a 4-barrel carburetor with all four barrels WFO. The initial lunge of the RV sent all of my passengers sprawling to the rear with the women screaming.

Grubbs was pleading, "Oh shit, Sills, don't!"

As I'm chasing this guy with my foot flat on the floor and gaining speed, I can see that cars in the pitside lane have blocked his exit plan. He came to a stop; I only slowed until contact was made. I slammed the RV into Park and raced out my door and ran to the Camaro, where the driver's door was just starting to open. I grabbed the driver and yanked him out of the car with all my strength.

The driver weighed in somewhere around the 100-pound mark, and he flew right out of the car. At that moment I turned my ankle under, just as Grubbs arrived to keep me from getting any deeper into trouble. This, ironically enough, was a reversal of roles for Grubbs.

He managed to get me calmed down, and as I walked back toward my RV some of the people nearby were cheering my sense of right and wrong. The other people, those who weren't cheering but just stood there and stared, I don't really want to know what they were thinking.

I bent down and picked up my bumper, and as I'm walking I'm beginning to realize that my ankle is really, really hurting and it's making me madder with every step. By the time I got back to the RV Grubbs had everything under control, but I was back on the rev limiter and decided I needed to ram my vehicle back into the enemy one more time just for the hell of it. However, since I had my bumper in my hand I figured that might suffice so I ran down and jammed it into the guy's back.

Which kinda got things fired up once again. The saving grace of the day was that nobody wanted to hang around until law enforcement showed up. So once again the angels of mercy were protecting me from myself.

I had high hopes for my chances at the 1979 Gold Cup at West Capital in September, which was a World of Outlaws race. Things started out just as planned and we won the opening night, but our time trial put us back a couple of rows on Saturday.

Tim Green started on the front and took off running the top rim, while my car was good on the bottom. I caught Tim and we swapped the lead for a good fifteen laps, running as hard as either of us could run. Finally my motor blew up and I was done, and a few laps later Tim dropped out after using up his car as well.

That was a real disappointment, because I wanted to win the Gold Cup. That's a race that forever eluded me, even after the venue changed and the event was held at Silver Dollar Speedway in Chico. The days were numbered for West Capital, and the track closed the following spring after running just one race.

An interesting footnote is that we held the track record at West Capital at the time of the closing, so that's a mark we'll hold for all time.

I mentioned Tim Green, and I should elaborate a little bit more about Tim.

Tim was a guy who would be in my life for, basically, the rest of my life. He is married to my sister Marcy, but in 1979 they were just going together. Tim was driving the Jensen Construction car out of Des Moines at that time, with Kenny Woodruff turning the wrenches.

Tim and Kenny were very fast together. At Knoxville that year they were just bad, scary fast. Most races you watch will have maybe one "Oh, shit!" moment during the entire race. If you were watching Tim race around Knoxville that year you got at least one "Oh, shit!" moment each lap, maybe more. The entire time you were thinking, "How did he get away with that?"

Later that summer Tim returned to California for a rest after a bad flip at Knoxville, nursing the worst case of red-eye/raccoon eye you'll ever see.

Tim and I were great friends for a long time. He would be racing in the Midwest and I would be in California, and we would talk every Monday about what happened over the weekend and discuss set-ups, race cars, and race tracks. Then he would race for a season out west, and I would race somewhere else.

We had a lot of the same car owners through the years; Duke McMillen, the Lovell Brothers, Virgil and Anne Owen, and Bob Trostle.

In 1987 Tim was driving for Virgil Owen in California and I was chasing the Outlaws in Lenard McCarl's car. Clyde Prickett, a well-known pavement supermodified car owner, invited Tim to Madera for a test session in his car.

It did not turn out well. Tim crashed hard and was knocked out with the car on fire. His legs were severely burned, and he spent some agonizing days in the Fresno hospital getting skin grafts. I came home to visit Tim in the hospital and he was in a tremendous amount of pain and very concerned about what his future might be.

Doctors there gave Tim some sobering scenarios about his recovery and his outlook, but like most athletes Tim healed more quickly than expected. Tim was concerned that while he recovered, Virgil might lose interest and move on. Tim graciously offered me his ride if things weren't going well for me out on the road, and I later took him up on the offer.

The final race of the season came at Baylands Raceway. Tim was able to walk at that point, although he looked like Frankenstein as he shuffled along. The tendons on the back of his legs were burned apart and had been stapled together (yet to this day this still gives Tim problems) and walking was not only difficult, but terribly painful.

Tim lined up fourth in the A-main, and I was sixth. Steve Kent got the early lead and Tim worked his way to second, and I was right behind them in third.

With just a couple of laps remaining Tim mustered all of his strength to make a run at Steve. This guy had been lying in a hospital all summer, his body burned up and atrophying, and here he is not only racing but fighting for the win.

Tim got up on the wheel and passed Steve to take the lead. I don't know what the rest of the crowd was doing, but I was cheering so hard that my shield fogged up. Tim won the race and the top three cars were directed to stop on the front straightaway.

Steve and I both rushed to Tim's car, and with tears in our eyes we helped him get out of the car. Then we helped him stand steady while David Vodden interviewed him on the PA.

To this day, that was one of the most powerful moments I have ever experienced. To see the courage of a man who had been down-and-out, nearly burned up, and written off as done…and to see him rise up to triumph like that, it was just very emotional and special.

Tim was a very good mechanic, and he paid attention to detail. He designed an axle birdcage setup in 1987 that was really ingenious, and only recently has someone figured out how to build something similar.

Virgil later passed away and Tim managed Virgil's business, All Weld, for several years until buying it from Virgil's widow Anne which allowed her to retire.

My relationship with Tim and Marcy had some troubled times and I probably hold some responsibility for that. The first episode came when

Tim and Marcy were making their first trip to Australia, and they stayed with Karen and me until they left. We set up a slot car track in a spare room, and we raced them until we got bored and decided to go dirt bike riding.

We borrowed a couple of bikes, and along with Rick Hirst decided to go riding. One of the bikes was an RM400 Suzuki which was known to be light in the front. With a 400cc engine, that was a perfect recipe for big wheelies. That's exactly what Tim experienced, and the problem was that his leg was sticking out on the side when he slid off the back of the bike and it blew out his knee.

Marcy was less than pleased with all of us. Tim was afraid of getting fired by Trostle for being irresponsible, so he told him he fell off a ladder while cleaning out a gutter at his mom's house. Tim spent the next few months in a cast and we raced slot cars at my house all winter.

Another stressful episode came at the Missouri Nationals, where we were all staying at the Ramada Inn. I was driving Bob Tuttle's car, and his son Rob and I finished up the car out in the hotel parking lot. I was walking Scooter, my black Chow dog, to our room.

We stopped at Tim's room to find him in the shower and learned that Marcy had left to go to the swimming pool. Her blouse and shorts were lying on the bed and we thought it might be funny to put the shorts on Scooter and let him walk around.

It was hilarious to see Scooter's little butt swaying in those shorts as we walked out to the pool. He looked like a bear cub with a diaper (which later inspired a really ingenious and memorable Halloween costume).

The humor went to a new level as we got Marcy's attention from our laughter, and she looked our way. Right at that moment Scooter hiked his leg and pissed in Marcy's shorts. She, it could safely be said, was not the least bit amused.

Another factor could have been what happened at the 1985 Dirt Cup at Skagit Speedway. The format there required all drivers to help wheel pack the track, and then attend the driver's meeting. This was followed by a pill draw to determine the qualifying order, and then we had hot laps.

The track was so wet during wheel packing that the bottom lane was complete slop. After the driver's meeting an official was doing the pill draw by himself; he had a bag of numbered pills and a clipboard in one hand and a coffee can in the other. He had each driver draw from the bag, then he put the bag under his arm as he wrote the pill number and corresponding car number on the clipboard.

I offered to help him and he welcomed my assistance. I reached into the bag and drew out No. 73, and then Brent Kaeding took over holding the bag and drew No. 75. Tim guessed that—like the previous night—an early number would be faster so he carefully pulled out pill No. 3.

We went out for hot laps in no particular order, so several of us waited for the last session. I managed to run down in the slop and hit the throttle, spitting lots of mud and moisture up into the groove for the qualifying session that would immediately follow. After the checkered flag waved I noticed that Brent was doing the same thing and the groove was pretty much covered in mud.

Needless to say, Tim didn't set fast time that night. I apologize, Tim… it was all in good fun, but no wonder you were pissed at me.

10

Hurt, win, fired

Marriage came into my picture in 1978, and I immediately discovered that a married guy has a slightly different agenda than a single guy. As a single guy, you can tolerate starving for a few days so you make decisions—financial decisions, racing decisions, life decisions—accordingly. However a married guy has to filter those decisions through another person, and she might not be in agreement on the willingness to starve for a few days when necessary.

For the 1980 season I was that married guy who had changed his priorities a bit. In addition to really wanting a good ride, I needed a job. That's the three-letter word most ambitious racers run away from: J-O-B.

My friend Joel McCray had the promise of both. Joel was a plastering contractor, and he also owned a race car. So I took a job during the week with Joel, hauling material and putting up scaffolding, and would drive Joel's car in the coming season.

Joel loved to talk about which driver in the pits had the biggest balls, and that's who Joel wanted in his car. He had nothing but contempt for the cautious driving approach. One of his favorite ways to describe a conservative driver was to say, "That guy loves his body too much!"

Duke McMillen was wrenching Joel's car, and that was a plus.

We started the season at Ascot, then headed for Texas where we would connect with the World of Outlaws. I needed some help driving to Texas, so my friend Tex Countryman tagged along with me. Interstate 5 was not yet complete through Stockton, so you had to take Charter Way across from Highway 99.

Stockton rivals Chicago for gang violence—in 1980 that was true and it's still true today—and in hindsight we should have planned better because we were right in the middle of Stockton when we needed to stop for fuel.

We were towing a 30-foot enclosed trailer with an RV, so we needed lots of fuel stops.

I was pumping the gas when a black man walked up to Tex and said, "Are you a racist?" Tex was a little confused and he asked the guy to repeat himself. The guy did, and Tex still thought he said, "Are you a racer?" So Tex pointed at me and says, "No, but he is!"

So now the guy walks up to me, waving his hands and speaking in Ebonics, and I tried to explain that I'm a racer, would you like to see my race car? Now the guy was even more confused than we were, and he finally walked away, shaking his head.

We stopped in Odessa, Texas to see some of Tex's relatives, and I discovered that his real name is Robby Dale Countryman. He's gittin' more country by the dadgum minute!

Joel and Duke flew in to meet us, and we headed for Devil's Bowl Speedway. We were in the middle of a ton of traffic on the freeway and I saw an opening I could get into, but an asshole in a pickup truck was speeding up to close the gap.

As luck would have it a guy was walking along the shoulder right then so my moves were limited. I was hoping the asshole in the pickup truck had brakes, because I'm coming over. He apparently didn't have enough brakes, because he lost one of his mirrors on the side of our trailer.

At this point we're in a hurry to get to the track, so we viewed the exchange as collateral damage. We rolled along to the turnoff to the track and had to stop for fuel, and the guy confronted us there. He's a black man, so I'm in the middle of my second interracial exchange in three days. I explained my position that he should have left room for my trailer and if he wants to pursue it further, we'll be at the track.

Sure enough, he showed up with the Texas Highway Patrol at the pit gate, where all the racers were lined up at the sign-in window. We managed to get everything smoothed over, which was good. I didn't want to be viewed as the guy from California who had the cops on his trail.

We raced without wings the first weekend, and the following weekend put the wings on. We did okay, and on the Sunday of the second weekend my crew flew home.

I stayed in the RV at Norman Martin's shop. Norman and his friends had a motorcycle race on Sunday afternoon so I tagged along.

It was a Hare Scramble, with a five-mile lap. The race began but after just two laps everybody apparently needed a pit stop for rest and beer. Somebody asked me if I wanted to make some laps, and I borrowed some boots and took off. It was a fun track and a really fun weekend with Norman and his buddies.

John Travolta and the movie *Urban Cowboy* had been a big hit a year or so earlier, and everybody was familiar with Gilley's Bar in Pasadena, Texas where the movie was filmed. Shortly after the Devil's Bowl race we traveled to Houston and some of us decided to head over and check out Gilley's place.

It was an amazing layout, probably an acre of mechanical bulls, roping contests, country music, bars with beer, bars with shots, bar-b-cue stands, and fights. That seemed to be a central part of the attraction at Gilley's. I wasn't looking for a fight but in due course one found me.

We were in the parking lot when we ran across a couple of cute girls with a flat tire. Rendy Boldrini, Scott McMillen and I did the right thing and changed their tire. I was talking with one of the girls when a guy came up and started cussing the girl (probably the guy who flattened their tire). As a chivalrous gentleman I insisted that he stop talking to her like that. A few more words were said and it was time for a good 'ol fight in Gilley's parking lot.

As a prelude to the fight I asked the guy to put down his longneck beer bottle, and he replied, "I don't fight fair," and broke the bottle across my left eye. The blow almost took me out but as I got over being dazed and confused I could see him running for the front of Gilley's, and that's where I caught him. When the security guys stopped the fight I had him down on the ground kicking his head, and I believe based on Texas rules that constitutes a win.

By the time I got back to the car the tire was changed, and at this point we realized that our ride back home had long ago departed. The girls seemed hesitant to offer us a ride, knowing that the bleeding over my eye was likely to make a mess in their car. Their sense of fairness finally prevailed and they gave us a ride back to our RV.

So for the third time in recent memory I showed up at the track with a black eye, and there was definitely a pattern here. Evidently I was doing something wrong in my self-defense.

Our season back home hadn't started yet, and my sister Marcy came out to visit with Tim Green. She rode home with me, and on the way back we stopped at Manzanita for a CRA race. We started 16th and ran second, which felt really, really good. I hold a lot of respect for the CRA guys and to run well at Manzy was a great thing.

Our next stop was at Chula Vista, a big half-mile right on the Mexican border. The joke was that if you flipped out of turn one you would need a Green Card to get back into the U.S. Sure enough, that's exactly where I flipped, but evidently I didn't land on foreign soil.

Like everyone else at that time I was using a seat that wrapped around my body, just under my armpits. During a crash they had a tendency to dig into your side and back, breaking your shoulder blade.

After my crash I crawled out of the car and walked back to our pit, and as the adrenaline went away I realized I was hurting. I asked an official about getting an x-ray, and he pointed at the spare ambulance and said they could take me to a hospital.

Karen and I climbed into the back of the ambulance and discovered that the two medical attendants were teen-aged boys with no medical training at all—just a driver's license. We went bouncing off across the infield, and all the way to the hospital the kid was either wide-open or stopped. It was a painful ride, for sure.

The x-ray technician informed me that I had a broken scapula. He seemed very enthusiastic as he explained that in 14 years on the job, this was the first broken scapula he had ever seen. Yippee! I guess I should have won a prize or something.

I was out of action for a little while and the next night we stopped at Ascot to watch the races. This tells you a lot about the seats of the day: a bunch of people at Ascot asked me what happened, and when I told them at least three drivers said, "Oh, yeah, I broke mine, too. You'll be out about three weeks."

They put Lealand McSpadden in our car while I healed up. It's hard to watch someone else drive your car; it's like watching someone kiss your girlfriend. It's especially hard watching a really good driver like Lealand run your car.

Sure enough my recovery timeframe was three weeks, and once I healed up I managed to get back up to speed pretty quickly. We won three races in Joel's car and it was time to head north for the Dirt Cup at Skagit.

The 1980 Dirt Cup is a win I'm really proud of. As a racer you know that some wins come to you by chance, and some wins you've worked your ass off to get. This was one of those wins.

On the prelim night we broke a rear end in our heat race, which really hurt us because you have to be in the top two spots in your heat to make Saturday's main event. We went on to win the A-main that night but were slated to start in the back of the C-main on Saturday.

The C-main was the first race of the night, and the track was still greasy and slick. We were loose and finished one car out of a transfer position. However, a car didn't make the call for the B-main so we tagged the tail and proceeded to win the race.

That put us on the tail of the championship race. We worked our way up to second place and had a caution with two laps to go. During the yellow the track had just enough dew falling that the center would be fast for a lap, maybe two, on the restart.

The green dropped and I put a big slider on my buddy Gary Patterson and made it stick. I held on for the final two laps and won the Dirt Cup from the C-main, which was a very big deal.

But my days in Joel's car were numbered.

Two races later we were at Chico, and Jimmy Boyd and I got together and it tore off my brake line. We both went to the tail, and without any brakes my car was less than perfect. We managed to get back to third, and Jimmy won the race.

When I got back to our pit, Joel was pissed that I didn't try to crash Jimmy after we got together. It was just a racing deal, and there was no reason I should be mad at Jimmy. Joel insisted that I needed to go down to Jimmy's pit right now and whip his ass, which was stupid. Jimmy was my friend and there was no way I was interested in starting a fight with him, especially when it wasn't right.

"You're not going down there and fight him?" Joel demanded.

"Nope."

"Then you're fired."

"Thank you," I said, and I meant it.

Hurt, win, fired, and it's only June. Now that's racin'!

By now the racing season was in full swing and that meant there might be opportunities to run somebody's car in the Midwest. My first phone call was to Bob Trostle, who offered me a ride for a couple of races. Bob explained that he had already made arrangements for Kramer Williamson to run his car in a couple of weeks, so once Kramer arrived I would be on my own.

We went to Sedalia for the Missouri Nationals, where we had a good race with Tim Green for the win. We were running an experimental in/out box that kept jumping out of gear and that sealed our fate as we finished behind Tim.

Bob had one of the best sprint cars in the country, but the fact is that he was always down on horsepower. Looking back, I realize now that Bob was truly outstanding on chassis issues because even though his motor budget was far less than everybody else he still won a lot of races. A *lot* of races.

Bob got us an appearance deal to run at Lake of the Ozarks Speedway, and his wife Dorotha joined us as we drove down. It was a typical summer day in Missouri: very hot and very humid. The air conditioning in Bob's truck wasn't working, so when we arrived at our hotel room we cranked up the air conditioning to full blast and had a siesta. We woke up and piled into Bob's truck, but it wouldn't crank. We did the usual stuff you did to a Chevy motor: bang on the starter to free it up, jumper cables, and so forth. No dice.

We called the track and explained our situation and they sent a wrecker out to tow our truck and trailer to the speedway. Bob and I were in the front seat of the truck and Dorotha was in the back seat and as the tow truck pulled into the infield we could hear the track announcer say, "Ladies and gentlemen, we promised Jimmy Sills in the Bob Trostle car, and here they are!"

We blew our motor in the heat race, and I climbed out of the car. It was still hot as hell outside, and Bob and I just looked at each other and started to lower the trailer ramps to load the car. The track announcer said over the PA, "Don't worry, ladies and gentlemen…these guys are professionals and they'll have a spare motor in that car before the B-main!"

Other racers started walking up to our pit to offer help, and I asked Bob if he had a spare motor. He nodded, so we changed it and were able to race the feature.

A couple of days later we went to Mason City, Iowa, where we had 'em covered. As I went past the flag stand I saw the light flashing that signals the flagman that there are two laps to go. The car suddenly started shaking and my first thought was an impending motor explosion, so I took it out of gear and pulled to the inside. Just as I'm coming to a stop I noticed that the left rear tire has come apart and is flapping against the nerf bar. There's your vibration. Well, crap.

Pretty soon Kramer arrived and I was out of a ride again. But there were always lots of cars in the Midwest…just stick around, and something will open up. That's what I always told myself, anyways.

In racing, the unfortunate reality is that somebody else's misfortune usually leads to an opportunity for somebody else. That summer of 1980 Mike Pinkney was badly hurt in a crash at Knoxville, and with Mike out of action that opened up the seat in the Tuttle-Easter Ace Lines car.

I landed the ride and it was a good fit for me. It was a Trostle chassis with decent motors and enough money to run plenty of races. Bob Tuttle took care of the car in the back of his business in West Des Moines where

With Grandpa Sills, 1958. Five years old. Finally got a riding mower!

With my sister Val at our little dirt track, 1958. Ready for hot laps!

My mom Marilyn on her 650 Triumph in 1947. Isn't this just cool as hell?

My dad, Jimmy Sills Sr., in Bill Johnson's midget in 1955. (George Bray Jr. photo)

My dad with his Piper Cub in 1947.

My step-father Dick Johnson in 1961. The trophy girl's husband was Walter Ross, a successful car owner in our area.

Dick Johnson's stock car at the 1967 Daytona 500.

At the wheel of bus No. 33, I hold the school bus qualifying record for Buscomb County, North Carolina. That's our dog Bosco, named after stock car racer Bosco Lowe.

My first ride, Ed Watson's supermodified. This is my second year of racing (1974) and I'm shouting to Jack Hunter that our cross-weight is good.

Winning at West Capital in 1974. In the back are Chuck and Jack Hunter; in front with me are my nephews (L-R) John Rankin, Scott Hall, and Tommy Hall.

Bob Davis owned this Lloyd chassis sprint car. It's 1975; the hair is getting bigger and so are the wings.

My second trip to Australia in 1975. Team USA consisted of (L-R) Sills, Gary Patterson, Larry Burton, and Larry Rice. Kneeling out front is Bob Davis. We're at the Sydney Showgrounds. (Bill Meyer photo)

Australia, 1979. Posing for a photo with Doug Wolfgang at the Sydney Showground. (Bill Meyer photo)

Australia, 1979, and I joined Steve Kinser, Doug Wolfgang, and Richard Burton (Larry's son) on a little track outside Sydney where we had a blast racing Honda Odyssey ATV's.

This is what we looked like afterwards! Sills, Richard, Doug, and Steve.

Knoxville, 1981.
(John Mahoney photo)

We ran this car quite a bit out of Columbia, Missouri. This is 1978, and the car owners were Jerry Smith, Larry McCown, and Archie Simpson.

Knoxville Nationals, 1981. I'm in the Tuttle-Eastern No. 10, racing with Larry Gates on the outside. (John Mahoney photo)

A classic sprint car pose in the Bailey Bros. Stanton car at El Centro in 1983.

With Fred Marks and Les Kepler in 1986. I'm explaining why I didn't win.

The World of Outlaws championship banquet in 1986. From L-R: Steve Kinser, Sills, Mark Kinser, Ron Shuman, Bobby Allen, Jac Haudenschild, Brad Doty, and Tim Gee. (Dave Lawless photo)

On the gas at Kokomo, Indiana in 1987 in Lenard McCarl's car. Boy, traveling with Lenard...what a fun adventure! (Mark Miefert photo)

I'll always remember my 1987 Dirt Cup win with mixed emotions. We walked the track prior to the race with Dave Bradway; sadly, Dave was killed in a crash later that night.

What a great night! Winning against the World of Outlaws on the Indy Mile at Indianapolis, 1987. Lenard McCarl gave us a great car and it was a big night.

Our crew chiefs for Ohio Speedweek in 1988: Sonny Kratzer's daughter Janet (back) and my daughter Stephanie.

Running Bob Weikert's Beefmobile at Knoxville.

Winning at Williams Grove for Bob Weikert in 1988. Nothing compares to the experience of running sprint cars in Pennsylvania! (Marty Gordner photo)

Warmwater Captures BCRA Midget Go at Silver Dollar

By RON ALBRIGHT

CHICO, Calif. — Luke Warmwater became the fifth different winner in as many events by storming to victory in Saturday night's 30-lap Bay Cities Racing Ass'n midget main event on Silver Dollar Speedway's banked quarter-mile clay oval.

Warmwater, a nom de guerre for a former national sprint car driver, throttled the potent Jim Wellington-owned Diego/Rennsport Stagger-Fire Chevy V-4 No. 05 to victory after starting ninth in the 20-car lineup. Warmwater roared past Ray Derby for the top spot during the 14th circuit.

Derby, who had a clean sweep going until the feature race, settled for runner-up money after starting 10th aboard the Stoffer & Derby Gambler/Autocraft No. 5. However, Derby's effort was good enough to place him atop the latest BCRA standings ahead of defending champ Gary Koster.

Second starter John Cordell grabbed third, followed by Koster and Tim Joyce.

The BCRA vintage midget division also ran an exhibition event with Dickie Reese and Mel Azevedo pacing the field in Offenhauser-powered midgets.

The summary:

Fast Time: Ray Derby, Stoffer & Derby 5, 14.125 (new track record).
Trophy Dash: (3 laps): Derby, Floyd Alvis, Luke Warmwater, Rick Haugh, Jr.
First Heat (8 laps): Derby, John Cofer, Terry Tarditi, Glenn Carson, Tom Esposito, Leonard Lopez.
Second Heat (8 laps): Warmwater, Gary Koster, John Cordell, Tom Dupont Jr., Bob Gare, Burt Foland Jr., Lou Baglin.
Third Heat (8 laps): Haugh, Greg Nelson, Bob Schneider, Marshall Mathews, Sterling Pratz, Michael Pettibone, Billy Garcia.
Fourth Heat (8 laps): Tim Joyce, Bruce Thurston, Alvis, Mike Appio, Victor Mencarini, Ken Lyle.
Semi Main (12 laps): Mencarini, Pratz, Gare, Foland, Pettibone, Lopez, Scott Dupont, Lyle.
Feature (30 laps): Warmwater, Derby, Cordell, Koster, Joyce, Nelson, Mathews, Carson, Cofer, Thurston, Foland, Gare, Schneider, Pratz, Haugh, Tarditi, T. Dupont, Appio, Alvis, Mencarini.

National Speed Sport News, May 10, 1989: Luke Warmwater makes his national media debut.

This was a big day! My first USAC Silver Crown win at Sacramento, June 3, 1990. Jeff Gordon ran third, and Jeff is obviously in awe of my amazing driving ability. Or...maybe trophy girl Leslie Bremer has captured Jeff's imagination.
(Cyndi Craft photo)

Driving Bob Consani's beautiful Silver Crown car at the Indy Mile in 1993. (REM Racing photo)

Silver Crown racing at its best! I'm leading Ron Shuman and Lealand McSpadden at the Hoosier Hundred on the Indy Mile in 1993.

With George Snider (left) and Bob Consani in 1994.

Ready for the 4-Crown Nationals at Eldora in 1992, wheeling
Dave Calderwood's sprinter. (John Mahoney photo)

Racing with Dave Calderwood was a lot of fun and we had good success. Dave was a good friend as well as a hard-working car owner.

Driving Dave Calderwood's midget at Phoenix in 1995. Phoenix was one of my favorite tracks, and the Copper World Classic each February was something to look forward to.
(Bill Taylor photo)

The Hoosier Hundred at the Indy Mile, 1992. We were leading with six laps to go when a bolt broke on our tie rod, costing us a $23,000 win. Disappointment like that stays with you for a while.

Close quarters at Phoenix with Ron Shuman to my outside in 1993. (Bill Taylor photo)

When Gary Stanton spoke, I listened. Teaming up with Gary resulted in some of the most successful years of my career, and also allowed us to share a lasting friendship.

Western Springs Speedway in New Zealand, 1996. As part of the Hauka native opening ceremony, if you pick up a knife they have placed on the ground you have accepted the challenge. Dave Darland (left) and Tony Elliott look on.

Keith Hall at Manzanita Speedway always had a surprise for driver introductions. And yes, I did ride this Brahma beast to the grid in 1997. That really is a lot of bull.

With car owners Don and Janet Berry after a Mini Gold Cup win in 1995.

With True Value's Tom Cotter and car owner George "Ziggy" Snider (right) in 1998 after our Sacramento Silver Crown win. (Greg Tyler photo)

With daughter Stephanie at Phoenix in 1998 as Stan Fox photobombs. (US Photographics photo)

Our racing school begins, 1991. Race ours or bring your own!

California racing legend Johnny Boyd visited our school in 1995. No, he didn't need any instruction, but we were honored that he visited.

Our booth at a PRI show at San Jose in 1992, joined by Rod Tiner and Randy Frank.

Calistoga, 1999, and we're wheeling our two-seater built by Rod Tiner. Many people got the ride of their life in this car!

With legendary Eldora Speedway owners Earl and Berneice Baltes after our 4-Crown Nationals USAC sprint car win in 1996.
(John Mahoney photo)

With one of my all-time favorite people, Jack Hewitt.

2004: Look, ma! I'm about to take my second trip to Tulare Hospital!

Knoxville Raceway in 2012, where I joined longtime friend Kenny Woodruff to coach Natalie Sather.

Running Tony Stewart's sprint car at the Masters Classic at Knoxville. In our three visits we ran 2nd, 1st, and 1st.

George Lasoski was a big reason for our success at the Masters Classic. Thank you, George!

Jeff Gordon invited some of his friends to join him at his final Brickyard 400 appearance in 2015. (L-R) Steve Kinser, Randy Kinser, Rick Ferkel, Kelly Kinser, Jeff, Gary Stanton, Sills, Jack Hewitt, Kenny Jacobs, and Rodney Duncan.

Quality time with granddaughter Shelby, and her pink tutu is the perfect outfit for motorcycle repair and maintenance.

I love moments like this...with daughter Stephanie and granddaughter Sophia.

Cheryl enjoying time with grandchildren
(L-R) Jack, Nixon, Aidan, and Shelby.

Jimmy and Cheryl...life is good!

they manufactured basement windows. Bob's son Rob is still one of my best friends, along with his mom Janan. Their friends Tom and Marilyn were part of our crew.

Janan had a cool dog, Pancho. Pancho was a Yorkie terrier and he had the express understanding that the last bite of anything being eaten was his. One day we got a carryout pizza and were riding down the road having our dinner. Pancho was studying Rob, watching intently as the last bite of the pizza approached, inching closer to Rob. Just as Rob got to the last bite of crust he pitched it out the window, and Pancho almost went out the window after it.

One day we were working on the car at an abandoned gas station in West Memphis, Arkansas. We could hear Pancho barking and whining, but couldn't see him. We started looking around and discovered that he had fallen into a hole where the cover had been removed. Bob and I had to hold Rob's feet and lower him into the hole to rescue Pancho.

As we got into autumn the Midwestern season was winding down so we decided to head out west. Rapid City, South Dakota had a big race that paid $5,000 to the winner, and this was on my way home to Sacramento. Bob towed the race car out, and we ran well on Friday night.

It was freezing-ass cold that weekend and the crowd turnout was pretty sparse, which would be an important factor in the weeks to come. I'll explain that in a moment. Cold or not, after the Friday night races I decided to celebrate with some adult beverages. Rob headed back to the motel in the early-morning hours, and I should have followed his lead. Instead, I decided to ride with some local girls to a party.

I had a major hangover the next morning, and when I got to the track I realized I didn't have my uniform with me. I trusted a guy with my room key and he retrieved the uniform while I attended the driver's meeting.

We were fast, and had a great race. We swapped the lead with Shane Carson in the Speedway Motors No. 4x and Rick Ferkel in his famous No. 0. During the course of the race a local racer stopped for a flat tire and they gave him his spot back. An important development, it would turn out.

A few laps later I gave Ferkel a slide job in turn one and he gave me one back in turn three, but we got together and both spun. We pushed off and naturally went back to where we were running before—second and third—because just a few laps earlier they gave the guy from Sioux Falls his spot back.

The officials were waving us to the tail, and our crews signaled us to stop on the front straightaway. We argued so passionately that they actually red flagged the race to get it sorted out. Ferkel asked to talk to the track owner and he asked the guy if they had two sets of rules: one set for the locals and one set for everybody else. The track owner asked the officials about the guy from Sioux Falls getting his spot back, and they were a little red-faced as they explained that they had made a mistake in doing so.

The owner said, well, if you did it for him you have to do it for these guys. Put them back to second and third.

We damn near had a riot when they announced over the PA what was happening. Shane won, Rick was second, and I was third. We didn't linger too long in the pit area after that one.

Bob and the race car headed back to Iowa and I worked out a plan to get myself back to California. Earl Kelly had raced with us at Rapid City and was driving back to San Jose by himself, so Shane Carson and I rode with Earl. Before we left, Shane crawled up on the hood of Earl's truck and drew a goofy face on the wind dome and wrote "EARL" in big letters across the top for fun.

Because of the light turnout of fans, the promoter didn't have enough money to pay everybody in cash. Shane got half of his money in cash and a check for the rest. Bob Tuttle got a check for our winnings, and was at the bank when it opened on Monday morning and the check cleared. Ferkel traveled on to California and by the time he got to Tognotti's speed shop his check bounced, and Earl Kelly's check bounced as well. Such was the life of a racer in 1980.

Karen and I bought our first house in Sacramento at the end of the 1980 season. It was fun to get settled in, but it wasn't long before we had to leave in February 1981 to go racing in Florida. We flew to Des Moines to reconnect with Bob Tuttle. I was pumped, because we had heard all about the beautiful new 30-foot trailer Bob and his friend Dick Easter had put together.

I had considered moving to Iowa, because in the summer it's the center of a lot of great racing. But getting off the plane that January day was an eye-opening experience. It was maybe 20 degrees, and snowing. Not the normal kind of snowfall, either; this stuff was coming down sideways. Five minutes out in that weather forever cured me of any thoughts of living in Iowa.

Rob and Dick Easter picked us up at the airport and drove us out to see the trailer. I was very excited, but was stopped in my tracks. There we found an ancient old carnival trailer with a roll-up door in the back and a big side door. This thing was not only an antique, it was a broken-down and ugly antique. "What do you think?" they asked. I was at a loss for words when everybody started laughing. They had set me up on a good joke, and then they showed us the *real* new trailer and the beautiful new race car that went with it.

We spent two weeks in Florida at East Bay, racing without wings the first week and with the wing—against the Outlaws—the second week. We ran fourth and fifth with the Outlaws.

On one of our trips to the track we had a very close call. We were crossing a bridge that was built with a lot of arc, and on the downhill side of the bridge found a line of stopped traffic in our lane. Bob's RV had a tag trailer with a lot of tongue weight, and his front tires locked up under hard braking. We were sliding the front wheels just as a semi-truck was getting closer at a high rate of speed. I was braced for impact when a space opened up and Bob somehow missed the trailer.

So Bob has saved my life, right? Now we're bonding as only a family can bond, right? Not so!

The very next day we were sitting at a traffic light in Tampa when the guy next to us rolled down his window and started a conversation about what's in our trailer. Bob explained that we had a race car and were heading for the track to go racing. Just as the guy asked, "Is it just you and your son doing this?" the light changed and the guy started to pull away. Bob says, "He's not my kid," but the guy didn't hear so Bob has his head out the window shouting at the top of his lungs, "He's not my kid! He's not my kid!"

So much for bonding like family!

I always went to the pay window to pick up our money while Bob and Rob loaded the car. One night we finished loading up and piled into the RV, and Bob and Janan's granddaughter was riding with us. As we headed down the road I counted out the cash and separated our percentage and handed Bob's share to him.

His granddaughter said, "Grandpa, what do you say to Jimmy?"

"About what?" he answered.

"He just gave you some money, what do you say?"

"I don't say anything…it's my money."

"Grandpa, that's not nice. Tell Jimmy 'thank you' for giving you some money."

That one was a Mexican standoff; no clear winner.

From Florida we towed out to Devil's Bowl in Mesquite, Texas to run with the Outlaws. The Bowl has an elevation change as you go through turn one, and the track surface is usually very sticky. The cars would often lift the inside wheels going through the corner, trying to flip over. This is not a good feeling for a driver.

However, a few guys had really figured out Devil's Bowl, and Doug Wolfgang was one of those guys. Doug gave us some good ideas on setup, and we proceeded to win the race with Doug finishing second.

This was a huge win for me. To beat the Outlaws away from home—a long way from California—was a major victory. It's the kind of win that can make a real difference in your confidence, and in this business confidence is almost everything.

However, Wolfie laughed and let us know that here would be no further setup advice from him, especially at Devil's Bowl.

Karen and I traveled back to California and made arrangements to rent out our house for the summer. We borrowed her father's 18-foot camping trailer and we were all set to tow to Iowa for the summer.

The day before we were scheduled to get on the road Karen's mother JoAnn died suddenly. That made for a very sad summer; Karen was devastated and I was very sad as well. JoAnn was a huge racing fan and she was very much missed. We finally headed east several weeks after her services, and it was a hard period for all of us. One footnote is that we brought our young dog Scooter, the first of a countless number of racing trips he would take with us.

We were set to continue driving Bob Tuttle's car. Our sponsor, Ace Lines, was a trucking company owned by Dick Easter. Dick was a dynamic businessman, tall and handsome and outgoing. He looked like a guy who could take charge at a corporate board meeting, and then be just as comfortable drinking a beer at the local dirt track.

Dick gave me a job to fill in our open time between races, which meant it had flexible hours. I would shuttle flatbed trailers to Fort Dodge, then bring back van trailers. It paid well and I could make two trips a day when I was working.

Dick was very good to Karen and me. We were racing a two-day event at Granite City, Illinois when Karen got sick, and Dick arranged for her to have insurance to cover her medical expenses until she could get back to California.

We traveled to Lakeside Speedway for a Friday night race, finishing second to Shane Carson. When we finished racing we loaded up and headed north on I-35 toward Des Moines. We had worked out a traveling arrangement that called for me to drive the RV at night while Bob and Rob got some sleep, and then I slept in the morning while they cleaned the race car.

I have made many bad decisions in my life, and nearly all of them were very minor things that wouldn't hurt anyone. But that night I messed up and it could have had terrible consequences.

We were rolling along with me behind the wheel, and Karen was sitting in the passenger seat. I had to pee, and of course I didn't want to take the time to pull over and stop. So we began a transition that we had done a hundred times in our van: I kinda stood up in the seat and Karen slid into the seat behind me, resuming the driving without slowing down. Simple, right?

The only problem was that Karen hadn't driven a vehicle with this much tongue weight, and she wasn't used to pulling a trailer with so much sway. About the time I got unzipped we started swaying and Karen was chasing the steering and she's way behind. By the time I could run to the front of the RV, tripping over people who had fallen to the floor, the RV was swerving from one shoulder to the other.

I grabbed the wheel and got us back under control and pulled off the shoulder. By then everybody was wide awake, and we stepped outside to look things over. The tires were gone from the left side trailer wheels; just rims directly on the pavement and no sign of a tire anywhere.

We opened the trailer and it looked like a tornado had swept through it. We only had one spare tire for the trailer, so we chained the other axle so the hub was off the ground and limped on to West Des Moines, where we arrived home around daylight. But at least we were still alive.

We dodged a bullet that night. I still think about that episode and shake my head about what terrible things might have been.

Racing with the Tuttle family was a good, fun experience. We won some races and made a little money—at least the driver made a few bucks—and had a great time doing it.

By this time my schedule consisted of a lot more Midwestern races than anything out west. There was just so much racing in the Midwest—compared to around home—it made sense to make the trip. When you race for a living you look at how many times you can race, and the Midwest was the place to go racing.

In the early 1980s the Midwestern season was a little more abbreviated than today. Knoxville, for example, usually raced only once or twice after the Nationals in mid-August. Throughout the region nearly everything had finished up by September, so I would start making my way back out west.

In California we could race well into November, and could usually pick up a few rides in local cars before we finished the season.

In August 1981 I made the Saturday night A-main at the Knoxville Nationals in the Tuttle car, starting 7th and dropping out early to finish 22nd. After just a few more races they parked the car for the winter and we said our goodbyes. I figured we'd race together again the following year, but that wasn't in the cards.

One of the best sprint car teams in the country was right in my back yard, and after watching that great race car for several years I was about to get my chance at the wheel. One of the most enjoyable and successful chapters of my career was coming up.

11

Sam and Fred

One of the best race cars in the country in the early 1980s belonged to Sam and Fred Bailey of Vallejo, California. Sam and Fred were two really neat guys with differing personalities that made their relationship really work. They operated a speed shop and built racing engines and were very successful, and they also had a top-notch race car that any driver in our area—really, almost any driver, anywhere—would be eager to drive.

Fred Bailey was outgoing and personable, and he took the lead in dealing with customers and suppliers. Kind of the front man, you might say. Sam wasn't much on talking and socializing, so he handled a lot of the behind-the-scenes duties. Both men were very good at what they did and everything really worked, in all areas.

In early 1982 I connected with Fred and Sam and was hired to run the famous Bailey Bros. No. 01. It was an exciting time for racing in our area, with a lot happening. A new track—Baylands Speedway—had just opened near Fremont, California, and it was an important addition to our racing scene.

1982 was a great year for both me and our team. We started off with a win in NARC competition at Petaluma, California, then went on later that season to win five in a row at Baylands.

In June we headed north to Skagit for the Dirt Cup. This was one of Sam's favorite races, because it was well-organized and had rules—which were made to be broken. Sam loved to figure out the best way to do so.

Skagit required us to run SuperTrapp mufflers limited to 15 baffling plates. The more plates, the more noise and power, so the racer wanted more plates. However, to control this, instead of counting the plates the officials simply measured the length of the muffler in contrast to the rock shield. Sam responded by building a longer rock shield so it looked like we had the proper sized muffler.

Before we had bead locks to keep the tires snug against the wheel, the officials mandated a minimum of 15 pounds of air pressure. Sam built a wheel with a hose that went the entire circumference of the inside of the wheel. The hose would hold 18 pounds of pressure, but was only good for one test, which was usually enough. The actual air stem was on the inside of the wheel.

Sam also tried a trick hood of pliable fiberglass, which he figured wouldn't be so brittle and would resist chipping. He found some neat rubber hold-downs—versus the traditional Dzus buttons—so the hood could be removed quickly to work on the engine (with Sam's engines this was rarely necessary).

We won the preliminary night at Skagit, and the following night race promoter Jim Raper had the track very heavy for the championship race. I was following eventual winner Jimmy Boyd when he peeled a big piece of mud off his right rear tire and it smacked my car, dislodging the rubber hold-down for our hood. I spent the next 40 laps holding the hood with my right hand and steering with my left, eventually finishing fourth.

We made the trip to Knoxville in August for the Nationals and did pretty well, winning the Wednesday night qualifying feature. We finished 6th on Saturday night. You might have heard of the guys who finished in front of us that night: Steve Kinser, Doug Wolfgang, Jac Haudenschild, Brad Doty, and Sammy Swindell. That's a pretty talented group, I don't mind saying.

Winning at Knoxville is always an exciting moment, and I felt great on Wednesday night. My friend Robby Tuttle and I celebrated with some adult beverages and sometime in the wee hours Robby decided we needed to take a couple of victory laps in his car, a Ford Country Squire station wagon with wood paneling on the sides. (The fake wood always got lots of comments, and Robby told everybody that his car was so new that it was still in the crate.)

We grabbed a couple of beers and headed out onto the Marion County Fairgrounds track. Most of the partiers had gone to bed and the place was quiet, and we starting cutting some fast laps on the dirt. We probably would have gotten away with our little adventure but Robby discovered that if he shut the key off then flicked it back on real quick, the gases in the muffler would set off a huge "BOOM!"

Of course he started doing this several times a lap at frequent intervals, and it wasn't long before we drew a crowd, which included several irate officials and sheriff's deputies.

They were waving their arms and shouting but since nobody showed us a yellow or red flag we figured we were still under green. Finally they got enough people together that they blocked the entire track and we stopped for an official consultation.

I don't remember exactly what was said but it was something along the line of, "What the hell do you think you're doing??!!" It wasn't actually phrased like a question, but Robby was very polite and calm as he answered.

"I'm just showing my buddy how to run the cushion!" he said.

It was obviously very thoughtful of Robby to want to help me like that, and I'm sure that's why they let us go. However I think they did say something about getting our ass out of there and no more "booming" tonight.

The Outlaws headed west in September after Knoxville, so that was a good transition for us to return home. We were running well and that's when we got on a roll to win five straight at Baylands. The fifth was against the World of Outlaws there on Sept. 17, and we would have also won the finale that weekend but for a bad racing break.

We were leading late in the race and were under caution. The starter, Ken Garcia, turned out the yellow light to let us know that we would see the green flag next time past the flag stand. However, Ken flicked off the switch after I had already passed the light, and I had no way to see that the restart was coming on that lap. But everybody behind me apparently saw the light go out.

Sammy Swindell was running second, and as we came to the fourth corner Sammy stood on the gas and drove right by me. I heard Sammy's motor pick up and couldn't believe my eyes when I saw Ken waving the green flag.

I was pissed. There is no other way to say it. I'm not sure an official can fully understand how such a crushing mistake can affect a racer. This was the second time this had happened to me; the first cost me the Australian title race.

We won four more races that autumn before heading for Phoenix for the Western World Championship at Manzanita Speedway. At that time the Western World was easily as big and as prestigious as the Knoxville Nationals.

I was eager to get to Manzy. I had watched Lealand McSpadden in the Bailey Bros. car there in the past, and he was always hauling ass. So I figured I had a car that definitely could win the Western World. I was further encouraged and pumped up when we finished second to Ron Shuman on the opening night; Shuman was another racer who could really fly at Manzy.

The promoter at Manzy, Keith Hall, decided to add a special race to the Friday night program. This was an invitational race, something added to provide the fans another chance to see us race. Sam and I decided to try a different setup in the invitational and just run a few laps to get the feel of that setup and then pull in. We looked at the race as a test session.

We drew for starting position, and I pulled a two. Steve Kinser pulled a one. I felt confident that I could beat the King with the 01 car, but as we picked up the throttle my motor made an unusual stumble and Steve beat me to the corner exit. I got up on the cushion and ran him down. Steve thought he had me cleared and drifted up.

I ran out of track and tagged the wall with my right rear. I began one of the wildest flips I'd experienced at that point in my career, and I closed my eyes tightly. I actually realized that this was going to be one of those crashes where your eyeball can literally pop out of the socket and I was scared of that possibility. Things got quiet for a few moments and I thought it must be over, so it's probably safe to open my eyes. But I was still in the air and the ground underneath me was still flying past, so I closed my eyes again and held on and braced for more hits.

The best way I can describe what it feels like to crash like this is to imagine somebody putting an air hose to your head and pumping a hundred pounds of pressure inside your skull while a gorilla shakes you as hard as he can. The car finally stopped flipping and I crawled out, immediately realizing that I needed to sit down for a moment on the left rear tire to get my bearings.

Sam came running up and asked if I was okay. I just said, "How's the car?"

Sam pointed down the track. "Do you see that yellow piece way down there?"

"Yeah."

"That's the front half of the frame."

"Oh…not good, huh?"

"Not good."

Lealand McSpadden insisted that I needed to go to the hospital, and somebody drove me there in a private vehicle. When I got to the hospital it seemed like there were more drivers there than in the pits back at the track. Some were there from my wreck—I landed on Jeff Swindell and got him wrecking along with a few others—and some were there from crashes earlier in the night.

They kept me overnight, and I was eager to get out. I needed a doctor to sign my release form, and finally a doctor came in to talk to me. He explained that I had to answer some questions so that he could evaluate my condition. I had a bad case of "red eye" but honestly I don't believe I hit my head. So he started with the usual questions: Where are you? What's your address? What day is it?

Then he asked me, "Who's the president of the United States?" Well, I wasn't into politics, and that one stumped me. He could see the worry in my eyes and he must have figured I was okay because he signed my papers and out the door I went.

I had a good season in Sam and Fred's car, winning 15 races. My daughter Stephanie was born just after the Gold Cup—October 2—so that made for a *great* year.

In spite of traveling to Eldora and Knoxville that summer we managed to win the 1982 Baylands track championship. That was a very satisfying title, because in a way I felt like we had the best of both worlds: we could compete on good footing with the Outlaws on the road, and we could also win at home.

I believed we were as good as anyone in the country. Let's hit the road and win some Outlaws races—on their turf! This made perfect sense to me because we could have done it. We lacked nothing in terms of our race car.

So I went to the race shop in Vallejo and handed Sam the World of Outlaws schedule. Sam just smiled and handed the schedule back to me.

"Yeah, Lealand used to bring me those all the time," he said.

Sam wasn't afraid to go on the road, but he couldn't spend that much time away from his shop. He was very busy with engine work and it wasn't feasible to have all that work waiting for weeks—maybe months—while he was on the road racing.

Chuck Delu built our cars, and we started the 1983 season with a brand new chassis. My crash at Manzanita had marked the expiration date of the previous car, for sure.

We started the season at Ascot, where we ran in the top-5 both nights. At Devil's Bowl we ran third, then ran second at Oklahoma City. We soon headed back to California and won a couple races at Baylands.

Although we were having success with Chuck's chassis, Sam wanted to try a Stanton. This was the hot setup at the time. Gary Stanton was—and is—a very smart and successful man. Gary was also interested in having Sam run his chassis and they made it happen.

One day in the spring of 1983 I was reading *National Speed Sport News* when I saw an ad for a brand new racing event. They put together a series of races over a few days in July and called it Ohio Sprint Speedweek. I figured it would be cool to talk Sam into hauling out to Ohio to run that deal. So I took the advertisement into the shop and started my sales pitch.

Surprisingly enough, Sam liked the idea. So in the middle of July we loaded up and hauled 2,400 miles east to the opening event at Millstream Speedway in Findlay, Ohio, only to get rained out.

The following day at Quad City Speedway in McCutcheonville we had more bad weather. Just as time trials were finishing the wind began to blow and everyone loaded up moments before a huge downpour drenched the place. Everybody headed for the motels to get some rest, and our motel was only about three miles up the road. It was pouring so hard we were driving 10 mph as we made our way there.

Around 11 p.m. I looked out the window and noticed that all the race car haulers had left. I woke Sam up and we hurried back to the track and arrived just as they were getting the track ran in. We raced until 4 a.m.—Steve Kinser won it—and then hauled a couple of hours east to Cortland, Ohio.

There is such a thing as somebody being incompatible with something. I should have seen this coming but, basically, Sam was incompatible with Ohio Sprint Speedweek. That would become evident very quickly.

Sam likes cold weather, and that's why his shop is on the edge of the San Francisco bay. He had figured out a way to cope with the Iowa heat in August because he found a hotel that had dueling air conditioners on opposite sides of the room. He would crank them both up to full blast and you could keep the beer cold by just setting it on the table. Sam loved for things to be nice and cool.

Sam also liked to work on his car in a nice, clean shop. None of that happening here; it is hot, humid, dirty, and with the haul between race tracks every night and maintaining your stuff you were on-your-ass tired.

Oh, there is one other thing Sam found distasteful: crashing. By the time we got to the third night—Sharon, Ohio, near the Pennsylvania state line—we mastered the trifecta and covered all the things Sam hated.

We snapped a left front radius rod and I hit the fence at a pretty good speed and spun around and collected every corner of the car. We dragged it into the trailer and went back to the motel, and the next morning we dragged it out again. We had torn up a lot of parts but we got it fixed and towed a couple of hours to Mansfield, Ohio.

Did I mention that this series had the baddest racers in the country? The Outlaws were there, the Pennsylvania Posse guys were there, and all the tough guys who ran the All-Star Circuit of Champions were there. Most of the races were on big, fast tracks and it was an extremely competitive deal.

Mansfield was one of Earl Baltes's tracks, and they had it a little dusty that night. It was one of those nights when you basically followed the top of the wing of the guy in front of you, hoping nobody was parked on the race track ahead. Late in the race Steve Kinser had a flat right rear and that brought out the yellow which turned into a red and they decided to rework the race track and put down a little water.

Unfortunately they got carried away with the water truck and when they finished it was so sloppy and muddy you could hardly get your wheels to turn over and fire the motor. But they fired everybody off, and just when we figured we were going to roll around and pack for a little while they turned the yellow light off and waved the green flag.

At this point everyone was follow-the-leader because if you got an inch out of line it was all slop. However, the groove came in quickly and it was wide-ass open. Jeff Swindell and Brad Doty got together in front of me on the front straightaway and I turned down to avoid their wreck. Just as I got there Brad came shooting straight across the track in front of me.

I was in the grease and was basically a passenger at that point, and I t-boned Brad right at the motor plate. It almost broke his leg and it bent his car in a big "U" and my car was bent in the shape of an "S".

Both our cars and our teams went to the house. Sam explained that he had seen enough of Ohio Sprint Speedweek and he was heading west: tonight.

It was just like all the other times I've had a divorce with a car owner: he got the car, the spares, the truck, and the trailer, and I got my helmet bag. It was actually quite simple how that worked.

So I was without a ride and basically homeless in Ohio in July. Ah, the solid, dependable world of a sprint car driver...

After parting ways with the Bailey Bros. car in July 1983 I rode around with Tim Green for a while, hoping something would open up. Tim had a big crash at Chicago and I actually thought that would be *his* seat that was about to open up. I rode with Tim to the hospital in the ambulance but he was just too tough and was right back in the car a day or so later.

Right after that race Jeff Swindell moved out of the "penalty box." That was the 80x car owned by the late Crockett Tomlinson of Missouri, a man who owned B&L Electric. The car was really not bad and the reason it got the nickname was because Danny Smith pointed out that from a distance the number—80x—looked like it said, "BOx." The name stuck.

The team was an odd situation, because Crockett had died some months earlier and his widow honored his wishes and kept the race team going. In early August we ran the Eldora Sprint Nationals and did well against a stout field, scoring a 5th and two 3rd-place finishes. The track was so dry each night that an early qualifying number was a premium, and I talked the guy with the bucket into letting me find a low pill each night when we entered the track.

That week we worked out of the automotive repair shop of the Ohio Hillbillies: Harold and Don Nichols. The Nichols Brothers were from Lima, Ohio and they were two of the least sophisticated people I have ever known. They were great guys but they were what some people would describe as, "rough around the edges." They had a race car and were well-known in the Ohio area.

It was an eye-opening experience to hang out with Harold and Don. They loved to play cards—not really gambling, just cards—and every day there was a big game. They'd be wrapped up in a game and their phone would ring and one of the brothers would get up and answer the phone. Somebody would ask about a repair job and they would say, "We're just swamped today, there's no way we could get to it until next week." They'd hang up the phone and hurry back to the table and the game was back on.

They used a tow truck to wrap the cable around a car to lift it on its side to remove the starter to use on another job. I asked how long the wrecker had been holding the car up and one of them said, "Since last fall."

The 80x had two crew members, and although both were young kids they were very hard workers. One of the kids, Marty, still had braces on his teeth. We stayed at his parent's house a couple of days between running Eldora and Missouri, where we won the Jayhawk Nationals at Lakeside. We went on to Knoxville and finished 5th in the Saturday night main.

The car was hauled with a Trans Van, which was a one-ton truck of sorts with dual wheels and a unique look to the front; like a mix between an RV and an oversized van. It was short but it had room to rest and a toilet in the back, which made it kinda nice for getting to the track.

The trailer was a different story. It began life as 40-foot 18-wheel unit but had been reworked with the rear axle removed and other lighter axles attached to the frame—at the wrong place, too far forward. The combination was not a good thing. The trailer was heavy and it pulled the Trans Van all over the highway. That thing towed like hell at any speed, and these kids were 80 mph on two-lane roads. They acted like we were late for the Indy 500 and were starting on the pole. I'd try to nap on the way to the race track, but there was no napping in this vehicle. After piling out of that truck anything the car did on the race track seemed tame by comparison.

I told myself, "Self, as soon as you can find another ride to the race track, take it." After the next race I caught a ride from Lakeside to Knoxville with Russell McNish. Sure enough the kids got off the shoulder and jackknifed the truck on Hwy. 163 near Knoxville. Nobody got hurt but they had to get the trailer hitch welded on the Trans Van.

It was fun hanging around with the two kids, however. When we had time between races we did "kid" things like going to the drive-in to watch monster movies. But late in the season I parted ways with the 80x and went back home to Sacramento.

The final World of Outlaws race of the 1983 season was at Knoxville. I-70 Speedway scheduled a big race one week after the Knoxville finale, and I called the Nichols Brothers to see if they would bring their car to both races. They agreed and I connected with my buddy Bob Miller, who was hauling his car out east with Bobby Brutto driving. Bob enthusiastically said that I was welcome to ride along with him and the car to Knoxville.

Bob had a huge International truck with four-wheel-drive and bunks for sleeping in the back. It looked like it had formerly been an Army troop carrier and had earned the name of "Kong."

Bob picked me up in Sacramento and after I tossed my gear in the back I climbed into the cab with him and he looked over at me and said, "You got anything to say?"

I gave him a puzzled look and said, "I don't know...let's go, I guess? Why?"

"Because I'm about to start this truck and I won't hear a word you say for the next 2,000 miles."

He turned the key and that Detroit Diesel engine fired up and it was immediately clear what he was talking about. That thing was loud! The truck had a 10-speed Road Ranger transmission and none of the other guys could shift, so Bob and I were the designated drivers. Suddenly it became very clear why Bob was so eager for me to ride out with them.

We got to Knoxville just fine and I found my sprint car at the Hy-Vee parking lot across from the track. Don Nichols had his hands wrapped in a lot of white gauze, and he explained that on the way out they lost a fan belt on their van. They got another belt and as Don was putting the belt in place Harold bumped the starter to let the belt roll onto the pulley. Might have been a good plan, but Don's fingers were still in the way. Don apparently left a couple of fingers lying on I-80.

Come to think of it, I don't think his hand was wrapped in gauze; I think it was red grease rags and duct tape.

I knew when Harold and Don hired me that they weren't bringing a showpiece out to Knoxville. The car looked like they removed the wheels and headers and sprayed everything bright yellow, then painted a No. 31 on the tank. However, the car had won some races in previous years, including the World of Outlaws season finale at Eldora in 1978 with Shane Carson at the wheel. I was hoping that history could repeat itself at the 1983 finale, too.

The first thing I noticed was that the seatbelts looked like a faded gray color, like they had maybe spent a couple of winters in the outdoors—alongside the car their tow-truck was holding up. I demanded that if I'm strapping into the car it would at least need a new set of lap belts. Harold grudgingly walked over to Shirley Kear's truck and bought a lap belt.

We rained out on Saturday night and the race was pushed to Sunday afternoon. As expected, the car was much faster than it looked, but I had to run the B-main. When I pushed off for hot laps the magneto switch didn't work and the wheels were bucking and chattering. Harold said, "Don't worry about it, just go race it!"

Which I did, all the while hoping the throttle didn't hang wide open. We were leading the B-main when we had a restart. At that time the Outlaws allowed the race leader to pick up the throttle somewhere entering the third turn. I did that, and everything was going great until I reached turn four where the magneto switch decided to work and shut off the engine.

My first thought, of course, was, "Oh, shit!" Or something along that line. Then I remembered the trouble with the switch and figured it was worth a try. So I flipped the switch and it worked; the motor fired up and we were back in the racing business.

However, the rest of the field had caught up with me, and Rick Ferkel was running second and he bumped my rear bumper. I was able to keep going but the cars behind Rick were having a helluva pile-up with three cars upside down and one car clear over the fence.

There was also some debris into the stands with a slight injury to a fan. The red came out and when I saw the carnage I apologized to Rick and explained about the faulty magneto switch.

A few people thought I did it on purpose and they were pissed, writing letters to *National Speed Sport News* to complain. Nowadays they would just cuss you out on social media.

The next week Bob Miller and his crew went with me to Russell McNish's place in Sedalia. We had a few days of idle time until the I-70 race. It rained all week, which kept us inside most of the time. Russell cooked breakfast each morning; all the good cardiac food including biscuits with gravy, bacon, sausage, the whole deal. Every afternoon was a card game with Russell's big brother, Heavy.

One day instead of playing cards we decided to go bowling. And, as if they go together, we decided that we would all drink excessively. I will be the first to admit that drinking heavily is not a plus for my game. At one point I went to the bar to get another round and the bartender asked if I was the guy who had bowled a 47. I said, "Yeah…you've heard of me?"

On Saturday we traveled to I-70, and all the rain had made the track rough but very fast. I noticed at the start of each heat you could go way up top above the holes and the traffic and pass a few while everybody is all bunched up. Good plan! The green flag came out and we roared into the corner and all the cars left a lane for me to drive around.

Everything was going according to plan and I figured I should be running second by the time we hit the backstretch. A moment later the center broke out of the right front wheel and that was all she wrote. I-70 was formerly a paved track, and was well known for a very low fence on the outside. For an instant I was thinking I might be okay but I happened to hit in a spot where the wall actually kept a car in the track and wiped out our front axle.

We should have cut our losses but Harold and Don had a spare axle so we ran the feature. It was so rough that during the feature it pulled the tops out of both rear shocks so we were done for the weekend. We actually finished the race, and the tank was covered with oil from the shocks and parts of the shocks were hanging from the mounts.

(That little wall at I-70 brought about one of my favorite stories. One day Jac Haudenschild left the track and flipped clear out to the ticket booth. Luckily the tickets had all been sold and nobody was in the booth when Jac made contact. Jac crawled out of the car and walked back inside the track to the pit area, and when he arrived back at his pit his mechanic Kenny Woodruff asked Jac if they made him buy a ticket to get back inside.)

After helping Harold and Don load the car I piled into Bob's truck and we started toward home. I was driving through Wyoming at around 3 a.m. when Bob woke up and said, "Let's pull into this truck stop…the trailer lights look kinda funny."

The tongue had broken almost all the way off the box and was about to disconnect. Bob found a hardy welder who didn't mind spending a few hours lying on his back in 20-degree weather with a 20-mph wind at 3:30 a.m. This guy did a great job—he put braces and gussets on all connections and was a very good welder. When the job was finished Bob inquired, "How much?"

The guy kinda shrugged and said, "Oh…how about fifty bucks?"

Our jaws dropped open and Bob reached into his pocket and pulled out a hundred-dollar bill.

"Here, take your girlfriend to the Dairy Queen!"

We made our way home without any further trouble. It was good to be home, as our daughter Stephanie was a little over a year old. It's tough being away from your family for long periods; especially when you figure your kid is growing up and you're missing everything.

But I wasn't cured of this deal, not by any means. As soon as I got home I was trying to line something up for the next season. In due course it would be like returning to my roots: Duke McMillen and I were going to be back in business together for 1984.

12

Chasing the Outlaws

If my life was portrayed in a television series, a number of people would play what is known as a "recurring role." That's been a real plus in my life, because I've managed to stay friends with people to the point that, when the opportunity arose, we could work together again. And again, and again.

Duke McMillen is one of those recurring roles. He was there almost at the beginning and at different times in my life he was there again. In the mid-1980s Duke and his shop played a big part in a good run in my career.

In 1984 I connected with the Ronnie and Richard Lovell to drive their car. The Lovell Brothers raced out of Duke's shop, which was good because it was close to home and of course I had already worked with Duke many times.

We won 26 sprint car races in 1984, including my second Jayhawk Nationals. I also won six midget races, including a winged midget race at Bakersfield that was promoted by the great car builder, Don Edmunds. It was all the better since I started at the back and whizzed past everybody on the outside at the start of the race to go on and win. Winning in front of Don Edmunds meant a lot to me.

My friend Rick Hirst was living with me at this time, and he had a van with a 4-speed transmission on the floor. There was just something that felt wrong about a van with a 4-speed. After the post-race celebration at Bakersfield we left the track, and I was driving Rick's van and I'd always forget the fact that it wasn't an automatic. Every time I'd slow down for a stop sign the van would start shaking and Rick would yell, "Clutch! Clutch!"

One of the reasons for our success in sprint cars during this period was a new coil-over car built by Duke and his son Scott. We hauled it to our first race of the '84 season at Casa Grande, Arizona.

Ron Shuman and Duke Cook were the race organizers. I had known Ron for several years at this point, and we had raced with each other a lot. Ronnie is from the Phoenix area and he won a lot of races in his career.

Most race drivers I've known are thrifty out of necessity. You're never certain of a steady paycheck; you're not even certain you'll make *anything*. Shuman, however, had perfected the art of "thrifty." He was one of those guys who was born with good sense about money.

Shuman was razzed a lot about this, and probably is still razzed about it. But there was no denying that he had a good mind for money. It was always joked that if you radioed Ron at any stage of the race and asked him how much his current position made at the payoff window, Ron could tell you the amount instantly. In fact, as the joke went, he had even figured his percentage.

Ron was driving Gary Stanton's car at Casa Grande, which made for a very formidable team. I'm sure Ron was figuring on winning his own race, therefore he would keep first-place money close to home.

We wheeled past Ronnie on a race restart and went on to win, but the best part came at the payoff window. I got to the window and Ronnie looked across at me; the look on his face as he counted out the winner's purse was priceless. He tossed the money across the counter to me and I was grinning like a fool. Ron was not grinning, however.

After the race we got something to eat and were coming back to the freeway. Chuck was driving, and he had a big head of steam and was about to miss the on-ramp. We yelled to get his attention but Chuck was so laid back that, in his world, he had plenty of time to make the turn.

Not so! As soon as he turned the wheels the front brakes locked up and we skidded straight into the guardrail. We would later replace the bumper and grill, but after a quick adjustment of the headlights as a temporary fix we were back on the road and headed for home.

I was still driving Duke's car at the start of the '85 season, and we put together a new car that winter. Scott McMillen was helping, along with Terry Grubbs and Johnny "Chewy" Medina. Terry and Chewy had spent time on the road with World of Outlaws teams, so they were good help. We knew those guys as "Grubbs and Chewy."

Duke was also helping at times, but his son Jason McMillen was starting his racing career so Duke missed some of our shows to go with Jason. We had a deal with Brand X engines and a sponsorship deal with Bud Light that I had put together.

We started the season at El Centro, a track with a ton of history. We beat the CRA guys down there, which was an excellent way to start a racing season. We continued with six more sprint car wins, including two at Baylands where we also won a midget race on the same night's program.

We had a big weekend coming up at Hanford and Baylands in mid-May, and I happened to come down with the flu. Grubbs and Chewy were with us, and we had to stop several times for me to get rid of apparently unneeded bodily fluids. I was definitely not feeling great, but in hot laps we discovered that John Bickford's kid was going to hot lap with us. The kid was only 14 years old. His name? Jeff Gordon.

Jeff was too young to race with us, but they allowed him to participate in a hot lap session. I followed Jeff in the session and could immediately see that he had a good feel for the car and definitely had some talent. I couldn't get past him until we came up on a slower car that I used as a pick, driving by Jeff.

A half-lap later I drove wide open into turn one and something broke in the right rear of the car. The car dug in, and now I'm going for a ride. When it finally stopped I was upside down, and I have crashing soreness to add to my flu soreness and misery.

My first thought was, "Okay, at least now I can go back to the truck and sleep."

Getting out of a car that's upside down can be difficult, because you have to wedge yourself against something so that when you unlatch your seat belt you don't fall on your head. The wing was crushed down around the cage but there was an opening so I managed to crawl out.

I was sitting on the race track when I heard a voice say, "I don't know how you feel after that, but do you want to drive my car?"

Well this is a unique situation.

"Which car is it?"

"It's the No. 9 car…Milan Garrett is at the hospital in Fresno with his wife, she's having a baby. I need a driver for today!"

That was my introduction to Les Kepler, who had partnered with Fred Marks to field a sprint car team.

Milan beat us at Baylands two weeks earlier in their car, so I knew it was fast. Plus—and I have shown this tendency throughout my racing career—I have a hard time saying no when someone asks, "Do you want to drive my car?"

We started the feature in the fourth row and I got to second within a lap or two. But the track was dusty, and the officials were concerned.

When I say dusty, I mean, "California dusty." Not "Midwestern dusty." In the Midwest when it's dusty you can't see anything, and I've driven lots of races where it was dusty as hell but you could actually make out a few shapes in front of you. But in California the standard was very different, and they didn't have the tolerance for dusty conditions like they had in the Midwest.

So after maybe seven or eight laps the officials decided to call the race. That was unfortunate, because I could see well enough (if I had been running 10th I probably would have been very thankful they called the race). Plus, I think we would have won. At any rate it was a good experience with the Marks and Kepler team and we exchanged phone numbers.

We drove over to Brent Kaeding's shop that night to fix our car for the following night's race at Baylands. It was an all-day fix but we got to the track in time to run third, which wasn't bad. My flu was getting a little better; I wasn't running to the toilet every 10 minutes, but I was still feeling weak and dehydrated.

However, the Lovell Brothers were very upset when they heard I gave up on their car after crashing at Hanford and immediately drove another man's car. On Monday Richard Lovell called me to tell me they are divorcing me and I was no longer driving their car, despite the six wins together.

This was actually the right thing anyway. Richard wanted their car to run at Chico every Friday night so he could have local bragging rights, and that program wasn't interesting to me. I wanted to travel.

I was out of a job, so I immediately got on the phone to Les Kepler and asked if he and Fred Marks wanted to hire me as their steady driver. Milan Garrett was a fine racer and was doing a good job in the car, but obviously he had a new family to think of.

Les said that sounded okay so he hired me right there over the phone. Milan was pissed at me for a very long time and wouldn't even speak to me when he saw me at the race track. I understand, totally. But Marks and Kepler wanted to travel with the World of Outlaws, and so did I. Plus I brought the Brand X engine deal and the Bud Light sponsorship. I *AM* sorry, Milan.

This looked like it was going to be a marriage made in heaven. Everybody was nice to each other, and we ran well. We won six of our first eight races midway through the 1985 season, including the Pombo-Sargent Classic at Hanford, the Baylands Summer Nationals, and the Dirt Cup at Skagit.

Fred Marks and Les Kepler made some money as real estate developers in Grover City, California, which is located next to Pismo Beach and is famous for its sand dunes. The story of how they came to own a sprint car is very interesting.

Fred and his wife Bobbie and Les and wife Susie were great friends, and they loved traveling to Baja, Mexico. On one of their first trips they were in an RV and the roads were so rough that the RV literally shook apart. The refrigerator fell out on the floor and the air conditioner on the roof was dislodged and eventually the motor blew up.

Fred and Les took the engine apart and found a broken piston and some burned valves. They needed some parts so they chartered a small airplane to fly back north to get what they needed.

On the return flight they met with disaster. As Bobbie and Susie looked on in horror, the pilot landed short of the airstrip and crashed. As the plane skidded to a stop Fred and Les and the pilot realized they weren't hurt but could smell a strong odor of gasoline. Thank God the fuel didn't ignite, or all three would have been history. They scrambled out of the plane and were okay.

Their brush with death greatly affected them. From that moment Fred and Les decided to enjoy life as owners of a sprint car team. It might be an odd path to choose but it worked for them.

They had a long trailer, and they hired Jim Thorpe to finish the trailer and work on the race car. Once completed we loaded everything up and hit the road. Les, Susie and Lester rode in the rig; Fred and Bobbie rode in their RV; I traveled in our RV with wife Karen and daughter Stephanie. Eventually Jim Thorpe had a trailer, too.

Our travel costs were probably more than any team with the Outlaws. It was a fleet operation, you might say.

We finished the year together with 11 wins, and we decided to take on the World of Outlaws full-time in 1986.

That winter Karen and I bought a new RV from Jack Gordon. On New Year's Eve we went to Pismo Beach to celebrate.

Things had been pretty good for me that season, so I had some money to spend. I purchased a new Yamaha 250 dirt bike from Keith Cullen, Les's son-in-law. I loaded my new Yamaha into the trailer for the trip to Pismo Beach, along with my older Yamaha 465.

Keith was a dealer in Delano, California, and he arrived at Pismo Beach with a flatbed trailer loaded with quads. Tim Green and my sister Marcy bought a new RV and they came along as well. We spent two days riding and drinking around a bonfire, celebrating our upcoming adventure. Keith blew out his knee in a crash, so he was self-medicating to kill the pain.

Finally we loaded our RV and headed for home. We stopped for fuel when we reached Interstate 5, so while everybody got out and stretched I replaced a fuse for the radio. It was too dark to see the fuse so everybody piled back into the RV and off we went, headed north toward Sacramento.

After about a hundred miles we switched off and Karen took over the driving. I kind of looked around the RV and realized something was missing.

Scooter! Our beloved dog was nowhere to be found.

We found the first exit and made a U-turn. I took over behind the wheel, and I was in a full-blown panic over Scooter. We ran into some fog and even 50 mph was really pushing it. My mind was racing with bad thoughts. It would be at least two hours before we could get back to the station, and by that time Scooter would surely wander out onto the Interstate. He looked like a little black bear and nobody would see him in the dark. Scooter was an innocent little dog with no regard for cars and the damage they could do to his furry little body.

I was almost in tears, thinking this was going to end very badly.

We found the exit and wheeled into the gas station. There was Scooter, lying patiently at the side of the building like nothing at all had happened. He was very confused, however. You could look into his little eyes and almost read his thoughts: "Where did these dumbass people go? And now they're back here hugging and crying like it's a miracle or something!"

When you're driving a good car with a great motor and there is excellent chemistry between you and the crew and the car owner, the World of Outlaws is still a brutally tough deal. You're racing against the very best and it beats you down very quickly.

So you can imagine what it's like when you're out there and things aren't anywhere close to right for you and your team.

In 1986 Gambler had a new chassis that was the hot thing, but it didn't work for my style. Just didn't fit. It felt like it was loose all the time, and I just couldn't get going.

Les hired a mechanic who had worked for Karl Kinser, and the mechanic knew what Karl used to run in terms of setup. Well, what worked for Karl and Steve Kinser didn't work for me, and the new mechanic and his wealth of knowledge wasn't helping me at all.

Les was a good guy, but he had a short fuse at times. Once you pissed him off, it was never the same after that. Our first real exchange came at Devil's Bowl, where I pulled in after I got lapped.

Les was outraged that I would pull in when the car was still running. I wasn't used to the idea of points racing, and once we were lapped I figured we were better off getting out of everybody's way and let's fix this thing.

Things got worse.

We were at Port Royal in Pennsylvania, running in the back. I tried everything to pass somebody, including jumping the restarts. However, the guy I jumped just drove back by me in the next corner.

After the race Les asked me, "Why didn't you jump more cars?"

I wasn't very diplomatic and I said something like, "What the fuck, they would all just drive back by me anyway."

A lot of car owners feel like if they're spending as much money as Karl Kinser to go racing, they should have equal or better results. It's hard to make somebody understand that this deal is much more complicated than just buying parts and then you win races. It's about getting everything and everybody working together, and money can't buy that chemistry or that combination.

So in due course Fred and Les lost faith in me, and I was tired of banging my head against the wall. In that situation it becomes obvious that your days together are numbered, and in our case it was a small number. We said our goodbyes and went our separate ways.

13

Traveling with Lenard

When you're exiting a ride you're immediately plotting your next move. There is a nationwide network of sorts—and this was before smartphones or social media—and you monitor any open seats or any teams that might be thinking about making a change.

Randy Smith had just vacated the Cahill Brothers ride, so that was my next move. I talked to their mechanic Lenard McCarl—who was a part owner of the team—and we shook hands and decided to give each other a try.

What a way to start: in our first race together—July 5, 1986—we beat the World of Outlaws at Black Hills Speedway in South Dakota. Interestingly enough, it was the same night that Lenard's young son Terry won his first race at Knoxville. The following night we won again at an unsanctioned race at Sioux Falls so we were definitely getting started on a positive note.

Ken and Larry Cahill owned a bunch of Holiday Inn and Hilton hotels, and a company that refurbishes hotels "inside and out." They also owned some fast food restaurants. Ken and Larry were doing very well in business and they worked hard to accomplish their success.

They would fly into our races on their Citation jet, then fly home to Cedar Rapids, Iowa. Most of the time they owned a hotel property near the track, and we had free accommodations. If they didn't own a property nearby they would contact the owner of a local hotel and ask for a room for themselves. The hotel owner would almost always provide a free room for the Cahill Brothers.

On those trips when they didn't come, that meant Lenard and I would pose as Ken and Larry Cahill in order to use their free hotel room. We would show up at different times and I would tell the girls at the front desk that I was Ken Cahill. They would look at each other and study my dirty jeans and racing t-shirt and say, "Yes sir, Mr. Cahill, your brother is already here."

Sometimes when I got to the room there was a chilled bottle of wine or a fruit basket. This was a first-class deal!

Ken and Larry were both married, and their spouses played a big role in running their business. They were all fun people; even the pilots were fun to hang out with.

We were at Fargo, North Dakota when it rained and we had to pit on a road outside the track. The security was pretty lax and the girls had a great time picking up pieces of wristband from behind the pit shack, then taping them together so they wouldn't have to buy a pit pass. When the race was over they got on their private jet and flew home.

I remember thinking, "Maybe that's why they have millions, they see every possibility."

My experience in the car was good, and my experience working with Lenard was great. He was such a fun guy, had a great sense of humor and was fun to be around. He taught me a lot.

After the 1986 season Lenard and the Cahill Brothers split up and they were no longer part of the team. That changed a few things, especially the hotel situation. Once we were traveling on Lenard's nickel—he was a typical racer, scrimping and scratching along to survive—our accommodations were less, shall we say, *palatial*.

I remember one fleabag hotel in Colorado where the parking lot was dirt—not gravel, but dirt—and a couple of junkyard dogs were running loose right outside our door.

Lenard had a wicked sense of humor, and that's probably why we got along so well. After a little while we could figure out what each other was thinking, especially when it came to pulling tricks and pranks on people.

We were traveling to Fargo and stopped at Watertown, South Dakota to spend the night. We left the rig parked and Lenard, Billy and Virgil jumped into my RV and we rode down the street to look for something to eat.

We landed at a typical Chinese restaurant with an Asian family running the place. We were the only customers there, and as we were finishing our meal the mother looked out the window at the parking lot and saw my RV.

"Is that you really big car?" she asked with the usual heavy accent. I'm thinking this poor woman has never seen an RV, so I asked if she wanted to see the inside.

Her eyes lit up and off we go, and as we got inside the RV I realized her entire family—waiters, cashier, cooks, everybody—had followed us out and were in the RV with us. I didn't mind but I immediately realized that meant Lenard and the guys were in the restaurant alone, and I knew that was not a good thing.

In the back of my mind I could imagine Lenard opening the register and cleaning out the till, just as a prank. As a matter of fact, at that moment he was in the restaurant stuffing napkins down his pants and he had already worked everything out in his mind. When I came back inside he was going to show me the bulge in his pants and imply that he had rifled the register and that we needed to get the hell out of town, now. He figured he'd have me in a panic.

When we got back inside I immediately pulled Lenard aside and looked him right in the eye without a hint of a smile on my face.

"Did you clean out the till?" I whispered.

He almost fell out of his chair laughing, and he showed me the bulge of napkins in his pants and I cracked up, too.

That's an example of how we would think alike. I knew what prank he was likely to pull, and he could usually guess what I was up to. It was fun because we really got after each other.

When we stopped at a restaurant Lenard would insist that we sit at a booth, and he would always sit at the back of the booth. If we had anybody new on our crew we sat them at the front of the booth, closest to the waitress.

The waitress would come to the table and as she was taking our order Lenard would reach under the table and extend his tape measure and rub the end up her leg. Of course she would jump back and slap the guy closest to her. (This was obviously many years before the #MeToo movement.)

Lenard had a unique brand of wisdom, and a quick wit. We were at the track one day and rain was threatening, and some guy asked Lenard, "Which way does the rain usually come in here?"

Lenard pointed his finger straight up and said, "Up there."

One day I was calling home and giving our race results to someone and Lenard called from across the room, "Tell 'em you ran third. It doesn't sound too bad and nobody ever checks to see if you ran third."

We were at the race track and someone was helping us push the car up to the line. The guy said, "This car sure rolls easy." Lenard immediately replied, "Don't say that around my driver!"

On a serious note, Lenard explained to me that turn one is the tightest turn at nearly every race track, because turns two and three nearly always has a longer radius. It's true if you think about it.

It was August, and we were working in Lenard's shop to get ready for the Knoxville Nationals. I looked outside to see my dog Scooter walking in small circles and falling over. I ran outside to discover a big knot on the side of his head and a red eye, and it looked like he might have been hit by a car out in the street.

From that moment everything is fuzzy for me. I remember being rained out that night at Knoxville, and the next thing I remember is being awakened by Karen in the middle of the night. I was very confused.

"Where are we?" I asked.

"We're in Des Moines, and you got hurt tonight," she explained.

"Who am I driving for?"

"Lenard McCarl."

"Am I fired for crashing?"

"No," she explained. "Lenard thinks you're great."

Just as I started to ask my next question she handed me a piece of paper that had the answer to every question I was about to ask.

The paper said, "You drive for Lenard McCarl. No, you're not fired. Yes, you were fast. No, you can't have anything to eat because your stomach is upset from the concussion you suffered. No, we're not going to have sex."

I was never more amazed in my life.

"How did you know I was going to ask those questions?" I asked her.

"Because I have to wake you up every hour, and you ask me the same questions every time I wake you up. So I wrote down the answers for you."

My short term memory was basically out, and I would ask each of the questions and she would point at the paper, and I would look at it and be amazed all over again.

The following day Karen wanted to find my Mom—she was in town for the race—and let her see that I was all right. Karen left Scooter and I in our RV and told us to stay put while she walked over to my mom's hotel.

Scooter and I sat in the RV for a while and then our ADHD kicked in and we looked at each other and decided it was time to take a walk and off we went. Karen and my mom came back to the RV to discover that we were gone, and a full-blown panic set in.

They didn't quite know what to do. Here were two head injury cases—me and Scooter—wandering around somewhere in Des Moines, with no idea even what day it was. But after a little while Scooter and I came walking back to the RV like nothing had happened.

Karen and Mom were quite relieved to see us. In fact, I think Karen might have even shed a tear of happiness when she saw we were okay. That occasion was notable.

That night, and that episode, signaled the beginning of the end of our marriage. At the end of the season Karen basically said, "You can kill yourself in one of these cars, but I don't have to watch you do it."

I understand where she was coming from. The racer's lifestyle looks exciting sometimes, especially to young women who think it would be fun to be involved with a racing person. That life looks exciting until you have to live it.

We did not instantly divorce. It doesn't usually work like that anyway; it's a painful process and both parties have to find their way through it. We were apart, then tried again a couple of times, and finally both accepted that it wasn't going to work, and that was the end. We finally sat down and worked out the details and filed for divorce and took care of the legal stuff.

The worse part of everything was that it made life more complicated for our daughter Stephanie. For the rest of her life, her parents were two separate entities.

Plus, strictly from a logistical standpoint, it made it much more difficult for me to spend time with my daughter. I was out on the road racing, and Stephanie and her mom were stationary in California. The only way I would see Stephanie is to go back to California, or figure out some way for her to travel out to see me, wherever I might be at that moment. That's a challenging proposition for a single dad, traveling with a small kid while you're chasing up and down the road and racing 100-plus nights a year.

It was a really dark and painful time for me. I was lonely, I was scared, I missed Stephanie. It's hard to get fired up about another racing season when you feel like everything is lined up against you.

The grind of racing was starting to wear on me. For the first time in my life, I began to realize that things couldn't go on like this forever. And they didn't.

Lenard McCarl and I kicked off the 1987 season together, chasing the World of Outlaws schedule. Things started off pretty well and we continued to work well together.

In April we had a couple of days off in Indiana and Karl Kinser invited us to work on our car at his shop in Oolitic, just south of Bloomington. Karl apparently had a lot of respect for Lenard, and they shared a passion for engine building and car construction.

Karl and his driver Steve Kinser were on the verge of a monster season, winning 51 World of Outlaws features. 51! It's hard to grasp that number all these years later, but at the time it was tough for any of us to match that level of performance. Steve and Karl had found some advantages and they were just that much better than everybody else.

It was a great experience that April, spending time at Karl's shop. Karl had built a log home out of timber fallen from the nearby woods, then built a lot of his furniture as well. What an amazing craftsman!

Tow rigs were still pretty basic at this time, and Karl towed with a crew cab dually Chevy pickup. You couldn't buy a good diesel engine in a full-size pickup, so Karl installed a Caterpillar V8 diesel with an Allison transmission into the Chevy. It was a helluva project, and required some very creative engineering. But it towed like a champ and got much better fuel mileage as well.

On the second day of our April visit I stayed back at our hotel, the Knights Inn (we definitely weren't on the Cahill deal anymore) in Bloomington. I decided to get some rest, and after I showered I noticed that someone had left a woman's nightgown hanging on a hook on the back of the bathroom door. I kinda laughed and didn't give it a thought, but it led to some inspired thinking a few minutes later.

I walked through downtown Bloomington and got a haircut, enjoying the day. As I was walking past a sex shop an idea popped into my head and I couldn't help but smile.

I went inside the shop and bought a life-sized blow-up sex doll and walked back to our hotel. I inflated the doll and put the nightgown on her and tucked her in. When Lenard and the guys came back to the hotel I quietly mentioned that there was someone waiting for them in my room, and when they looked inside and saw the doll we all had a great laugh.

But that was only the beginning.

The doll needed a name, and we thought it over. Whenever Lenard told a joke it seemed like the lady's name in the joke was always "Mildred," so that was the name we chose.

All of the other teams had at least one woman at their trailer every night—wife, girlfriend, mom, sister, whatever—cheering the team on during the races. So we brought Mildred with us and put her on top of our trailer in a lawn chair. The other wives and girlfriends in the pits didn't seem to share our sense of humor but hey, Mildred got right into the spirit of things. The shape of her mouth made it look like she was shouting, "GOOOoooo!"

No, we did not actually use the doll for the purpose intended by the manufacturer. None of that. We all respected Mildred far too much for that sort of thing.

A few days later we were hauling down the road near Chicago, and our mechanic, Virgil Brandt, was driving our truck. Virgil is a super-nice guy, very clean-cut and respectful. He's also very shy.

As we rolled up to a toll booth Lenard reached up and placed Mildred on the seat next to Virgil. The woman in the toll booth called out the fee, and now Virgil is so nervous and embarrassed that he can't find the toll money and he can't speak. He finally fumbled and counted out the change and as the lady handed him the ticket she smiled and said, "I like your girlfriend."

In May we traveled to Indianapolis to race on the one-mile track at the Indiana State Fairgrounds. The Indy Mile is a bad fast race track; today the World of Outlaws doesn't race on any one-mile tracks because the cars are simply too fast and too light for these conditions.

Our straightaway speeds in 1987 were in the 165- to 170-mph range and you ran wide open through the corner. I had raced there once before but only ran a few laps, and I wasn't very comfortable on that earlier visit.

Lenard didn't put any special aero elements on our body, but we did have a new set of wings with a clean leading edge and no rock dents. Lenard stiffened all four spring rates and put more tow in the front wheels to make for a better feel.

We qualified on the pole, with Steve Kinser on the outside and Sammy Swindell right behind me. That's two of the baddest sprint car drivers in history. As we lined up I could tell that Steve's motor was loading up and with those tall gears at the mile, probably wasn't going to take off very well. We were rolling to the start, and Steve was trying to clear his motor on the backstretch before we took off in turn three.

I let Steve go, which caused a false start. On the next try I was the pace setter, so I brought us to the start a little slower than normal to try and take advantage of Steve's situation. I throttled down coming out of four and left Steve trying to get his motor to run.

It worked out perfectly, and after eight or 10 laps I started to feel pretty good. I was beginning to get used to the high speeds and our car was perfect.

We came up on two or three lapped cars that were scattered all over the track. I wasn't sure how much of a lead we had, but I do know that with the caliber of racers following me that if I followed the lapped cars on the bottom as we go into turn one I'm gonna get smoked.

I left the throttle wide open and drove to the outside of the lapped cars. I was very pleased to discover that at that speed the wing was providing a huge amount of downforce and you could drive almost anywhere on the track you wanted. I whipped past all three lapped cars before we got to the back straightaway.

Steve got stuck for an instant behind the lapped cars, and that was the difference. On the mile, just lifting for a moment will kill your momentum. When I hit turn three I had a lead of a half-straightaway.

After that I was cocky, knowing that my car could run anywhere on the track. If I came up on anybody I just drove past them on the outside and never lifted.

We lapped up to sixth place at the finish, which was Brad Doty in the Marks and Kepler car, my old ride. That was just an added bit of satisfaction, I must admit.

In July the Outlaws headed for Minnesota, where we got rained out at Jackson. A group of people decided to head down to Lake Okoboji and Spirit Lake, about a half-hour south into Iowa.

I fell into a disreputable group that included Danny Smith, Kelly Pryor, Jamie Kepler, Les Kepler, Fred Marks, Jac Haudenschild and his soon-to-be bride Patty Sweeney, and Greg Rule. It was great fun and I knew there were good times to be had.

We started the journey at a strip club where they were having a contest to see who could find the most creative way to present the dollar tip to the dancer. Greg Rule tied a folded dollar bill to his penis and he won the contest by universal vote.

The following day we rented a ski boat with an inflated torpedo to tow, and we had some spectacular crashes. If you were riding on the front of the torpedo and everybody from behind crashed into you, that was a tough experience. I had sore ribs for two weeks after that.

We also had a couple of Jet Ski's, and as I was handing off the Jet Ski to somebody and was swimming in to the dock something hit me and shoved me down into the water. For an instant I thought it was the ski boat. But it was only Patty, coming in for a landing on skis. After bouncing off me she piled into the dock, as well.

When we turned everything in we were told there was $3,500 worth of damages. Greg Rule always seemed to have plenty of cash, and he stepped forward to cover our damages. I am, to this day, still thankful for his kind gesture. Unfortunately we lost Greg a few years later when he drowned in San Francisco Bay while swimming with friends.

Although Lenard and I worked well together, we had lots of challenges as the 1987 season began to wind down. Our stuff was getting worn out and we weren't running well. Which meant that I wasn't making any money, and when that happens I start getting very concerned.

It isn't a matter of greed; it's a matter of survival. I was a professional racer and I had no other source of income. In business they would call it a "revenue stream" but regardless of how you put it, if I didn't make money at the pay window it wasn't going to be long before I was flat broke.

Lenard and I decided to go our separate ways for a little while. I returned to California and see if I could find somebody's car to race, and meanwhile Lenard would work on his motors and try to get things freshened up.

Karen and Stephanie were living in Placerville, so I went over for a visit. Afterwards I drove down to Fresno to see Tim Green who was hospitalized after suffering serious burns in a racing crash at Madera.

I would visit Tim several times while he was recovering, and we tried to cheer each other up. We'd sit in his room and talk about racing, and he offered me his sprint car ride if I needed it.

That was a hard thing for me to consider. I didn't want to benefit from Tim's misfortune. So initially I wouldn't consider it but after a few weeks I was beginning to think more seriously that it might be an option.

Life does that sometimes. You get beaten down to where you are willing to swallow your pride and do something uncomfortable because you're out of other choices.

As the great philosopher Doug Wolfgang once said, "I have been humbled to the max."

That perfectly describes how I was feeling at that point. There were a few bright spots; I went with Sam Bailey to Baylands and we won, which helped boost my confidence a little. Sam had a new car built by Lee Osborne, and everybody who had driven the car the past 6 races had won; luckily I maintained the streak. But Sam didn't want to race much, so it didn't present a long-term opportunity.

So I finally told Tim that I was willing to take over his sprint car ride until something else came my way. I finished out the 1987 season with Virgil and Anne Owen.

I knew Virgil and Annie spent the money it took to have a winning car. I also knew that Tim would put in the time and effort and expertise to put the pieces in place to win. And that's what we did, leading through the late stages of the season: we won. We started out by winning six of our first nine races together, including a terrific run in June at Skagit where we swept the Super Dirt Cup weekend.

Virgil wasn't interested in running the Outlaws schedule, but he did agree to take the car to Knoxville. So I ran some races out west with Virgil, then reconnected with Lenard in July and ran Omaha, Erie, Rapid City, and Jackson, Minnesota.

In August 1987 I reconnected with Virgil and Anne to drive their car at the Knoxville Nationals.

If anyone tells the story of the 1987 Nationals, they'll talk about the rain. Several inches of rain fell throughout the week and it completely disrupted everything.

Wednesday night was washed out early, and on Thursday we rolled out to qualify and set a new track record. That was an exciting deal but just as qualifying was finishing—I think there were two cars left to go—it began to rain and the officials had no choice but to postpone the program, which meant that we would all qualify again.

That wiped out our track record. However, on Friday night we drew another good number and set another new track record of 16.263 seconds, a couple of tenths quicker than we had gone the night before.

Carrera talked us into putting a trick shock on the left rear for our heat race, and it made the car so tight I missed the transfer by one position and had to run the B-main, which we won. We started the race and didn't make one lap before the skies opened up, and the balance of the show was postponed to Saturday. But our track record stood. That was a unique situation, because on the opening lap turns one and two were fine but when we got to turn three it was like a cloudburst. Everybody was sliding all over the place, bouncing off each other, and it was amazing that nobody got torn up.

We got to 9th in our preliminary feature, and lined up 6th for the championship event, which was pushed to the early hours of Sunday morning. Although Steve Kinser had everybody covered in the main event, we had a great run in Virgil's car. Bobby Davis Jr., Jeff Swindell, Mark Kinser, and I had a terrific race, and we were all over each other.

We ended up fifth, which was a good weekend. Virgil decided we would stick around to run Memphis, about a week following the Nationals. We were leading when a king pin came out of the right front, allowing the wheel and tire to leave us. The right front corner of the car dragged the ground and I thought I would just glide to a stop, but when I was almost stopped the inertia of the car spun me around to face traffic.

That made for a memorable moment: I was looking the entire field in the eyes as they came smoking right at me. Luckily everybody missed and after a minute or two I actually started breathing again.

The 1987 season was a good one for me, but as the season drew to a close I knew I would be moving to a different car. Tim Green recovered enough that he was anxious to return to racing, and that meant I was out of Virgil and Anne's car. They were nice enough to put together a second car for the last race of the year at Baylands.

That was the Hollywood ending I mentioned earlier in the book. Although Tim was still really weak and hurting, he did a helluva job and won the race. Steve Kent ran second and I was third, and we had to help Tim from the car because he was just whipped.

But man, what a moment. It was just so emotional. Tim Green is a tough son-of-a-gun and I was extremely proud of him that night. I guess it meant so much more because I had witnessed firsthand what a battle it had been for Tim to even climb into the car, never mind racing and winning.

Tim's win was a happy moment, but there weren't a lot of those for me in late 1987. My tenure with Lenard had come to an end, and I didn't have anything lined up for 1988. There was a nagging feeling, too, that something was wrong. Not so much physically, but *mentally*.

Karen and I had tried a reconciliation, but in late '87 she told me she just couldn't watch me race anymore. It was time to split our stuff; I got the RV and my dog Scooter, while Karen got the house in Placerville and Stephanie would be staying with her.

I had to face reality: if I continued to race nationally and follow the World of Outlaws schedule, I would see very little of my daughter back in California.

It was not a fun time. I was lonely, I was worried about finding a ride, and I missed Stephanie. It's hard to get fired up about another racing season when you feel like the pieces to the puzzle are all jumbled up.

I made two trips to Australia that winter, and that helped pick up my spirits. It's hard to be sad and depressed when you're around Aussies.

I had made a deal to go racing for a guy from Ohio who wanted to make a serious effort at the 1988 All-Star Circuit of Champions title and had lined up all the pieces to make it happen. We would have brand new Nance race cars, he hired Marshall Campbell as the mechanic, and a local Chevrolet dealer had offered a tow vehicle. Warren Johnson promised a new trailer, and an amusement park from northwest Ohio was supposed to provide some sponsorship.

I called LaVern Nance to inquire about the guy, and Mr. Nance said that as far as he knew everything was okay.

Things didn't turn out nearly as well as anyone had hoped. When I returned from my second Australian trip I traveled to Wichita, but Marshall hadn't arrived yet. Carroll Nance and I began building the cars, and Marshall arrived to help us put the motor in our first car. There was a snag with the Chevy dealership so we had to use Marshall's truck instead, but luckily Warren came through with a new trailer. The amusement park apparently backed out, and that meant we weren't able to get an aluminum engine. The All-Stars were still running steel blocks, and the lack of an aluminum motor meant that we would be seriously handicapped at Outlaws events.

We were behind from the get-go. We missed the opening race at Jacksonville because we didn't have everything finished, and that immediately put us in a hole from a points standpoint. But we won a race at Volusia, and felt like we were getting it together.

We headed for East Bay and Marshall accidently filled his truck with diesel fuel. I was driving a few minutes later and was drafting a semi-truck ahead of us because our truck acted like it didn't want to run. After a few minutes Marshall pointed out that our heat gauge was rising, and that I needed to back off and get some air to our radiator. That's when I noticed that we were blowing black smoke.

"Did you put diesel in this thing by mistake?"

"No, it was gasoline."

"Then we need to go back to the station…something is wrong with their fuel."

Sure enough it was fuel from a green outlet, and we went to scramble mode. I will confess that we were not good to the environment at that moment; we flushed the diesel and dumped it out alongside the road and then filled our tank with gasoline.

We were leading on the final night at East Bay when a bolt came out of the panhard bar and we ended up fourth.

Now we were already at a crossroad. Without the aluminum engine we couldn't race again until the next All-Stars race in the Midwest, which meant a two-month layoff. Marshall and I already didn't see eye-to-eye on things, so I made a clean break and decided to go back home.

However, the experience was worth it because it allowed me to spend a week in Wichita at Mr. Nance's house with him and his wife Marvell. They were truly amazing and gracious people.

When I made it back to California I connected with Clyde Lamar and we won at San Jose, and then beat the Outlaws at the Mini Gold Cup at Chico on March 5. I was living in the RV so it was truly a mobile home at that point.

The Outlaws were headed for Oklahoma and Texas the following week, so I called Daryl Saucier to ask about running his car. Darryl and I had raced together pretty well a couple of times the year before, and he told me to come on down to Tulsa. But when we reconnected everything went wrong over the next couple of races; we cut a tire, we got caught up in somebody else's wreck, just the standard deal of not having an ounce of good luck.

I was driving to Oklahoma City when I had a revelation. Several months earlier Doug Wolfgang had told me that if I ever needed a ride, I should give Bob Weikert a call. Weikert was a hugely successful car owner who ran locally in Central Pennsylvania. He was big in the cattle business and his car was known as the Beefmobile.

At the next exit I wheeled off the Interstate and found a pay phone. I dialed Bob's number and sure enough Bob answered the phone. He said he was glad to hear from me and as a matter of fact, he needed a driver.

"When can you be here, son?" he asked.

I explained that I would head east after tonight's race and could be at his place by Tuesday.

"That's good," he replied. "We'll run Port Royal on Wednesday, then."

Boom. Just like that, I had a ride in Pennsylvania.

14

My friend is hurting

Bob Weikert had a reputation as a tough, gruff guy. But my experience with Bob was quite good, and he was very supportive. He allowed me to live in the house where Doug Wolfgang and his family had lived, and the place was even furnished with a few trophies Wolfie had won.

One of the things you learn pretty quickly in Central Pennsylvania is that the fans there are passionate and, well…kinda nuts. If they don't like you, they are relentless. And they openly resented the fact that a guy from California was driving a local car—not just a local car, but *Weikert's* local car—and they let me hear it every week.

One night I was standing on the track in turn one, checking to see where the holes were forming up. I heard a voice from the stands yell, "Hey, Sills!"

I smiled and raised my hand to wave, and the voice said, "Fuck you!"

I slowly lowered my hand, and my head.

But when the Outlaws came to town there was an amazing transformation. I was suddenly a member of the Pennsylvania Posse—Placerville, Pennsylvania, maybe—and they loved me. They cheered their guts out when I was introduced.

Posse fans are a different breed. Definitely.

Davey Brown Sr. and Davey Brown Jr. were both legendary mechanics. They had been working on the Weikert car, but apparently departed shortly before I arrived. Davey Sr. was still doing our motors, however. Fred Grenoble was my mechanic initially, and later it was Sonny Kratzer.

The All-Stars scheduled a race at Wilmot, Wisconsin on May 18, a Wednesday night. That's a long tow from Central Pennsylvania, but we were getting $1,000 to show up so we were definitely going to make the trip.

Fred and I were scheduled to leave the shop at 1 a.m. I had the first shift to drive the hauler and climbed behind the wheel of our Ford Centurion Van—basically a large van-type vehicle with dual rear wheels—and we started rolling west while Fred got some sleep in the shotgun seat.

It was almost dawn the following morning and it was time for my driving shift to conclude. I was really tired, and the plan was to stop at the next exit. However, before that could happen another road adventure was taking shape. It was one of those, "Wake up, Fred! You don't want to miss this!"

We came upon a construction zone across a bridge where the eastbound lane shifted over to share the westbound portion of the bridge. You've basically got Interstate traffic funneled into a two-lane state highway. Just as we approach the bridge I felt a shudder and heard a loud bang and the truck was trying to go sideways across the bridge.

I'm not sleepy anymore and I'm yelling at Fred that he should wake up and brace for a crash. I managed to get the truck under control and we limped across the bridge and as I tried to ease onto the shoulder on the other side of the bridge the truck would no longer move. I pressed the gas pedal and the engine revved up without us moving, and that is a sure sign that something is not good.

Fred opened the back door of the van and noticed that the right rear wheels had left the vehicle. I hopped out and had a look and not only were the wheels gone, but the brake drum and shoes had departed as well.

A guy on the construction crew yelled that one of our wheels was up in the trees across the bridge. Fred stayed with our vehicle and waited for the State Police while I walked back across the bridge to look for our wheel.

That's when I made an interesting observation. Bridges on the Interstate Highway System are not designed for pedestrians. The sidewalk is about 18 inches wide, and traffic—including semi-trucks—is brushing past you running about 60 mph and kicking up shrapnel from our vehicle.

I crossed without injury and discovered that one of our wheels was indeed up the hill amidst the forest. Now I had the task of rolling the wheel and tire back across the bridge.

Anyone who has ever tried to roll a dually wheel has found that the wheel has a huge offset to allow the wheels to mate together on the hub. This offset causes the wheel—which you're now trying to roll—to pull very hard in one direction. I had a choice; I could roll the wheel where it wanted to pull out into the traffic, or I could roll it so that it wanted to pull toward the wall of the bridge.

I chose wall. But at least now the road shrapnel was hitting me in the back instead of in the face.

I made it back across and found the State Police waiting. They explained that our other wheel had its brief moment of freedom cut short when it collided with an eastbound Fiat. The officer explained that this poor guy in the Fiat had been driving all night when our wheel fell out of the sky and impaled itself into his grill.

We tried all day to round up the parts to put the truck back together and make it to Wilmot, but the Centurion used an adapter to mount the wheels that was unlike anything else. We had to travel to the manufacturer, located in White Pigeon, Michigan, to get the part.

We were a no-show at Wilmot. But the good news is that nobody was hurt and I don't think the guy in the Fiat sued anybody. I'll bet he had some interesting visions for the next few nights, however.

Pennsylvania racers are some of the very best and most dedicated in the world. I got along with all of them…except Joey Gravino. For some reason Joey and I just didn't have the right chemistry.

Not long after I arrived in Pennsylvania in early 1988 we were starting an A-main in the fourth row, and at the start the guys in the row ahead of me split to go to the top and bottom of the track, respectively. I drove between them when one car dropped to block and caused a big pile-up coming for the green.

Everybody got stopped and as I'm sitting in my car I hear Joey yelling and cussing like a madman and I'm thinking, "Yeah Joey, you tell them sons-a-bitches!" Then I looked over and he's yelling at me! Somehow he figured all this carnage was my fault.

It seemed like every week after that he started in front of me, and he made my life a living hell every time I tried to pass him.

During the 1988 season Fred Grenoble departed as crew chief and Weikert hired Sonny Kratzer. Sonny is a neat guy, a Vietnam veteran from Fresno who is kinda low-key but definitely knows his stuff. Sonny later went on to enjoy many successful years as a crew chief with a variety of drivers on the World of Outlaws circuit.

It was a mid-week race at Eldora when I discovered what Sonny Kratzer is made of.

Our motor wasn't running quite right and we found ourselves in the

B-main. The engine was getting hot and after the B-main we quickly had to change torsion bars, tire stagger, and get the car cooled down. We pulled the hood off and Sonny cracked the radiator cap to let off some pressure and then ran into the trailer to get the other torsion bars. I got our tires ready.

As Sonny came out of the trailer he saw that the radiator had stopped hissing and as soon as he touched the cap it blew off, hitting him in the forehead and spraying him with boiling water.

Sonny yanked his shirt off as quickly as he could, but I can see that he was badly burned. He toughed it out and we made the call and got to the lineup chute.

By the time the race had finished Sonny was already starting to blister. I remembered seeing a bottle of pain pills in the glove compartment, and Sonny took a couple of pills and washed them down with water.

On the way to Sidney, Ohio I told Sonny we were going to stop and get him some accelerant that would help those pain meds get working. I bought a 12-pack of beer and a bag of ice. The beer worked and Sonny lay down and I packed the ice around him.

The next day after we got back home in Pennsylvania, Sonny took a bottle of hydrogen peroxide into the shower with him. As he poured the peroxide down his chest I could hear his screams through the bathroom door.

Sonny did the peroxide treatment every day for a week. As the days progressed he screamed less each day. Well, a little less. But the peroxide must have helped because he healed up very quickly, and avoided any infection.

After listening to Sonny as he endured his treatment, I would not recommend this therapy to others.

Sonny Kratzer is a tough, tough guy.

In July we geared up to race Ohio Sprint Speedweek, a series of All-Star Circuit of Champions races on consecutive nights in Ohio. It's quite a grind and very tough but if you love lots of racing it's for you.

My split with Karen had really changed things with regards to spending time with our daughter, Stephanie, who lived with her mom in California. I really missed Stephanie but it was tough to schedule visits when I was off racing all summer. So I had to be creative to find ways to connect during the season.

Karen's dad Frank Jeffreys brought Stephanie out for a visit in late June but when it came time for Frank to go home I wanted Stephanie to stay for another week.

It isn't feasible to have a six-year-old kid hanging out in your pit area when it's only you and your mechanic taking care of the car. With just two of us we were spending every possible minute on the car, leaving very little time to watch a kid. Sonny's daughter Janet was old enough to babysit, but she was back in California. So I proposed a deal. I would split the airfare for Janet to fly out and join us, and she could travel with us and help take care of Stephanie while we worked on the car. It actually turned out to be a lot of fun and Sonny and I really enjoyed having the girls with us. Janet was an absolute beauty, and we had to chase off a few interested young racers a few times.

My friends from Chico, Tom Wrinkle and Terry Gilbert, traveled from California to hang out with us, which added to the fun. We also had Frank, a retired American Airlines pilot, helping with the car and driving the truck. It was a wacky bunch rolling up and down the highway. Bob Weikert took a liking to Tom and Terry, because they had everybody in stitches just about every minute.

We started the tour off right by winning the Eldora Anniversary—celebrating the track's 34th birthday—event on Saturday night, July 2. The track was rough; we started 12th and it seemed like every car I passed had the front wheels toed out from the rough conditions. We had the ace, as we were using a big, heavy tie-rod setup developed to accommodate the bumps that formed up at Williams Grove going into turn one.

With just two of us working on the car Sonny and I were constantly running late. With the maintenance required it really taxes two guys to get everything done. We'd work on the car in the hotel parking lot until the last minute, then load the car and hustle to the race track.

Sunday night we raced at Millstream and spent Monday morning and early afternoon working on the car. We piled into the hauler and Sonny was really hustling down the interstate. We kept looking at the clock because we were going to be cutting it close for hot laps at Buckeye Speedway (now Wayne County Speedway) in Orrville.

Sonny was making great time and we were literally within sight of our exit when a state cop pulled us over for speeding. He wrote Sonny a ticket, and naturally Sonny was pissed about this development. When the cop was finished Sonny pulled the truck into gear and took off, and we drove right past our exit. A mile or two later we realized what had happened and made a U-turn at the next exit to head back the other way.

Now Sonny was in especially fine spirits, and he was *really* making time. That's when a second cop pulled us over and, you guessed it, wrote Sonny up again.

We managed to get to the track on time for the driver's meeting, and All-Star leader Bert Emick had heard about Sonny's misfortune. At the driver's meeting Bert said, "Guys, we need to give Sonny Kratzer a round of applause. Sonny set fast time with a new track record on the way to the track today, then turned right around and broke his own track record!"

We ended up winning the Ohio Sprint Speedweek title, and that was a very satisfying moment. If you look at the list of Speedweek champions, it's a helluva list of racers. I was—and am—really proud to have my name on that list, especially since we did it with just me and Sonny and our daughters right there with us. It's a very cool memory, probably for all of us.

Later that July we traveled to Eldora for the Kings Royal weekend. Our win at the Eldora anniversary show gave us a good feeling going into the weekend, but everything turned out bad. In so many ways.

The Friday night race was sanctioned by the All-Stars, and it's a good tune-up for the big show. I was passing Joe Gaerte down the front straightaway and got squeezed into the wall, folding up the front axle. It parked me sideways entering turn one and Rocky Hodges drilled me right in the side of the cage.

Guess what, Ma? Another concussion!

The first thing I was aware of was waking up at the hospital, and a doctor was telling me that my CAT scan didn't show any fractures. So he was releasing me to the care of my girlfriend, who was sitting in the waiting room.

My first words were, "I have a girlfriend?"

"Right here she is," he says, and a very attractive girl walked into the room.

"I'm sorry, do I know you?" I said.

She explained that her name was Cyndi Craft and that she rode out from Pittsburgh with me.

Then my brain kicked into gear. "Oh, that's right," I said. "I know you!"

The next morning Bob Weikert called to check on me. I explained that I had a headache and I was a little dizzy, but I'm definitely good to go for tonight's race.

"The doc says you should stay out of sprint cars for a while," he said.

"Nah, it just feels like a hangover and I've raced with those a lot of times," I insisted.

Bob finally agreed that I would be allowed to race and the guys started cutting the frame of the wrecked car to get the motor out to put into our spare chassis. I helped with the car for a while but got to feeling bad and went back in and slept until it was time to leave for the track. That is not recommended in a concussion case, but oh well.

We got qualified on the third row inside, and they lined up the starting field on the front straightaway. Somebody handed me a watch that said "Knoxville Raceway."

Brad Doty was starting alongside me, and he saw me looking at my new watch. He started teasing me about my head injury.

"Hey Sills," he said. "You look confused…are you trying to figure out what track you're running tonight?"

I showed him the watch. "It says right here it must be Knoxville!"

We laughed and each got buckled into our car. After our motor fired I looked down and saw that our oil light was on, and the oil pressure gauge was showing barely five pounds.

I pulled back into the infield, and Davey Brown Sr.—he had been Weikert's mechanic, and had built the engine—ran over to try and help us.

"It's probably the bypass," he yelled. "Take the green, and if the pressure comes up go ahead and race it."

Because I pulled in I had to move to the tail for the start. The green came out and everybody was running hard—you run hard for 50 grand—and somebody way up front went high and turned down into the pack. By the time I got there three cars were upside down and another bunch of cars are scattered across the track.

I drove back to my pit and stopped. One of the cars in the crash was Brad Doty, and it was taking a very long time to get him out of his car. That's not a good sign. The word passed swiftly through the pit area that it looked like Brad had suffered some paralysis of his lower extremities.

The race was restarted after about 45 minutes, and we made our way up to 8th at the finish.

I'm not big on visiting hospitals, especially if there is a racer there. But this situation was a no-brainer; I had to try and see Brad, to see if there was anything I could do for him and his family.

As I arrived at the hospital I ran into Richard Brown who was working for Gary Stanton. Brad was driving Gary's car and the crash really affected Gary and everyone associated with the team. Richard confirmed that Brad had definitely suffered a spinal injury and the news was grim. He was paralyzed from the chest down and doctors were not optimistic that the situation would improve.

I got into the hospital room but Brad was sleeping. His wife Laurie was sitting with him, right beside the bed. There were lots of racers hanging out at the hospital, and the mood was somber. It was a hard reality for everyone to face.

After a couple of weeks they eventually moved Brad to a convalescent center in Columbus, Ohio. There was a mid-week race scheduled in that area and I talked Weikert into letting us go run it; the truth was, I wanted to go visit Brad.

Brad was down and depressed. He wasn't sure of his future and he actually told me he wished the crash had taken him out. It was a tough visit but I'm glad I went. Maybe it was good for Brad to have someone to talk to, and vent a little bit.

"Let's get you in your chair and go outside," I suggested. "The sun will do you good."

Brad's body was adjusting to his injury, and small things like heat changes really affected him. He actually got sick from going outside; that was just about the worst thing I could have suggested. I felt really badly about that.

We took the Weikert car to Knoxville in August for the Nationals, and ran 9th on Saturday night. The next day, as we made the long haul back to Pennsylvania, my mind was working overtime.

One of the things I kept thinking about was the night of Brad's crash at Eldora. I was supposed to start alongside him, but because of the engine problem I moved to the tail. That enabled me to completely miss the crash; I could have very easily been right in the middle of everything.

How'd I get so lucky? I was okay, but my buddy was lying in a hospital bed. I couldn't just shake that off; it felt really *wrong*.

It was late August and pretty soon the weather would be turning colder. The Outlaws would soon make their swing through California.

Karen wanted us to try to reconnect. Again. I missed my little Stephanie and I suppose I was homesick. Brad's situation was very much on my mind and everything in my head seemed jumbled and uncertain.

I called Bob Weikert. I thanked him for the opportunity to drive his car but it was time for me to head for California. He was very gracious and told me that, you never know, maybe we'd go racing together again someday (which we did).

Over in Gettysburg a few months earlier I spotted an IROC Camaro that caught my eye and made the purchase. So I borrowed a car dolly from my friend Frank and hooked the Camaro to the back of my RV and put Pennsylvania in my rear-view mirror.

As I rolled east on I-70 I stopped in Columbus for another visit with Brad. This time he was in much better spirits; his courage and determination had made it back to the surface and he was on the way to becoming one of the most beloved and admired people in all of sprint car racing. He was smiling and cheerful and showing the spirit that made everyone around him better.

Kenny Jacobs and Jac Haudenschild were in Brad's room when I got there. Kenny was looking for a ride, and I suggested that he call Bob Weikert.

"Davey Brown Jr. is also available, and maybe you could get him and Bob back together," I said.

That's exactly what Kenny did, and they won a bunch of races together over the next few months.

When our visit finished I walked outside to the RV. I opened the door and Scooter was standing there wagging his tail. Good ol' Scooter. I slid behind the wheel and reached for the ignition.

I was looking at a 2,400-mile ride, which makes for 40-plus hours of highway time. Time to think, reflect, and let your deepest thoughts get to the surface.

Before I even started the engine, I was tired. Even though I was still young, at that point I had been beating up my body in race cars for 15 years. That's a lot of concussions, a lot of bumps and bruises, a lot of hits. That's only part of it; it's also a lot of sleepless nights, countless hours on the highway, and lots of crappy food.

For the first time in my life, I wasn't certain that racing was my destiny. I was questioning everything I was doing, and had ever done. I wasn't sure of anything, not even myself.

A long drive gives a guy time to think. It gives you time to work through things, and gives you clarity. I'd like to say that this trip helped me sort out everything, but that isn't exactly true.

But I was sure of one thing: my spirits couldn't have been any lower than they were at that point.

15

Luke Warmwater

By the time I reached California on my long drive from Pennsylvania, I had made up my mind that it was time for me to put the lifestyle of a full-time professional racer behind me. I had been beaten up physically, emotionally, and financially for long enough. It was September 1988, and I was all set for a complete change of life and lifestyle.

I started running through various ideas of where I might go to work. You have to understand, when you've spent the previous 15 years chasing sprint cars all over the country you haven't exactly built a resume and acquired a skillset most employers are looking for. So I figured the most logical path would be to find a job doing something related to racing.

I had seen a lot of guys try to step away from the sport, and I knew it wouldn't be easy. But I was determined that I was going to completely retire from driving a race car, once and for all.

Conflicted? Damn right I was conflicted.

On one hand I liked the idea. I had visions of maybe reconciling with Karen, and we could have a normal life as a family. That appealed to me, a lot. We had a young daughter and I was excited about the idea of time at home with her, living like a normal person.

But there was a ton of uncertainty in my mind. It was like this emotional battle inside my head; for an hour or so I would be content with the idea of quitting, and then a voice took over my thought process with something along the line of, "Are you crazy? You are a race driver and that's all you'll ever be! It's what you're *supposed* to be. How dare you think you could ever be anything else!"

Back and forth, all day and all night, for the next few months.

I landed a job with Dick Anderson of Carrera Shocks, and also James Standley of DESIGN 500 Racewear. Neither position was a 9-to-5 job in the traditional sense; I was a factory rep, traveling to the races to represent each company and would earn money on sales.

It was painful to be on the sidelines at most of the World of Outlaws races the next few weeks in California. As the days passed I started to formulate an idea about how I might end my career in style.

Doug Wolfgang had just split from the Marks & Kepler ride, and they inquired if I'd be interested in running the car. The final event in the California swing was the Gary Patterson Memorial race at Baylands (not officially sanctioned by the Outlaws), a race that had eluded me the past few years. I finished behind Steve Kinser two or three times, and that bugged me. Gary was a friend of mine and I really wanted to win the race named in his honor.

I called David Vodden, the promoter at Baylands. I told him my plan: I wanted to run one final race, and then I would be retired. And, oh by the way…how about if the track kicked in $1,000 show-up money? I had won a lot of races at Baylands and I figured the fact that it was my final race could sell a few additional tickets.

Vodden agreed, but he was skeptical about the retirement part. "You'd better not be lying to me, Sills!" he said.

"I'm serious," I told him. "I am totally, completely serious. This is my last race."

"We're going to publicize the hell out of this," Vodden insisted. "You'd better not come back racing next March!"

The idea of running one final race made good sense, particularly since it was at Baylands. I had won 49 races there, and it would be cool to make it an even 50. The idea of it happening at Gary Patterson's race was even more special.

The night of the race they did indeed make a big deal out of my retirement. Dave Pusateri from Trophy City presented me with a plaque during a presentation before the race, and it was all very nice. I want everyone to know that at that moment I was completely serious about retiring. It wasn't a game.

I ended up finishing second, again to Steve Kinser. When the race was over I changed into my street clothes and stuffed my helmet and gloves and driving uniform in my bag and zipped it closed.

Just like that…as I zipped the bag closed it was like I was bringing an end to my driving career. After 14 years, I figured the whole deal had run its course.

Over. Done. Retired.

Winter came, and it was time to go on with my life. I was now a "normal person" (I have to admit, that label didn't work at that time, and it still doesn't work today) and I was going to make my way in the mainstream world. That was my plan and I was seriously focused on making it work.

For a little while.

It was not a fun period, as you might guess. For beginners, the domestic bliss that I was dreaming of is not how things worked out. After one final try at making our marriage work Karen and I ultimately went our separate ways, but we were still connected through our daughter Stephanie. I stayed in the area and was able to spend a lot more time with my daughter and that was obviously a very good thing, then and now.

I bought Karen out and stayed in our house and spent the winter working for Carrera and DESIGN 500. The racing season had finished, so I worked a few trade shows through the winter.

While working a show in Syracuse, New York I met a guy named Duke Southard who operated a stock car racing school in California. Duke was in the process of moving his operation to New Smyrna, Florida, and he invited me to come to Florida and help him with a school.

Duke had a guy bringing a sprint car from New York, so we were able to use the car to teach setup on a Friday afternoon. The next day we took the car over to Volusia County Speedway for some track time with the students. It was fun and listening to Duke's part of the class taught me a lot about stock cars.

Duke said I should start a school for sprint cars, but I wasn't quite ready yet for that part of my life. Maybe someday…

I was struggling financially at that time, mainly because it was the off-season. That made it tough to earn any commission, and it's not fun to watch your bank account steadily drop as the weeks pass by.

There were some issues as I tried to assimilate back into society, so to speak. One day I decided to fire up my dirt bike and go trail riding, which was one of the main reasons we bought a house in that area. My back yard had a section of old mining road running through the back, and that looked like a great place to start.

I rode around for a while and started to climb the hill up to my house when one of my neighbors came running out to stop me. He was clearly irritated.

"You can't ride that noisy thing up here," he insisted. "This is a residential area! Don't you get it…that thing is way too noisy around all these people!"

Well…I *didn't* get it. I didn't think it was noisy, not at all. Making noise and doing exciting things was just what we were supposed to do, right? It just kind of brought home the point that I was still, at heart, a different person than all my neighbors.

And there was no getting around this fact: Life was boring without racing. A racer looks forward to the weekends because they're exciting, and when you take those weekends away, life suddenly feels boring and empty.

Right about the time my bank balance was flirting with negative numbers I got a call from my friend John Kelly in Australia. John wanted to know if I would come to his track, Archerfield Speedway outside Brisbane, to drive a few races.

I told John that would be okay, but he had to keep everything quiet. I made the trip and ran several races, winning two—one of which was the Queensland State Championship.

So my official retirement lasted about three months, which is pretty much everybody's off-season anyways.

This deal is a lot like a guy who has a criminal skill—safe cracking, for example—and he goes to jail for a while. When he gets out he has every intention of going straight, but he is streamlined into the real world with no job skills—other than cracking a safe. He has no money coming in, and almost everyone in his circle—friends and former "co-workers"—is involved in illegal activity.

So pretty soon he's wondering where his next meal is coming from and somebody calls and asks if he's interested in cracking "just one more" little safe. What are the odds the guy is going to say yes? I'd say they are pretty high.

All I knew was racing. That's all I had done since I was 18 years old. When I tried to quit, I didn't have anywhere else to go. I was struggling financially, I was recently divorced—and maybe a little bit lonely—and I was just kinda lost. So when John called it made sense to take him up on his offer, because my bank account was in a desperate place.

I didn't want to quit racing because I didn't love it. I never stopped loving racing. It's just that it's so damned hard, it wears you down. You're on the road nearly all the time, and you're wracked with guilt because being gone so much probably makes you a lousy father. When you're home you're antsy because you aren't making any money, but when you're on the road you're feeling bad because you're away from your family.

You see what normal people do on weekends—camping, boating, family reunions, concerts—and that looks pretty attractive.

Plus, racing is hard on your body. Even if you're fortunate enough to avoid death and total destruction, you're old before your time. Concussions, broken bones, burns, highway accidents; I don't care who it is; racing sprint cars will eventually take a toll on your physical state.

That's what led me to try and step away. I was completely serious about quitting, no doubt about it. But what I discovered was that it's very, very hard to quit, especially when you're only 35 years old.

Just before I left for Australia I heard from Jim Wellington, who asked if I'd be interested in running his midget at Chico in May. I agreed to drive the car, but I told Jim that my participation had to be top secret. In fact, I told him I'd probably not even use my own name.

Lots of racers through the years have raced under an alias, for different reasons. Maybe you didn't want your employer to know you were driving a race car, or maybe you didn't want your wife to know you made an extra $300 this past weekend. Sometimes you used an alias because you'd get in trouble with another racing club for running outside their group.

In my case I was thinking about that big retirement ceremony they did for me at Baylands the previous September. I felt pretty badly about a retirement that didn't even last six months.

So I came up with a new racing name: Luke Warmwater, from Hot Springs, Arkansas.

May rolled around and I headed for Chico. The promoter, John Padjen, respected my privacy and agreed they wouldn't use my real name in any of the results or news stories. But I ended up winning the damned race and I had to go to the front straightaway for the trophy presentation.

I was still sitting in the race car when John came walking up with a big grin on his face.

"What are you going to do now?" he said.

"I'll just leave my helmet on," I answered.

"No, you've got to take it off," John insisted. "The fans will be wondering what's going on if you don't."

I reluctantly took off my helmet, and it wasn't five seconds before I heard someone up in the stands—as clear as day—say, "Oh, bullshit, that ain't no Luke Warmwater…that's Sills!"

But the wheels were in motion. The next weekend I drove Jerry Ponzo's sprint car at Chico, with Richard Brown wrenching. It was a NARC event, and Brent Kaeding was a board member with NARC and he insisted that we put rookie stripes on the car because he had never seen Luke race before. Well, Luke won again.

The following week it was another NARC race at Grass Valley. As Luke passed Tim Green for the lead the red flag waved, and by NARC rules they reverted to the previous lap for the restart lineup. But before the race could resume it was called due to a curfew, and Luke was officially scored second.

Now Luke has two wins and a "woulda."

A few days later my phone rang, and it was Jim Burrow of Washington.

Jim's son Bobby had punched an official and was suspended for a week, and they were leading the car owner points at Skagit and needed somebody to drive their car this weekend. Luke sprang into action and headed north, where he won a 360-ci race and finished second in a 410-ci race.

By this time everybody seemed to know that Luke Warmwater of Hot Springs, Arkansas was really a guy named Sills from Placerville, California. The PA announcers were starting to say, "This is Jimmy Sills, racing as Luke Warmwater…" and that took all the fun out of it.

One writer with little bits of bad information wrote that Jimmy Sills was racing under the alias of Luke Warmwater so he wouldn't jeopardize his ride with the Porsche Carrera team.

It was all in good fun, and it was a chapter of my life that I'll never completely put behind me. I continue to be amazed that all these years later, whenever my name comes up somebody inevitably refers to me as Luke Warmwater. It was a small episode, really, that lasted just a few weeks. But I'll never live it down.

Which is okay. I have no problem with people having fun with it. I have fun with it, too.

Who would have ever dreamed that an offhand alias—Luke Warmwater from Hot Springs, Arkansas—would stay with me for the rest of my life? Life with Luke has been pretty good.

My retirement from racing was short-lived, definitely. By June of 1989 I was once again driving race cars for a living, and I wasn't looking back.

But things were different. Things had changed.

I had finally started to realize that life didn't have to be lived at a wide-open, ass-kicking pace. I began to discover—slowly but surely—that there are enjoyable and interesting things to be experienced that have nothing to do with racing or race cars.

That sounds ridiculously obvious, I know. Of course there are many things in life besides racing! But believe me, racing has a way of sucking you in to the point where everything else in the world disappears. You wake up in the morning with this obsession that centers around your next race, your next ride, your next win.

People become so obsessed with racing that they neglect—maybe that's the wrong word, maybe the right word is "ignore"—anything that is not associated with the sport. And they tell everyone around them that this is the proper way to live.

"Okay, kid, you want to be a professional race driver? Then you've got to cut out everything in life that might interfere with your goal. Family, friends, finances, hobbies, interests…they've all got to go. Because if people in the sport see that you're not 100 percent—no, 1,000 percent—focused on racing, they're going to think you aren't fully dedicated. And if you're not fully dedicated, why would somebody want you driving their race car, or working on their race car?"

When you're young and impressionable, you accept that line of thinking as realistic. As you get older, most of us begin to realize—at one point or another—that it isn't the right way to live.

You learn that it's okay to "manage" your racing career. It is possible—I know this is true because I ultimately experienced it—to be a professional race driver yet also have hobbies and interests. It's possible to be a good dad, a good family person and race.

Of course, you need help learning how to do this. As life went on I began to listen and learn and figure out how to retrain myself. It's a learning process, and it took me a while. But I did it.

Not long after my divorce I met a woman named Charlene Corder who worked in the business of placing people in various jobs in the workplace. Charlene encouraged me to take a test that determines where a person's aptitudes lie and helps direct them toward the career that fits them. After I took the test the counselor looked over the results and told me I was already doing what was perfect for me. I thanked him and walked out of the office with a lot more confidence, because in a way that made it official.

So there you go. If you're already doing the job that fits your aptitudes, it doesn't make any sense to change, right?

This was an important step, actually. When I decided to retire I had convinced myself—*tried* to convince myself—that racing was not the best career for me. But I realized almost immediately that I still loved to race, and I was pretty decent at it. So it was okay for me to continue doing it; I just had to figure out how to do so without being gone all the time. I had to figure out a workable compromise between the demands of professional racing yet still be a normal person who has a life outside of racing.

I appreciated Charlene's career advice so much that I started hanging around with her just to see what else she might know. Charlene ultimately helped me understand that racing can be a big part of my life, but not *every* part of it. It's all about recognizing when you're in racing mode, and when you're not.

She showed me that snow skiing didn't have to be flying down a mountain at breakneck speed, but could also involve cross-country skiing. You could ski where people aren't around and get lots of good exercise and have fun.

It wasn't an easy transition.

One day I was on skis and trying to get my rhythm going up a grade when Charlene pulled up beside me. My immediate thought was that she wanted to race, so I started trying to go faster which only threw off my rhythm. So now I'm fired up and trying harder and harder and at one point I actually stuck my pole in front of her ski.

She got me stopped and said, "*Slow down, Sills*...not everything is a race. Learn to relax!"

That was a good lesson, and the concept began to get through to me.

We also did some wilderness backpacking, and she actually got me to literally stop and smell the flowers along the trail. We went together on a motorcycle ride with a group of people that included a driver from Northern California, Jim Richardson, riding with the group up to Canada. Charlene had her own Honda Rebel motorcycle and we both enjoyed riding.

It sounds crazy, but at age 36 I was learning how to live. I was learning to have a different kind of fun. Don't get me wrong, I had plenty of fun throughout my racing career. But in 1989 I began to learn that fun could be doing different things without flying around like a bat out of hell. I started to see and appreciate different things that I hadn't noticed before.

Charlene and I decided to take a trip to Italy, and Rome was our first stop. We had no idea how we were going to get around until we saw a scooter for rent at one of the little shops. We jumped on that thing and off we went. She was holding the map on my back and within ten minutes we found the coliseum, and continued to the Apian Way, Trevi Fountain, and Vatican City, all in one day.

I still had a racing mindset, no doubt about it. That came out the first time we were stopped at a traffic light. The setup was pretty chaotic, with tons of scooters and taxis and passenger cars all gathered together for a race across the intersection. If you waited for the light to turn green you were running about fifth before you crossed the starting line. Traffic was tight, and you could feel taxi's rubbing your leg trying to get position on you.

Hanging in Charlene's house was a watercolor painting of the home of her grandparents in Corleto. Off we went to Corleto to try and find the home. We started with a train ride to Potenza, then a three hour bus trip. As we traveled along we discovered that nobody spoke English this deep into the countryside. However, we managed to communicate with a man on the bus and explained that we were looking for a family home belonging to the Bonidies family.

We showed him a picture of the home and he was able to express that he knew of some people with that name. As luck would have it, as we stepped off the bus at the piazza (town square) the man spotted one of the Bonidies family members. He explained to him that this American couple is trying to find the family home. The man looked at the painting and immediately said, "Mia casa!"

We piled into the man's little car and drove through tiny alleyways until we pulled to a stop—right in front of the home in the painting.

The Italian people are very hospitable and they love a good drink. So they immediately invited us inside for a drink with Charlene's Italian relatives, and then we headed back to catch the bus to Potenza. We discovered there wouldn't be another bus for a couple of hours, so we stepped across the piazza to have lunch.

The restaurant was owned by an older couple, and we faced a serious language barrier. We managed to order some spaghetti and red wine—both of which they made themselves. As the wine flowed and we enjoyed the good food we asked about the next bus to Potenza. "There are many buses," they managed to explain. "Not to worry!"

There was obviously nobody in a hurry in this town, because life moved along at a much slower speed. There was laughter and friendship and it was wonderful.

Finally the evening drew to a close and we discovered that there would be no more buses to Potenza until morning. We were immediately a little panicked, but our hosts quickly reassured us and said, once again, "Not to worry!"

They offered us a room upstairs, and we would stay the night. Right away they brought out the grappa lemon liquor and we started roasting chestnuts and the language barrier melted away. It was great.

The following morning we caught the bus to Potenza. That's when I got another reminder of something. I had realized one day a few years earlier while scrubbing my race tires back and forth that I very easily experienced motion sickness, caused by the number of concussions I had suffered. As our bus navigated the twisting, curvy roads of the Italian countryside that morning, I felt the effect of all those concussions—maybe the grappa the night before didn't help, either. Regardless of the exact cause, it was tough getting back to Potenza without reaching for the puke bag.

Charlene was a part of my life for several years, but over time she drifted away. She traveled with me to several races: Indianapolis, Springfield, Richmond, Phoenix, even New Zealand. But at some point it became apparent that the racing life wasn't really her deal.

She started rock climbing with a fire chief from Chico, and pretty soon our deal was done. I understood; here was a guy who saved lives and property, climbed mountains and owned horses, and if that's not enough he also took in stray animals. (Hell, *I* wanted to hang out with him.) My driving around in circles in a loud car seemed mundane in comparison.

One of the practical elements that came from my brief retirement was that I had to find a more manageable schedule. I was no longer interested in chasing the World of Outlaws and running 120 races per season. I was looking for a schedule that allowed me to be home more, where I could watch Stephanie grow up and be a part of her life.

The ideal scenario would have me racing around home, throughout northern California. But the local races offered smaller purses, making it very challenging to earn a living as a professional race driver.

There was another idea circulating in my mind. The USAC Silver Crown division featured cars that were a little larger than sprint cars, raced without a wing, racing on larger tracks such as the famous dirt miles in the Midwest. Their purses were pretty good, and that intrigued me.

I called my friend Jack Hewitt, who was the series champion in 1986 and '87. Jack said the Silver Crown cars were the most fun cars to drive, especially at the one-mile tracks. Most of the races were 100 laps, which meant you got a lot more time in the race car. Jack explained that the Silver Crown races had become a big part of his annual income, even though the schedule was only around a dozen races each season.

To top it off, Jack said that if I called the USAC office they could probably help me land a ride.

How could you beat that? It sure sounded good to me.

That was my next phone call, to the USAC office in Indianapolis. A short while later my phone rang, and my career was about to experience a major change.

16

A slice of Americana

Kenny Jarrett was on the phone, and he wanted to know if I was interested in driving his USAC Silver Crown car at the Hulman Hundred on the one-mile dirt oval at the Indiana State Fairgrounds in Indianapolis. Kenny won the 1988 Silver Crown series championship the previous season with Steve Butler driving.

Steve had a ride lined up for the Indianapolis 500, and wouldn't be able to drive Kenny's Silver Crown car that weekend. Kenny was looking for somebody to fill in, and after a few minutes on the phone we agreed that I was the guy.

As the race approached I flew to Indianapolis, where Kenny picked me up at the airport. We drove to his farm, about an hour northeast of Indianapolis near the town of Elwood. I spent a few days with Kenny and his family as we prepared to go racing.

Kenny took me to breakfast at the local coffee shop in Elwood and a couple of farmers were sitting in the booth across from us. I couldn't help overhearing their conversation as they talked about this no-good kid who wouldn't work, avoided school, and was never going to amount to anything in his life. My California brain was thinking drugs; then I heard one guy explain that all the kid wanted to do was play basketball.

It was good to be in Indiana.

I also had a chance to fill in for Steve in his Stoops Express sprint car owned by Jeff Stoops and wrenched by Phil Poor. It was a one-night stand at Paragon, and we didn't do much.

On Friday we headed for Indianapolis, and the Indy Mile. They had an open practice session about an hour prior to qualifying, so I rolled out for my first experience in a Silver Crown car.

This was a big moment for me: May 26, 1989. I was stepping into a different type of racing, where tradition was a huge part of the experience.

The origins of these cars—upright chassis, 96-inch wheelbase, engine in front—can literally be traced to the very beginning of auto racing in America. The cars—and the tracks where they raced—are truly a slice of Americana.

The Indiana State Fairgrounds was like something you'd see on a postcard. Large buildings were along the front straightaway, covered by dark bricks that were clearly from the 1930s. Horse barns and exhibition halls were located outside the track, particularly outside turns one and two.

Man, if you closed your eyes you could picture A.J. Foyt and Mario Andretti and the Unsers and their knobby tires throwing dirt over the short little fence. The giant grandstand was filled with people and the pits were full of race cars, and there was just a prevailing sense that this was *special*.

You could feel the tradition in your soul, and I felt privileged to be allowed to race on the same track as so many legendary American racers. Although I was an outsider from California there for the first time, I instantly felt like I had discovered something new and very special.

In a way it was like the very first time I raced as a young guy. You're a little bit overwhelmed, a little bit intimidated, and you almost feel like you have to prove that you belong out there. I was now on the same track with guys I had idolized—Gary Bettenhausen, Jim McElreath, Larry Rice, Johnny Parsons—and it was like they were all in this special family. These guys had raced in the Indianapolis 500, and it really raised the prestige of being on the same track with them.

My first hot lap session was memorable. All of the other cars were running down on the bottom, which left the top groove wide open. This was strange to me, because it was much more fun to gas the car up and go to the outside. Which is exactly what I did, immediately. I'm having the time of my life, running around the outside of all these cars. It was super fun to hold the throttle wide open down those long straightaways.

Then I looked down at the temperature gauge; it was pegged. All of the other cars had been kicking loose dirt up into my radiator, and I quickly headed for our pit. As I came to a stop the engine was teakettling like crazy; it had gotten pretty hot.

They drew numbers to line up the heat races, and I drew the pole of the first heat. Gary Bettenhausen would be lining up to my outside. This was really cool, as I'm going to line up alongside a racing legend: Indy car driver, sprint car champion, midget champion.

However, we had overheated badly enough to blow a head gasket, and the car wouldn't take off on the start. Our night was finished, way too early.

I was disappointed, but I learned a valuable lesson about Silver Crown racing: stay out of that loose dirt and keep your radiator clear.

Still, I was hooked on these cars. They were fun to drive, and it was exciting to go fast on the big tracks.

The Jarrett ride was a one-off, so I wasn't sure when I might get another shot at a Silver Crown car. As it turns out my next opportunity was only a couple of weeks later, and it was right in my own back yard.

The one-mile dirt track at the CalExpo State Fairgrounds was the site of a renewed effort to bring auto racing to Sacramento. The old fairgrounds had been closed not long after that terrible day in 1970 when three drivers were lost in one afternoon, and a new fairgrounds was built north of downtown. Although the horse racing community had a monopoly on the new track, in 1989 a group of local people got together to bring auto racing back to Sacramento.

The principles were Tommy Hunt, Jim Naify, John Naify, Matt Campbell (my dentist), Artie Oji, and Gary Alvernez. They were successful in getting it going again and eventually turned over the promotional reins to Don Tognotti and John Padjen.

It was a pretty significant undertaking. One of the biggest hurdles was the need for a new crash wall, and the group purchased over 6,000 feet of concrete K Rail for that purpose. They lined the outside perimeter as well as the pit wall on the front straightaway.

On June 4, 1989 the CalExpo State Fairgrounds hosted the return of the USAC Silver Crown series. My old friends Tex Countryman and John Boy Sullivan built a Silver Crown car specifically for this race, and I was their guy to take the wheel.

We had a good starting spot—fifth—and I was all pumped up to run well in front of my hometown crowd. The car ran aluminum brake rotors on the front axle, and about 10 laps into the race the right front brake overheated and locked up. We were forced into the pits, where we pulled off the right front brake. We lost several laps in the process, but we went back out. Although we passed everybody on the track, we couldn't make up all those laps and eventually finished 10th.

George Snider won in A.J. Foyt's car, with Chuck Gurney second and Gary Bettenhausen third. The event was a big success, and the local fans were excited about Sacramento being on the Silver Crown schedule once again.

Our next start was on August 27, back on the Indy Mile for the Hoosier Hundred. The Hoosier Hundred is a rich and prestigious race, with a history going back to the early 1950s. You always want to run well at the

Hoosier Hundred, even when you're just getting started in Silver Crown cars.

For the first time in history the race was going to be held under the lights, on the final day of the Indiana State Fair. The track prep guys must have been a little excited because they overwatered the track, throwing in some calcium chloride for added measure. They put one final load of water on just before the feature, and when a few drivers spoke up the officials agreed the track was too soupy to race on.

I qualified 15th, and the officials sent the field out to iron out the track and allow for a couple of flights of hot laps before we took the green flag. Man, what a mess. I was hanging back, trying to stay away from other cars to conserve my tear-offs.

Hot laps soon commenced, and must have gone on for 60 laps. I ran out of tear-offs, and the dirt was so greasy it smeared when you tried to wipe your visor with your hand.

There was a red flag on the opening lap for a crash, and when racing resumed I began to get my rhythm in the car. Visibility continued to be a problem, and when we were under caution on lap 60 or so I ducked into the pits for some tear-offs. I had prepared another helmet with a full set of fresh tear-offs for just this situation, and we made a quick change and I was right back out.

(Tear-offs have come a long way since then. At that time we'd put 20 on, but the visor would be very dark and cloudy. Your vision didn't really clear until you got down to maybe 10 or 12.)

It was a pretty good night for us, overall. Jack Hewitt won the race, and we finished 8th. I felt okay about that, considering it was only my third Silver Crown race. I was starting to get the hang of this deal.

It was funny, I went to a post-race party and overheard one of A.J. Foyt's crew members (Larry "Flash" Humphries, whom I would later get to know well) say, "Hey, did you guys see that dude from California come in for a new helmet, and they didn't even put a new tire on?"

We were new at this type of racing but we were learning.

One week later we traveled to DuQuoin, Illinois, where we put Tex's car on the pole. That was a great feeling, and it was good for our confidence. We were relatively inexperienced and to post quick time proved to me that we could compete with these guys. We ran third behind Chuck Gurney and Rich Vogler and with every lap we were learning more.

Although we only ran five races in 1989, when the season finished we were named series Rookie of the Year. I thought that was kind of funny, winning a rookie award at that point in my career. Ironically enough, that was the same year Dick Trickle was the Winston Cup Rookie of the Year at age 50. So maybe a 36-year-old Rookie wasn't so crazy after all!

Tex Countryman and I agreed that I would run his Silver Crown car for the 1990 season, and our opener was at the Copper Classic at Phoenix Intl. Raceway in early February. We kicked off the season with high hopes, excited about the possibility of running more of these races.

Phoenix wasn't anything like we had hoped, however, and we only made six laps in the feature event when our engine blew up.

But fate has a funny way of changing the course of things. Our primary focus at the Copper Classic was the Silver Crown car, but there were three other classes there as well. It so happened that Bob Consani needed a driver for his midget, and we got together. We ran the B-main and got to second and transferred into the feature, then ran 14th in the main event.

Bob and I hit it off pretty well, and he asked if I'd be interested in running his Silver Crown car that season. He wanted to run all the races on the schedule; me too! I knew the deal with Tex was limited to just a few races, so I jumped at the chance to connect with Bob.

That turned out to be one of the best decisions I ever made. Bob was a good guy and we had a lot of fun racing together, and a lot of success. Bob was a great car owner and he campaigned a Silver Crown car along with a sprint car and midget. Bob was sharp on chassis setup, and his son Mike was a talented mechanic as well. Bob was a successful businessman, and he owned a trucking company and a concrete plant in Santa Rosa, California.

Our first Silver Crown race together was in May in Indianapolis, the Hulman Hundred on the Indy Mile. The race was scheduled for Friday night, but rain pushed it to Monday, the day following the Indy 500. We ran fifth, and that was a pretty good start. Jack Hewitt won it—running McCreary tires—passing Eric Gordon late in the race when Gordon's oil pump belt came off.

I had no idea at the time, but Eric's misfortune would loom large in a few months.

The following weekend the series was in Sacramento, and our team really shined. We set fast time (108.748 mph) and started on the pole of the 100-lap race.

Things got exciting in a hurry. On the first lap Gary Bettenhausen crashed on the backstretch toward turn three, backing into a concrete barrier that was set in place to block a light pole. Gary's fuel tank ruptured, spilling 60 gallons of methanol over a 20-yard radius.

The impact knocked the wind out of Gary, and he was trying to get himself out of the car. A passing car ignited all that fuel, and Gary suddenly realized he was on fire and fuel was everywhere around him. He managed to get out and as he was running away from the car he saw a puddle and figured that if he rolled in the puddle it would cool him off.

Unfortunately, it was a puddle of fuel. Gary suffered several broken ribs and burns on his arm and backside, and it was a miracle that it wasn't worse.

(Some years later we were sitting at IMS with Gary, one-on-one, and he talked a lot about that day in Sacramento. It was very interesting, he had a clear memory of how everything happened and it was almost like living the moment all over again.)

Gary's crash had sparked a melee behind him, and Steve Butler flipped hard and was also taken to the hospital. The race was stopped for about an hour while they cleaned up the mess and got the track back into shape.

We led from the start, but Rich Vogler was right there. Rich was driving for the Wilke team, running an A.J. Watson car that had a vintage look. Those guys were loaded for bear that day. A.J. Watson was in attendance, and it felt like we were racing against royalty.

Rich got under me on the front straightaway on lap 10 and took the lead, and all I could do at that point was chase him. We could gain on him some in traffic but on an open track he could pull away a little bit.

Our break came when Rich clipped a barrier on lap 72, blowing a tire and bending a radius rod. He headed for the pits and I was back in the lead.

Chuck Gurney made a run at me in that last handful of laps, but we were able to hold him off and win our first Silver Crown race. The hometown fans really let me hear it, and it was a great moment.

Winning that race felt really, really good. More than I can describe. A lot of my friends were there, along with some of my family, and it was almost like a homecoming. Everybody was celebrating and it was just a wonderful feeling.

It was an All-California podium, with Gurney second and Jeff Gordon third.

From Sacramento our next stop was a few weeks later at Indianapolis Raceway Park. IRP wasn't a great outing for us and we finished 17th, two laps down.

We came out of IRP leading the Silver Crown points, but at the time I didn't think anything of it. Some of that might be because the Silver Crown schedule was a little spread out, with a gap of several weeks between their early races. But as late-summer arrived we had five events over a span of about six weeks.

In August we were back in Indianapolis for the Hoosier Hundred. We qualified fifth, and were running well throughout the race. Andy Hillenburg, who had grown up on the south side of Indianapolis almost worshipping Silver Crown cars, led the first 96 laps before a flat tire sent him to the pits just four laps from the finish. It was an absolute heartbreak for Andy; winning the Hoosier Hundred in front of his hometown fans would have been spectacular for him.

We were right in the thick of things when Andy's tire blew, and I couldn't get away from him fast enough and had to get out of the gas. Gary Hieber got the lead and went on to win it, and we finished second.

Andy later told me that if he could have won the Hoosier Hundred that day it would have been the greatest highlight of his life. And I understood exactly what he meant.

One week later we traveled to Springfield, Illinois for the Tony Bettenhausen 100. We didn't qualify well and started 19th, and made our way to ninth at the finish. The day belonged to Chuck Gurney in the Plastic Express car owned by Junior Kurtz, as they led all 100 laps to win.

Eric Gordon was second, and he had made a big surge in points. I was still leading, but Eric had closed the gap quite a bit.

The next stop on Labor Day weekend was our final appearance on a one-mile dirt track, DuQuoin. Things got off to a wild start when Jeff Gordon and Gary Hieber crashed on lap 8 and Gordon literally went through the guardrail and down the outside embankment. On lap 14 George Snider was upside-down, tangling with Wally Pankratz and Jack Hewitt and knocking down another section of guardrail.

Johnny Parsons led most of the way, and we worked our way from 14th to the top-5. Parsons had trouble and Jeff Swindell won it, with Chuck Gurney 2nd and we were third.

Less than a week later we went to the Milwaukee Mile, a unique and very competitive paved track. We qualified on the pole and led the first 45 laps, but Eric Gordon got past us. We regained the lead 10 laps later, and it looked like we might win on our very first visit to Milwaukee.

That, unfortunately, was not to be. We picked up a tire vibration while leading on lap 66, and it shook so badly that it damaged our suspension. We tried to make repairs but ended up dropping out on lap 88. Chalk that one up to the "shoulda-woulda-coulda" category.

Dave Blaney made a spectacular move from third to first and nearly won it, but in the end it was Eric Gordon in victory lane.

We had one more race to run—Eldora's 4-Crown Nationals on September 30—and our point lead was just 25 over Gordon.

To be honest, I still wasn't thinking much about the title. I was never much of a points racer, and I just didn't have that mindset. I didn't give it much thought.

By the time we got to Eldora, however, the Silver Crown championship was in the front of my mind. After having a few weeks to contemplate the possibilities, I was definitely excited about our chances. Winning the championship would be very cool and as I signed the pit sheet at Eldora I felt like we could get it done.

Both Eric and I had experienced our share of bad luck at various points of the season, so the title was basically going to come down to who could run the best on the final day. Of course, my plan was to win the race and settle the subject that way. That was absolutely our plan and Bob and Mike Consani felt the same way.

That's not how it played out.

We were off to a good start by qualifying on the pole, but our good fortune didn't last. As we came around to take the green Jack Hewitt bumped me from behind and I spun across the track. Tray House had nowhere to go and he t-boned me, and we were bent badly enough that we were done for the day.

What a rotten situation. There was nothing I could do but climb up on our trailer to watch the rest of the race. The PA announcer said that if Gordon finished fourth or better, he would be the champion.

I didn't wish any bad luck on Eric, I really didn't. But I knew that if he had a strong day, we were sunk.

That was a tough race to watch. But as the laps clicked away it was clear that it wasn't going to be Eric's day either, and he eventually finished 7th.

We won the title by 11 points, the closest finish in the history of the series.

Obviously we were happy, but as I look back at that weekend I realize that I didn't fully grasp what it meant to win a USAC championship. I definitely didn't appreciate or understand what it meant to me, and my career.

In the weeks and months after winning the title, different things opened up for me. Dan Cotter, the President of True Value Hardware and a guy with a genuine love for racing, invited me to a banquet in Chicago that benefitted the Boys and Girls Club of America. This was a big deal with all sorts of big-time racing people in attendance, and I was seated at the table with Dale Earnhardt, Mark Martin, and Mike Helton of NASCAR, along with Walter Payton of the Chicago Bears.

They brought all of us up on the stage to be interviewed, and that's when I realized: winning a USAC Silver Crown title is way beyond just winning a series title somewhere else. It puts you on a much bigger radar screen and people view you—and your career—in a different light.

I was able to test at Daytona in an IROC car and raced the Long Beach Grand Prix celebrity race, which would have never happened if I hadn't won the Silver Crown title. It was among a lot of things—some small, some more significant—that happened because of winning the championship.

Winning a USAC race was a pretty big deal to me, and winning the title was off the charts big. At least in my eyes. The series was extremely competitive, and sometimes there were 60 cars in the pits at the Indy Mile or Springfield or DuQuoin, fighting for 30 starting spots. It was tough to make the race, with a lot of fast cars and top drivers from around the country. Doug Wolfgang, Jeff Swindell, Brent Kaeding, plus all the USAC regulars. So winning the title really meant something to me.

For the first time in my life, I was racing on my own terms. Two years earlier I ran 114 races in one season, and now I was running half that amount and making just as much money. Plus I had the luxury of variety: Silver Crown cars, winged sprint cars, non-wing sprint cars, midgets, pavement…I was able to race all of them, but I could pick and choose. It was a whole new perspective, both physically and mentally.

Going from 114 races a year to 40 or 50 felt great. I can tell you that for sure.

In the span of two years—from those dark days of late 1988 to winning the USAC Silver Crown title in autumn 1990—my life had come full circle. I was excited about racing again, yet my life now had something it had never had before: balance. Life was good and I was enjoying every minute of it!

17

Stanton and me

I raced with Bob Consani from early 1990 through the end of the 1993 season, and it was a great experience for both of us. We were proud to carry the No. 1 on our car in 1991 as the defending USAC Silver Crown champion, and we came very close to repeating our title. We got off to a good start at Phoenix, but blew a motor while leading. Jeff Gordon won the race and ultimately won the title, becoming the youngest Silver Crown champion in series history.

We were in the hunt all year, and finished second to Jeff in the points. But we didn't win any races that season while Jeff won two in the M&L Plumbing car, and that was the difference.

For us, it was a year of "almost." We finished second in three of the seven series races, but we just weren't able to get over the hump and win.

Whenever we had trouble, Mike Consani was always the guy to dive right in and fix the problem. At Milwaukee we had trouble right after practice and had to quickly change motors. Bob had different plumbing on each motor, and the fuel and oil pumps were belt-driven and required quite a bit of effort to get in place and adjusted. It was more work than you'd normally encounter, but Mike somehow came through and got us put back together in time.

One day at Springfield we had to do an engine change after practice, and it was particularly tough. It was close to 100 degrees that day, and the engine was still hot from our practice session. Don Tognotti and Mike Andreetta were there doing some PR work for the Sacramento race, and they rolled up their sleeves and pitched in to help us. Man, it was miserably hot and sweaty, just awful.

In 1992 I decided to move over to the M&L Plumbing car, leaving Bob's deal. Bob was very busy with his business and I felt like they weren't able to spend the time needed on the Silver Crown car, figuring the M&L car would be a good situation for me. Jeff Gordon won the title in the car the year before, then left to go NASCAR racing. As you might recall Jeff had a decent amount of success in NASCAR as it turned out.

But the M&L guys were a hard-headed bunch. We went to Phoenix and the car had all kinds of problems, but they didn't want to listen to my suggestions on what the car needed. We made just 11 laps before the driveline broke and were scored 29th.

Next stop was the Hulman Hundred in Indianapolis, where it was a little better. We qualified 16th and made it to 6th at the finish, but it still wasn't a good experience. They weren't interested in my input in how to prepare the car so I figured it was time to find something else.

Consani had raced with Brad Noffsinger at Phoenix, where they qualified on the pole but blew an engine 25 laps in. Ron Shuman was in the seat at the Hulman Hundred, where he qualified 2nd and finished 14th. I approached Bob and proposed that we get back together and run the rest of the year, and he agreed. Shuman eventually ended up in the M&L car a few weeks later, just in time to score a big payoff at the Indy Mile.

One of the best things to happen to Silver Crown racing during the early 1990s was the Foyt Group taking over the promotion of the Indiana State Fairgrounds mile. Dennis Wood of the Foyt Group worked his ass off and greatly elevated the purse and overall profile of the event, with a point fund for the two races at the Indy Mile. They also posted lap prize money of $100 for every lap led.

Bob and I arrived at the Hoosier Hundred in September 1992, looking for a good payday. It turned out to be one of the longest, strangest, and most tragic races I've ever been a part of.

The track prep guys got a little overzealous with the tiller and the water truck and put way too much moisture on the surface, and it was soup. They must have drained a small lake to put that much water on the big mile.

We were very late in getting on the track, and it took a major effort by all involved to get the track worked in to where we could hot lap. It took a long time to qualify 53 cars, and then a non-qualifier race dragged out the proceedings even further.

We qualified fourth, and it was late afternoon when we rolled out for the 100-lap race. For all the problems with the track, it turned out to be very racy. The inside groove was narrow and eventually got worn out, but the dirt was so loose it didn't lay rubber. The middle groove was very rough and no car was going to finish if they spent much time out there. The top groove built up a cushion right next to the wall, which provided an exciting and fun groove that was a throwback to Champ Dirt Car racing of old.

Shuman led early in the M&L car, but we got past him on lap 10 to take the lead. Shuman and I traded the lead a couple of times, and Lealand McSpadden got into the mix, but we were back into the lead on lap 56.

We were racing into the sunset when the race started, so I went out with a dark shield on my helmet. But as the sun began to set, it became very tough to read the track and miss the bumps. I absolutely had my hands full and a couple of times thought I might end up on the roof of one of the barns outside the track.

To complicate matters they were having trouble with the track lights along the backstretch and into turn three. There were a couple of cautions, and on lap 34 Wally Pankratz spun in turn three.

That's when things took a tragic turn. Carl McCormick, a 56-year-old longtime USAC official, was on the track directing traffic a couple of laps later when he was struck by a race car and was killed. The race was red flagged, and it was just a really, really bad deal.

There was another red flag on the restart for a crash, and several cautions after that. The race never got any rhythm, and just kept dragging out.

But we were still out front, and I kept thinking about that $100 for every lap we led.

I figured we had everything handled, but a rod end broke on our tie rod on lap 94 and I couldn't steer the car. I bumped into the wall and we were done, and as I climbed from the car and walked across the track to the infield I was completely disgusted. The only consolation was that we made about $5,000 in lap money.

The race ended up with a spectacular finish, with Shuman, Jeff Swindell, and Steve Butler having a helluva race on the final lap. Shuman won it, scoring about $24,000.

The race had taken just a few minutes shy of three hours, part of a nine-hour marathon program. It would be easy to say it was just one of those days, but with the death of an official it made for a very bad memory.

Despite changing rides during the season we ended up third in series points in 1992. Bob and I had now finished first, second, and third in series standings together.

We continued on for 1993, but the season was a bit of a struggle. We had a couple of decent finishes early on, but blew an engine at IRP and then blew up again at Milwaukee a few weeks later.

We closed out the year on a high note, however, when we won at

Sacramento in October. This would turn out to be our final race together, and looking back it was a great way to close out a very enjoyable and productive period in my career. A lot of my success came with Bob and that's something good to look back on.

We finished fourth in the series standings, so we kept our streak alive in Silver Crown points: first, second, third, and now, fourth. You could see a trend here, but unfortunately it was going in the wrong direction. So I decided it was time to line something else up going forward.

Bob was a really competitive guy and you couldn't always predict what would get him fired up. Everybody knew Bob's cars were particularly good on pavement, and he built a winged sprint car that he and I won some races with in Oregon. He didn't run the car a lot, but it was a very fast car.

CRA scheduled a pavement race at Bakersfield, and Davey Hamilton was looking for a ride. He called Bob and asked about running his car, but Bob was in a bad mood that day and told Davey he wasn't interested in running the race. A few days later Bob heard that Davey was going to drive the Morales Bros. Tamale Wagon, and somehow Bob came up with the idea that it would be great if we went to Bakersfield and kicked their ass.

It was a memorable day, marked by tragedy. During practice I was pulling off the track when I noticed a car coming hot into the corner, front tires locked up and smoking as he skidded toward the outside wall. It was Billy Vukovich III. Billy slammed into the wall sideways and was killed. It was a terrible loss for the sport and a very dark day.

The program continued and no other car was within a second of our two cars all day long; Davey in the Tamale Wagon and me in Bob's sprinter. We started the race and I was leading, with Davey poking his nose under me a couple of times. Finally he got under me and was drifting up, and we locked wheels and both crashed exiting turn two. Brad Noffsinger drove past us and won the race. It was a bummer ending for two good race cars on what should have been a good day.

Bob could also be a sick human being, God rest his soul. The first time we went to Milwaukee we set fast time and they presented us with a nice trophy. This was a good-looking piece, a large, bright and shiny champion's cup. Bob and I both had every intention of keeping it. So we decided to flip a coin to see who would take the trophy home.

I won the toss and Bob went into the trailer and got the trophy, set it on the ground, and pulled out his penis and pissed the trophy full to the brim. It took a lot of piss, but he got 'er done. He then stepped away and said, "There you go, Sills!"

I carefully poured the piss out and carried it by the edges back to my hotel room, where I put it in the shower to give it a good rinse.

Several years later Bob's wife Jona invited me to Bob's retirement party at a vineyard in Santa Rosa. I decided I would give Bob the Milwaukee trophy as a retirement gift. I set the trophy on the floor by my table and filled it to the rim with beer, letting the beer go flat so it looked like piss.

It came my turn to present my gift to Bob, so I carefully hoisted the trophy and gingerly walked up to the head table, letting a little fluid spill over the side so that Bob could see it. He immediately recognized the trophy and let out a worried moan as I got close, where I faked a stumble and let it spill right in his lap.

Good memories.

Thinking of Billy Vukovich's accident all these years later really makes me sad. We had not developed cage nets yet, which would probably have saved Billy's life. Not long after his accident, those nylon nets became a common part of racing.

There were so many things like this that trouble me today. We lost—and injured—so many people through the years, and it was only after such tragedy that we took steps to prevent those things. Roll cages, cage padding, cage nets, high-backed seats, fireproof uniforms…what took us so long?

More than anything else I am surprised and amazed that I survived. And sad for those who didn't.

Gary Stanton has made a huge impact on racing over the past generation. He has built race cars, established one of the first successful chassis-building businesses, owned race teams, and built racing engines. He is the type of guy who has been successful at anything he's tried.

Gary is a unique person, intense but also very funny. He's got a wry sense of humor and he can be very direct. Most of all he's smart; he's got a sharp mind and he has learned how to focus his thoughts on accomplishing his goals.

I was fortunate—and I say this very seriously—that our paths crossed in 1994 and we enjoyed several good years together.

At the end of the 1993 season I could see that the enthusiasm—and budget—was waning with Bob Consani's Silver Crown effort, so I was looking for a new deal when my phone rang. It was Stanton, and he explained the he had a new idea for a Silver Crown chassis. He was putting a car and a team together and was looking for a driver. Was I interested?

You bet I was interested. I knew Gary's motors were very strong from his experiences in sprint car racing over the past few years, and I was excited to drive for one of the premier car builders in the country. Although Gary had been out of the chassis business for several years I had no doubt that he could put a great chassis together.

Gary tried to explain the concept of the car, which would have torsion arms with push rods in the front and pull rods in the rear with coil-over springs tucked inside the frame rails. I tried to follow along but I just couldn't visualize what he had in mind. But I trusted Gary and during the winter of 1993-94 made plans to run the full 1994 Silver Crown season together.

In January I called Gary for a progress report on the new car. The Phoenix opener was about three weeks away.

"Hey Stanton, what's the new car look like?" I asked.

"Well, right now it looks like straight tubing on the rack," he answered. One thing about Stanton, he will give it to you straight with no bullshit.

At that moment I was wondering if I had made a mistake. Three weeks from our first race, and they haven't even bent a tube at Stanton's shop.

But they made it to Phoenix in time, with a strange-looking race car. Even after looking it over I still didn't fully understand all of the suspension dynamics; however it was cool that I was able to change the right rear spring while sitting in the driver's seat—it ran parallel to the main frame rail.

Phoenix was a bust, however, because we blew our motor in practice and didn't even post a qualifying time.

Two months later came the next event, the Hulman Hundred at the Indiana State Fairgrounds. I drove into the infield on Friday afternoon and walked toward the pit area, looking for our car. There was no sign of Stanton or the car, so I went to the driver's meeting and got suited up. Still no sign of Stanton.

Practice began, and Dave and Ruth Keperling arrived with the race car. We quickly unloaded and threw some tires on the car and went out with the last practice session. When I got out of the car I saw Gary walking up with a grin on his face.

"How was the car?" he asked.

"Well, Gary, it kinda just sat on the top and spun the tires."

He laughed and said, "It should, it still has the pavement springs and shocks from Phoenix!"

I think Gary enjoyed messing with his driver.

Because the car wasn't there in time to draw a qualifying pill, we were forced to qualify at the end of the order and only got one lap. The joke was on USAC, because the track cleaned up and laid a little rubber by the time we rolled out to qualify. We were quick time, and that put us on the pole.

(This led USAC to change to rule to state that if you were relegated to go out last, the best you could qualify was the front row of the consolation race.)

Randy Tolsma was on the outside of the front row and he led the opening lap. But we got past him on the outside to lead the second round and from that point we led the rest of the way. I worked on saving my tires, and took it as easy as I dared. I had no idea how big my lead was, but if the cameras started flashing as I went through the corner I figured somebody was getting close so I stepped it up a little.

At the end Ron Shuman was behind me for second and George Snider was third.

The Foyt Group had continued their program of a point bonus for the driver who finished best in the two races at the Fairgrounds, so Stanton and I left Indianapolis feeling pretty good about our ability to race together in his new car. Despite our trouble at Phoenix we left Indy riding third in series points.

We were back in Indiana in August for Indianapolis Raceway Park. We qualified 12th and made our way to 5th at the finish, and moved up to 2nd in points.

At that point we were starting to feel pretty good about our situation. Stanton's car was proving itself, and his engines were strong as well. Despite missing the show at the opener we were definitely in the hunt for the title.

If we could step things up a notch and keep winning races, we could get it done. When we left IRP that night I felt very good about how this season was going.

Then came a very painful appointment at Belleville.

Belleville, Kansas, is home to one of the most exciting and intimidating tracks in the country. The Belleville High-Banks is a half-mile track with steep banks and is almost circular. The old grandstand, and the area surrounding the town, just reeks of history.

They've been racing at Belleville for a long time, decades before I ever climbed into a car. No matter what era you look at, the track was one of the fastest places for contemporary cars. The steep banking and roundish shape makes for extreme speeds.

That factor—extreme speeds—is the reason fans have flocked to the track through the years. It's also the reason the track is one of the scariest tracks in the country.

Sprint cars have raced at Belleville for many years; I raced a traditional sprint car there in the 1970s and was present when a driver was killed, which I mentioned earlier. Through the years midgets began running

Belleville, and in 1978 the Belleville Midget Nationals began.

The Belleville Nationals became more than just another race. This great little town opened their doors to racers traveling in from all over the country—really, the world—and it was like a giant family reunion. One lady and her husband put together a huge lunch on the day of the finale, feeding dozens of people—old friends and complete strangers—for free. It was just the coolest thing.

The event was held in early August, the same time as the North Central Kansas Free Fair at the fairgrounds. Farmers and people from all over the region poured into the little town, adding to the aura of the event. It's always close to 100 degrees there in early August, and with the bright lights of the rides, the food vendors, people walking around enjoying themselves, it was exactly how you might picture small-town America on a summer night.

In 1994 I teamed up with Larry Brown to run his midget at the Belleville Nationals, a brand-new TCR chassis. The Nationals would be held over three nights—Thursday, Friday, and Saturday, August 4-6—and the Silver Crown race at IRP would conflict with the Thursday night show at Belleville. That was no problem, because the plan was to race at IRP and fly to Belleville for the remaining two nights.

I arranged to fly with my friends, Page and P.J. Jones, on P.J.'s airplane. P.J. was still learning to fly, and had hired a pilot to handle that end of things. When we finished at IRP we hopped over to nearby Eagle Creek Airport on the west side of Indianapolis and flew to the small airstrip just outside Belleville.

We qualified sixth on Friday night and started third in the 20-lap feature, and I got to the lead on the opening lap. On the third lap I cut a tire going into turn one, and suddenly it was flapping against the nerf bar. I tried to move out of the groove, but Robby Flock was right on me and he tagged me pretty good.

Throughout my career I had my share of crashes; I've suffered five concussions that I know of, and have taken my lumps. Whenever you crash your brain is processing things at a very high speed, and there are moments when you actually register thoughts that you'll recall later.

Usually you're aware enough to think, "Man, I hope this stops here pretty soon."

They say death is painless, and maybe it is. I've been knocked out and I can say from experience that it is just like somebody unplugged the television; things just go black and that's it.

Both Robby and I started flipping and at some point somebody unplugged my television. When you flip on a high-banked track you usually don't stop until you get to the bottom of the track, and that's exactly what happened. I dropped out of the sky right in front of Robert Dolacki, who hit me broadside at full speed and drop-kicked me another 20 to 30 yards down the race track.

Larry's brand-new car was absolutely decimated, and the cage had collapsed around me. As they used the jaws-of-life to cut me from the car I was in and out of consciousness, but mostly out. I was mumbling here and there but had no awareness of my surroundings. Yet to this day I have no memory of anything that happened that day or evening.

Like most of us, I was traveling alone that weekend. Even if a guy is married, it's tough to bring your wife along with the schedule I ran. If you're running just one series and nothing else, you can get a motorhome and bring your family with you. But when you jump around on different series and catch a flight here or there, you discover that traveling alone makes sense.

That makes for a lot of alone time. You sit alone at the airport, you eat in restaurants by yourself, you ride in the rental car alone, and you go to sleep and wake up in your motel room with nobody else around. Once you get to the race track you're in the middle of your community and surrounded by your friends, but all the rest of the time you're alone.

That's a difficult situation when you're badly hurt in a race car. Usually somebody from your crew, or maybe one of your other friends, will step up and try to help you. But it's a pretty lonely scenario when you're lying in a hospital bed all beat up and there is nobody there to pick up your spirits.

In this case they transported both me and Dolacki to the nearby Republic County Hospital in Belleville. Dolacki had a broken hand and lots of bruises, but was treated and released. I had a two broken ribs, a concussion, and severed nerves that led to the deltoid muscle near my left shoulder. That meant I had to stay for a couple of days.

It could have been much worse, of course. When you get clocked by another car at full speed at Belleville, that is an extremely violent collision. Although I was badly beat up, I was lucky. I'm not sure I realized it at the time, but I realize it today. I'm not trying to be morbid but that one could easily have been the end of ol' Jimmy.

A bunch of my fellow racers came up to the hospital on Saturday to visit me. Things are a little foggy but I specifically remember Page and Stevie Reeves coming by. They picked up my spirits, and as usual they were razzing me.

"You got pretty excited last night while they were cutting you out of the car," they teased. "You were kinda in-and-out and one time you came to and couldn't see anything. You got pretty excited as you were telling them you were blind!"

"Well, hell yes!" I replied. "If I came to right now and was blind, I'd get pretty excited, too!"

They released me on Sunday morning, and Larry arranged for someone to drive me up to Lincoln, Nebraska where I could catch a flight home. I wish I could remember who drove me, because I appreciate that they helped take care of me. But things are just so foggy I have no idea who it was.

That incident changed how I felt about visiting other racers in the hospital. For the longest time I refused to go see anybody who had been hurt. It probably stems from 1988 when I was so deeply affected by my hospital visit with Brad Doty; I was so badly shaken that it made me want to quit racing.

So I simply avoided hospitals. That's a crappy way to handle it, I know, because you're in denial. But that was my mode for several years. Seeing a guy laid up with injuries was a vivid reminder of what might happen to me, and I wanted to keep that out of my mind.

But having my friends come see me at the Belleville hospital made me realize what a huge difference a little moral support can make. When you are hurt, you're also a little bit scared. I don't care who you are. And it helps to have people around you who pick up your spirits and help you get through it.

From that point I had a different attitude about visiting people. Not long after that my friend Brian Gerster suffered a broken neck at Bakersfield and I remember going to see him in the hospital. Luckily Brian made a full recovery after wearing a halo for a while.

Even after what happened, and even though I knew it was dangerous, I still liked Belleville. The Nationals continued on for another 20 years or so, but as I write this the future of the event is in doubt. It was at Belleville where Bryan Clauson was killed in 2016, and the event has seen car counts drop steadily in recent years. Whether or not the event will continue is anybody's guess.

Actually, racing at Belleville wasn't as scary as *watching* there. Several years after my crash I went back there to help Bradley and Alfred Galedrige, and I was terrified as I watched the race. Seriously. I was thinking, "This place is way *too* fast!" I was in fear for everyone's safety.

There is also the fact that few midget engines can withstand the demands of Belleville. From the time you fire in the pits and roll onto the track, you never lift the throttle. All night long. That is extremely demanding of an engine, as well as everything else on the car.

Of all the years I ran there, I don't believe I ever finished a race. We blew up our motor, every time. One year I went to the Nationals with Dave Calderwood, and he brought three motors: our primary, our backup, and our backup-backup. We blew up all three of 'em.

Midget teams can't afford to do that. And when it gets to where you can't do it any more, you won't. That's the end.

Still, Belleville is fun and exciting. And the way the local people embrace racing is very special.

The other issue is that it isn't easy to get there. The nearest major airport is Lincoln or Kansas City, and it's a long tow from almost anywhere. You're in the heart of farm country, and it's definitely the wide-open spaces.

One night we finished racing on Saturday night and I had to catch my flight the next morning at Kansas City. I figured I'd just cruise on back to the airport that night, and I was driving south in my rental car on U.S. 81, running WFO.. Way off in the distance I saw a set of headlights, and naturally I assured myself, "Nah, there wouldn't be any cops out here in the middle of nowhere at this time of night."

As soon as he passed me I saw his brake lights come on, and saw him swing around on the highway. My heart jumped, and I knew I was in trouble. A moment later the red and blue lights came on, and it wasn't because it was Christmas.

"Why in the world are you driving 105 miles an hour!" the cop said when he got to my window.

"Because that's all she'd do!" I replied.

(Actually, I didn't say that to the cop. But I've always wanted to.)

He wrote me up for an even 100 mph and allowed me to put the $85 fine on my credit card. A minute or two later I was southbound in the night, looking for I-70.

18

A second title

My injuries from the Belleville crash lingered for several weeks, and that was a problem because we were in the middle of racing season. Two weeks after the crash, in fact, we headed for Springfield, Illinois for the Tony Bettenhausen 100 for the USAC Silver Crown cars.

My ribs were very sore, but the mile tracks are usually pretty smooth so I figured I'd be okay. The biggest issue was my left arm; because of the nerve damage I couldn't lift it more than a few inches, and if I needed to pull a tear-off I'd have to lower my head enough so that my hand could reach it. That doesn't sound like a great challenge until you're strapped tightly into a race car.

The concussion? Like I said before, that's like racing with a hangover. You ignore it and off you go.

It poured rain the night before the race and promoter Bob Sargent—one of the best promoters in the business—wasn't going to let a little rain get in the way. The track crew bladed off most of the slop, and we had a very racy track. The track was heavy early on, of course, but dried out considerably later in the race with a big ledge for a cushion in turn two.

The fast line would involve sliding your right rear tire hard into the cushion; this would straighten you out and shoot your car down the backstretch. I knew that was what I had to do, but with my broken ribs it took my breath away every time I bounced the right rear against the cushion. It would take me all the way to turn three to breathe again.

We qualified 10th and soldiered through the 100-lap race. At about 60 laps it became very hot in the car; not "fire" hot but very uncomfortable. Ten laps later the ignition failed and the engine shot a few ducks then died. We figured the heat came from the ignition timing retarding before it died, and thought nothing more of it. But the issue of "hot" would come back at a later date.

The big news at Springfield was Chuck Gurney, who came into the race 9th in series points. Gurney won the race and jumped into the point lead, with the top five drivers separated by less than 50 points.

We were right in the middle of another tight points race, which suited me. If you can launch a brand new team with a new-design chassis and contend for the championship in your first season, that's pretty decent.

In early September we returned to the Indy Fairgrounds for the Hoosier Hundred. We were confident, because we had won there just a couple of months earlier. There was also the matter of the overall bonus money that was up for grabs, and that was also on our mind.

Hoosier Tire was trying to displace Goodyear in sprint cars at the time, and they were steadily gaining ground and making a pretty good tire. Although it had been a long time since Hoosier Tire had won a Silver Crown race, Stanton agreed to run them at Indy.

As far as recovering from my Belleville injuries, the worst was behind me. I raced at Indy and my arm and shoulder didn't give me any pain at all. I had regained the ability to raise my left arm enough to pull a tear-off, so all was well with the world.

We qualified third and the racing was tight early. Just three laps into the race George Snider flipped end-over-end in turn three in a multi-car pileup that began with Mike Bliss hitting the wall. It was a scary ride but luckily George was okay.

Gurney took the lead on lap 25 but we were right there with him. When Chuck got tangled with a lapped car on lap 28 and suffered some damage—he lost a few laps but returned to the race—we took the lead.

Our car was great, and we clicked off the laps as we rode out front. But we soon had company, as Randy Tolsma began to pressure us on lap 69. We were in heavy traffic, and Randy got past us on lap 80. The traffic was tough, and two laps later I regained the lead when Randy slipped out of the groove and left the inside open.

We were running these big cars like sprint cars; I squeaked past Billy Boat on the inside by the thinnest of margins, and Tolsma somehow followed me through. I had to run as hard as I could, because I knew Randy was right there. It was fun racing, but nerve-wracking.

We had a couple of yellows over the last 15 laps, but I laid down good laps and kept Randy behind me. When we raced across the finish line we were leading by a little over two seconds, and the photographer's flashes lit up the straightaway. It was a great win and I didn't need some time for the gravity of this win to soak in—I knew it right then and there! I had won the Hoosier Hundred and I was one excited racer. Tolsma finished 2nd and Ron Shuman was 3rd.

Our win earlier that year in May assured that we were the top points guy, and between the race purse and the points money the Foyt Group handed us $26,000 at the pay window.

It was a fantastic win, from every angle. History, personal satisfaction, money, everything. An added bonus was that we were leading the points—not by much, just 10 points—but we were leading.

It was also a good night for Hoosier Tire, because their tires worked perfectly all night long.

It was one of those moments when you just feel like a million bucks. Racing has a lot of ups and downs, and nobody denies the downs. But the ups are pretty damn nice. And that night was a really good "up." We didn't mind savoring that one a little bit, hanging out in our pit after the race and drinking a couple of beers with people who came by to celebrate with us.

The following week we were at DuQuoin. We didn't qualify well, and started 22nd in the 100-lap race. About halfway through the race my ass—buttocks to those who are sensitive—was telling me that our heat issue had returned.

Race seats fit pretty tightly, so as my ass grew more uncomfortable there was no way to get away from the heat. I didn't use a lot of cushion in my Ultra Shield seat, so that probably didn't help. The heat grew more intense and it was literally like sitting down on a skillet on a hot stove. As the laps clicked away my ass was screaming for me to pull off and get out of the car before I burned to a crisp.

Pulling off was not an option; we're leading the Silver Crown points. And we did ultimately improve our position by a bunch, moving up to 6th at the finish.

When the race was over I drove to our pit and was out of the car in an instant. I unzipped my uniform and found blisters not quite the size of tennis balls on the side of my thighs where the seat belts come through, and my ass felt like it was on fire.

"Stanton!" I called out. "C'mere a minute."

Gary walked over and I lowered my voice.

"I need you to look at my ass and see if it's blistered."

He did not have a supportive expression on his face.

"I'm not gonna look at your ass! You're crazy."

"No, seriously. Look and see if I'm blistered back there."

"No!"

"I'm not kidding, I got burned on my ass. Look and see if it's blistered."

Gary looked around very slowly a couple of times to make sure nobody was looking. I turned toward the car and dropped my underwear and he glanced at my backside for about a millisecond.

He walked away very quickly and said over his shoulder, "Ya got two golf-ball size blisters on both cheeks."

Pretty soon some of my friends came by to visit our pit. My friends from St. Louis, Gene and Dave Fontaine, always brought water pre-race, and brought beer for after the races. After we visited for a few minutes I needed to head for St. Louis to catch my flight home, so Gene and Dave helped me get my stuff to my rental car in the parking lot.

Gene gave me a plastic bag of ice with four beers for pain meds, and put my helmet bag in the back seat. After he walked away I stood there looking at the bag of ice, and got an idea. I put the bag in the driver's seat and sliced the plastic open then sat my ass right down, directly on the ice. I fired up the rental car and headed for St. Louis.

On the way to St. Louis I made an amazing discovery: If you sweat all your fluids out and then drink four beers without eating anything, you might become intoxicated. So when I reached the rental car return at the airport my inhibitions were probably, uh, *compromised*.

I pulled up in line and got out of the car, and my pants were still down around my knees. I bent over to pull them up and exposed my bare ass to Lambert Intl. Airport and anybody else in the vicinity. The rental agent came racing up and asked if he could do anything to help me, and you could see that he was a little concerned about how I might answer.

"Get my helmet bag out of the back seat and point me toward the terminal," were my only requests. I thought both were quite reasonable.

I began wobbling on my own toward the terminal when I heard him get into the car to pull it forward. As he sat in my melted ice I heard him yell and cuss a little bit but I have to admit that I wasn't feeling all that sensitive to anyone else's problems at the moment.

By the time I arrived back in California all my blisters had popped so I walked through the airport to the parking lot with big wet spots on my pants.

We later figured out the problem with the cockpit heat. The headers on the car went straight back and ended in the vicinity of the seat, with no turnouts. We eventually figured out that the only source of the heat had to be the exhaust, and when Stanton installed turnouts on the headers it solved the problem.

Now that I'm recalling this story, the next time I see Stanton I should ask him to look and see if those blisters left any scars on my ass. I think that would be a good idea.

Chuck Gurney's win at DuQuoin had thrown the '94 Silver Crown title chase into a tight three-man race. Randy Tolsma was the point leader, and I was 30 points back in second. Gurney was third, 32 points behind me. We had three races yet to run.

We arrived at Eldora for the 4-Crown Nationals on September 25, a weekend that will forever have a dark place in my memory. Gurney set quick time in Galen Fox's Foxco car, and we were second-quick. Tolsma qualified 13th and had to race his way into the feature through the last-chance race.

I didn't have a ride in the sprint car or midget portions of the program, so I watched both races from the infield. During the sprint car feature Page Jones was leading the race in Team 6R Racing's V6 car, and as I watched him it looked to me that Page was losing power. While he was under throttle you could see the nose drop for a second and the car would turn toward the wall; if you lose power you lose the steering from your stagger.

The track was very treacherous; the cushion was just a couple of inches off the wall and if your front end sucked into the concrete you were in big trouble. Tray House and Danny Smith each took a hard end-over-end ride earlier in the race when that happened to them.

On lap 12 Page was between turns three and four when the car turned into the wall and flipped. The flip itself didn't look that bad, but Page was clipped by a trailing car. It was just one of those deals where nobody was at fault; Page was leading the race and the entire pack was on his back bumper. There was no way everybody could miss him.

It took them a long time to get Page out of the car; that's never a good sign. The grandstand got very quiet, and all of us racers in the infield were quiet, too. The ambulance whisked him away and everybody was hoping for the best and preparing for the worst.

But we still had a race to run. Kevin Doty won the sprint car race, and then it was time for the Silver Crown cars to take to the track.

It was one of those situations every racer dreads. Something terrible has just happened to one of your friends, but you have to push on. We were set to start on the outside of the front row, in the middle of a tight points race, with one of our closest challengers starting alongside us. This was an important race and we needed a good finish.

I tried to put Page's situation out of my mind as much as I could. There was nothing I could do at that point, I reasoned. Still, it's hard to say you're completely focused in a situation like that.

Jack Hewitt ended up driving past both Gurney and me to win the race. Gurney finished second and I finished third. Tolsma finished 17th. We left Eldora with a 22-point lead in the Silver Crown standings.

Page was very much on my mind as I got into my rental car after the race. I had an early morning flight the following day out of Indianapolis, so I wasn't able to go to the hospital in Dayton to check on Page. But as I drove back to Indy I thought a lot about the past few years and getting to know Page and his brother, P.J.

Our next series stop was Sacramento, right in my back yard. The fairgrounds had been good to us over the years, and we had won the past two races there. We were confident going into that weekend.

Gurney and I continued our duel; I set fast time, and he was second. We started side-by-side on the front row, and Chuck got into the lead at the start. We were right there on him, and on lap 54 I got past him in traffic. That was the story, and we went on to win our third race at the CalExpo State Fairgrounds. Gurney finished second.

During the race I tangled a little bit with George Snider. I was leading the race, and George had a faster car that night. He pulled up beside me on the front straightaway, and his right front was about at my header pipes. I figured I would stay on the gas until I saw him lift, then I would turn in for the corner.

George took us into the corner very deep, and by the time he lifted I had to get my car down or I'd slide across the track. I turned in, and my left rear went over George's right front tire. I got up on two wheels and for an instant I thought I was going out of the place, but my car got back on four wheels and I was okay. But George snapped a right front radius rod and he went into the wall a ton.

Randy Tolsma fell out with overheating problems, dropping him from title contention. Now it was between me and Gurney, with one more race remaining. We would travel to Mesa Marin Raceway in Bakersfield, California one week later holding a lead of 62 points.

Mesa Marin was not a regular stop for the Silver Crown cars, and in fact this was their first appearance there. The track is a half-mile paved oval, a little bit small for these cars. But at any rate the event was added to the schedule and they drew a very large crowd, although only 18 cars made the tow to Bakersfield.

Kenny Irwin Jr. was the class of the field that day, lapping everybody but second-place Tony Stewart. We started 10th and finished fifth, and clinched our second Silver Crown title. Gurney finished seventh, and our point lead at the finish was 82 points.

It was good to win the title with Gary Stanton. Gary and I worked really well together, and I think the championship meant a lot to him as well. This was a good stage of my career; the second title always proves that your first was not a fluke. Since coming to the Silver Crown series five years earlier it had turned out to be a really good place for me.

It was a good feeling, too, that we beat Chuck Gurney. Chuck was a bit of a rival throughout my career, and beating him was never easy.

Chuck was racing before I started, and I remember him at West Capital. This was probably during my first couple of seasons in a race car, and Chuck told me, "You're going to go places…you need to get out of here and start traveling. Go to the Midwest and do some racing out there."

I had read about Chuck in *National Speed Sport News*, and followed his career in those early days. He encouraged me a lot, and when he was back in California he'd tell me how good I was doing. At some point Chuck came back out west and we ended up racing against him a bunch.

Chuck ended up driving for Moller Brothers, and they had a fast car. When we went to Baylands—or anywhere out here, for that matter—I knew we had to beat Chuck if we were going to win the race. I could beat him more with a wing, and he'd beat me more without a wing.

Chuck was in Junior Kurtz's Plastic Express car when I arrived in Silver Crown, and they were bad fast. They had one of the first engines with down-nozzle heads, and they were making some major horsepower. At that time they were way ahead of almost everybody.

Chuck was especially tough on the dirt miles, particularly Springfield and DuQuoin. When I finally won at each of those tracks it was a genuine breakthrough for me. I not only won; I beat Chuck at those places. That was a big deal, really. To get those two under my belt was big.

Our rivalry with Chuck was never ugly or nasty; nothing like that. But it was just kind of "who can out-do the other." Listen, Chuck had some attitude in those days and he would let you know how fast he was. So in a friendly way I could get fired up about beating Chuck.

One day Larry Howard brought his midget to Baylands with Chuck in the seat, and everybody thought they were running for second that day. I was driving a car built by Chuck Delu and owned by Art Laski, painted in the same colors as the Bailey Brothers No. 01. We won the race, and beat Chuck. In my mind it was a huge win, because to beat Gurney in Larry Howard's car took some doing. And we did it.

Today Chuck and I are good friends. I see him all the time and I always enjoy our visits. We razz each other but we praise each other, too. We get along great and I'm glad.

The months of late 1994 were filled with concern and thoughts for Page Jones. After that terrible day at Eldora everyone was worried about him. The early news reports were that he might not live through his injuries, but as the weeks passed the prognosis shifted a little bit. He would survive, but was facing a long and difficult recovery.

Page and his brother P.J. were sons of Parnelli Jones, one of the greatest racing drivers in history. With those genes you've gotta be fast; they were.

One night at a USAC midget race at Oildale I got to watch one of the greatest "knock-down, drag-out" races between brothers in history. They were both running an Ellis chassis and a Chevy II motor. P.J. had already established himself as being fast and aggressive, and Page was just coming out of TQ midgets.

That night at Oildale you could sense that Page was out to show his big brother a thing or two. They were slicing through traffic and sliding each other in every corner. Page pulled off the win and everybody there saw that he was going to be a great racer.

Sometime later I flew into Indianapolis late one night and cruised by Kelly's Pub for a beer. Page, Stevie Reeves, and a couple other guys were playing volleyball out back and asked if I wanted to join them. I wasn't much of a volleyball player and was a little groggy from a long day, but I agreed.

Man, did they give me the needle. Every time I'd miss a ball, or blow a serve, Page would say something like, "Nice reactions, Sills…you race with those?"

Both P.J. and Page were racing some of the Silver Crown races in 1994 and we sometimes traveled together, particularly on our trip to Belleville. They were good friends and it pained me to think of Page being laid up with serious injuries.

I wanted to get to the hospital to see Page; I couldn't forget that he was one of the guys who came to see me in the hospital a few weeks earlier after I crashed at Belleville. These were the days before the Internet, so the only progress anyone heard on Page's condition were the news updates in *Speed Sport*.

In December I was booked to travel to New Zealand and discovered that Page was in a rehab hospital not far from LAX. I scheduled my connection in Los Angeles to allow for a layover of several hours, and when we landed I grabbed a cab and hustled over to the hospital.

I remember that afternoon like it was yesterday. I walked into the hospital room and there, sitting next to the bed, were Page's parents, Judy and Parnelli Jones. It was cool to meet someone I admired so much, but I would have given anything for the circumstances to be different.

Page was sitting there, and he looked normal. It was hard to understand, because he'd had this terrible head injury and he didn't look injured. But the brain is quite a mystery, and brain injuries aren't like a broken bone or burned skin.

Page looked at me with this blank stare, and at any moment I wanted him to say, "Hey, Sills…what are you doing here?"

Page just sat there, holding his arm very tightly to his chest. Judy explained that you couldn't get him to move his arm; he clenched it so tightly that it wouldn't move at all.

I stayed and chatted with Judy and Parnelli for a little while but there wasn't much I could say. It was just such a complete bummer. Finally we said our goodbyes and I left. My heart was heavy as I walked down the hallway toward the parking lot. It felt like my buddy Page was gone, yet he was still here. It was terrible.

But Page's story was far from over. *FAR* from over. The next time I saw him was the following February, at Phoenix. He was walking (with a limp) and talking (a little slowly and hard to understand). But he was there! It was an amazing thing, especially after seeing him look so hopeless in that hospital bed.

Page is really a helluva story. While he will always carry some lingering elements from his injury, he went on to get married, raise children, and work a full-time job. These days you see Page at the Chili Bowl and at other races and he still has that infectious smile and he makes everybody around him feel like a million bucks.

They made a movie about Page's recovery. *God Speed: The Story of Page Jones* has received some excellent reviews and I highly recommend everybody watch this movie about my good friend. You will be inspired, I promise you.

19

Title number three

Gary Stanton would not install a radio in his Silver Crown car. "There is nothing I want to say to my driver while he's racing," he pointed out, "and there's damn sure *nothing* I want to hear."

You've got to admit: Gary probably has a good point.

Still, a radio might have been helpful every now and then. In 1996 we were running real well at the USAC Silver Crown race at Richmond Intl. Raceway, and as the laps clicked down I thought we were running second behind Tony Stewart. But when the race finished I was amazed to discover that Stewart was actually a lapped car (that doesn't happen very often!) and we were leading.

There were lots of good moments like that in Gary's Silver Crown car. Of course, there are almost always some down moments as well, and we had a few of those, too.

Our USAC Silver Crown title in 1994 obviously falls into the "good" category, but the following year we weren't able to maintain enough momentum to repeat as Silver Crown champs.

Anybody who has raced knows that the margin between "championship" performance and "so-so" performance can be very small, and it's hard to pinpoint exactly why. That is how I would describe our 1995 season: we just didn't run nearly as well and I don't know exactly why.

We had a brand new Mopar engine—it was still being developed—but that wasn't the issue. Despite nearly all the same pieces from the year before we ended up 13th in series points and we didn't win a race. We had several different mishaps and a few outings where we were strong enough to win but it didn't happen.

Early in the year Gary decided that the check ball tank vent wasn't enough to properly vent our 75-gallon tank, so he tweaked the vent with a hose that ran from the top of the tank along the frame to drain under the tank.

This created a memorable couple of races. We eventually realized that when our tank was full—the early laps of long races—when you braked for the corner the vent allowed fuel to slosh from the top of the tank into the hose. The fuel would drain from the hose below the car.

Air blows forward at the bottom of the cockpit, and I would feel the cold fuel on the back of my legs. This was a serious problem and luckily we didn't have a fire—yet.

But losing that fuel cost us, because we ran out of fuel while leading at Springfield, and again later at Sacramento.

At DuQuoin it created a comical exchange among the race officials. We started the race and when I braked for the corner the inside of the car would get very warm and then cool off down the straightaway. A USAC official standing in the corner radioed, "The 75 car is on fire, better black-flag him!" But by the time I reached the observers on the straightaway the fire had blown out so the officials said, "No, he's okay…no fire."

Down to the corner again, and sloshing the fuel. "The 75 car is still on fire!"

"No, he isn't, he's okay."

"The 75 car is on fire again!"

And so on.

Then I realized that we might be running metallic brake pads, which often give off sparks. So instead of braking I lifted early for the corners and eased in, and at that point we weren't on fire through the corners any more. I did this until the fuel load burned down and I couldn't feel fuel splashing on the back of my legs anymore (after the race Gary confirmed that we were running metallic pads).

We eventually figured out the problem with the vent, but it was just one more factor in a weird, difficult season.

One of the new venues for 1995 was Richmond. Pavement was still a different animal for Gary—and for me too, really—and we had to study the topic a little bit. We used four-wheel brakes, so we ran four radius rods on the front. This would be a problem on dirt, because it would bind up the suspension and the car wouldn't transfer weight properly. So Gary installed a swivel on the right front to prevent binding.

We were 41 laps into the race at Richmond when the bolt holding the lower left radius rod failed. When I braked for the corner the axle rolled up inside the frame, tearing out the brake line, suspension, and steering. The front end dropped to the ground and I headed for the outside wall.

Richmond is a wide track, and I was a passenger as I watched that concrete wall approaching at well over a hundred miles an hour. It's amazing all the things you can think about in that situation! I had a good two or three seconds to contemplate things before a very loud and hard hit.

Luckily I wasn't hurt; we couldn't say the same for the car, as it was all but wiped out.

At the Indiana State Fairgrounds in September I learned a valuable lesson about tires. The Hoosier Tire engineers were always telling us we should run 11 or 12 pounds of pressure, and certainly nothing less than 10 pounds. But we were sprint car people, so we insisted on running eight pounds of air pressure.

We were pretty decent at the start of the race, but our tire blistered and began to lose air through the blisters. We came in and put a new tire on that carried 10 pounds of pressure, and I could feel that the car was no longer laying over in the corners because of the additional pressure. We were immediately faster, and I started passing cars and figured we'd be okay.

But that tire blistered too, and began to lose air. As soon as it lost some air the car was laying over, and I realized that we were slower and the car didn't want to drive forward. That was a revelation, because I finally realized those tire engineers knew what they were talking about. I quit arguing with them and began to listen.

When the 1995 season was over we were ready to forget it and move on. That turned out to be a good strategy because 1996 turned out much, much better.

One of the highlights was winning at Richmond, where we had crashed so hard the year before. We also won the final race of the year at Del Mar, California, and by winning the race we clinched our third USAC Silver Crown championship.

It went right down to the wire, in fact.

We had a lead of 20 points over Kenny Irwin Jr. coming into Sacramento in October, and we felt pretty good. I always ran well at Sacramento and figured we could capitalize on that. But we got tangled up with a lapped car while leading on lap 32, and were knocked out of the race. Kenny finished second and we left Sacramento trailing him by 138 points.

The next weekend we traveled to Del Mar—right on the Pacific coast just north of San Diego—to run the first auto race at the historic dirt mile since 1949. If Kenny finished 6th or better, he would clinch the championship.

We did everything we could do to prevent that; we set fast time to earn the pole, then led all 100 laps to win the race. But on lap 99 an incident dramatically changed the outcome of the points race.

Kenny was running sixth when he had a tire go down. He limped along for a moment but then collided with another car, ending his day one lap short of the finish. He was scored 11th and we won the title—our third—by 42 points.

The weekend of the Del Mar win was one of the greatest racing weekends of my life.

The Oval Nationals at Perris Auto Speedway was happening that same weekend, and Don Berry brought his sprint car down for me to run. We hadn't raced much without wings that year—although a few weeks earlier we won the sprint car feature at the 4-Crown Nationals at Eldora in Stanton's sprint car—so we had Don's car pretty loose and stable on that heavy track to help me get my confidence back.

We were fifth in points after the preliminary night, which put us in a trophy dash. How you finished the dash set your starting position for the feature. The track had dried out, and when they dropped the green flag on the dash I realized we were completely out to lunch with our setup. We had our feature tire on the car and I didn't want to chew it up, so I immediately pulled in from the dash and we went to work.

We changed all four torsion bars, all four shocks, put on a bigger left rear tire, changed the rear-end gear, the ride height, the wheel offset, and raised the motor in the car. Normally with that many changes you have your hands full sorting out the car, but when they dropped the green flag for the feature the car was perfect.

I got to second pretty quickly, then gave Richard Griffin a slider going into turn one to take command. After that we ran away from 'em. Ron Shuman got going good on the bottom in the last few laps and pulled beside me a couple of times, but we weren't going to be denied.

We won the Oval Nationals and banked $10,000. The Del Mar win the following afternoon was good for another $10,250, so it was a lucrative—and really fun!—weekend. Don Berry retired from racing after that weekend and went out on a totally high note.

My history with Don and Janet Berry was good. We raced off-and-on for several years, working around each of our schedules. Don was an easy guy to race with and nearly all of the time allowed me to choose where we raced.

We won some good races together in Don's sprint car. The Mini Gold Cup, the Cotton Classic, and the Oval Nationals come to mind. We had a lot of fun, too, and I have a ton of happy moments to reflect on. Don and Janet are still good friends today.

During our time together my schedule was fairly complicated, and they always tried to accommodate that. No matter what, we had fun. One year we decided to run California Sprint Week and were very good, but a series of weird things kept us out of victory lane. We traveled to Petaluma, and as we drove to the track I continued to tell Don that Petaluma was absolutely one of the tackiest and heaviest race tracks in the country. Naturally, the track that day was exactly the opposite; it was dry as a bone! There was some wind that night, but it also looked like the water truck driver had taken the day off.

To make matters worse we drew the last qualifying position and it was horribly slick by the time we qualified. We lined up last in our heat race and didn't make the transfer.

We went to work on the car, changing every adjustment on the car to tighten it up. Man, that thing was so tight that it should have turned over pulling away from the push truck. But it was just right for that slick track, and we won the B from the tail and tagged the tail of the feature race. We managed to drive up through the field and finished third, so we ended the night on a high note.

We had one more race before Don had to go back to work the following day. He wanted to race at San Jose, because that would be a much shorter drive home after the races. But I lobbied for us to race at Calistoga, even though it was much farther from home.

Finally Don yielded to my wishes, and we drove up to Calistoga. However, as part of the deal Don insisted that we stop at Satui Winery for a picnic lunch on the way to the track.

Jason Meyers was a fresh-faced young kid traveling with us that weekend. Jason was just getting started in his driving career, and he tagged along to learn everything he could about sprint car racing.

We had a very good time at the winery. *Much* too good a time. We had our picnic lunch on a blanket and sipped wine, and after our lunch nobody seemed to be in a hurry to get up and go to the races. Finally I stood up and looked at Don and Jason.

"Hey, can we get going?" I finally said. "We've got to go racing tonight!"

Don just looked up at me—over the rim of his wine glass—and said, "Sills...we let you choose where we raced, didn't we? Well, at least we've gotta have some fun before we get there!"

We finally made our way to Calistoga and unloaded. We fired up the car and I immediately discovered that my drunk crew had left the tuna cans—used to keep water out of the engine at the car wash—hanging on the headers. The cans went flying across the pit area like missiles, leading everybody to stare at us like we were racing for the first time.

We made a gear change for the big Calistoga track, and realized right away that the gear was way too high. Well, that was because the gears were in upside down. Strangely enough, we were quickest in hot laps, even with the wrong gear. So we qualified as-is and set quick time. After some debate they did agree to change the gear for the heat race so I could run traffic.

At the end of this very fun and eventful day we won the feature—in spite of ourselves. Even though Don had a much farther drive home, he was in a wonderful mood. After a win, of course, you can drive all night.

Looking back, it is obvious that Jason Meyers only used *some* of the things he learned from us; I say that because he went on to enjoy a great career in sprint cars. Luckily Jason didn't pick up the idea that every race team goes to a winery before going to the track! Jason went on to win two World of Outlaws titles and nearly won the Knoxville Nationals (he would have won it if Tyler Walker wouldn't have parked a dead car on the track to bring out a caution).

Jason, I hope we helped you in some small way and that you learned some good things from us. But luckily you didn't learn *everything* from us.

My time with Gary Stanton in the USAC Silver Crown series spanned five full seasons, and were some of the most successful and enjoyable of my career. We won two Silver Crown titles together, and five races. We had our ups and downs but we managed to avoid the personal conflicts that can spoil the good times.

We raced together as friends and we stayed friends when we were done. We're still friends to this day.

We ran fourth in series points in 1997, and again in 1998. Those were decent years but we had some setbacks, too.

In July of 1997 we traveled to Indianapolis Raceway Park. We were qualifying and were near the end of the backstretch when the universal joint came apart. I realized instantly what was happening and I could feel shrapnel hitting my feet.

Then things quickly got painful. And *scary*.

As the U-joint continued to disintegrate it broke a fitting for the fuel return line. Fuel spurted from the broken line and in an instant we are on fire. On *FIRE*.

ESPN was covering the race and their video showed flames blowing clear out the top of the cage. It was instantly hot and with the broken driveline we were freewheeling into the corner at about 100 mph. I applied the brakes and it immediately locked up the front wheels and the car pushed straight for the wall.

I don't want to crash *and* burn, so I lightened up the brakes and the car turned toward the infield. It was still on fire and as I was just about stopped I managed to bail out of the car onto the ground. Bobby Seymour's crew—and several other mechanics and drivers—were right there to pour buckets of water on my feet, which were literally covered with fuel and on fire.

IRP has a small medical building outside the track, and USAC official Bill Marvel took me over there on a golf cart. The medics got me up on the examination table and began peeling away my burned shoes and firesuit, and offered me a shot of morphine. Of course, I don't need morphine because I'm a tough, rough, strong racer.

"I'll pass," I said, very proud of myself for my incredibly high level of pain tolerance.

A few minutes later they started cleaning my burned feet. I felt sweat breaking out on my forehead and my voice was kind of squeaky and I asked the nurse, "Say, is that morphine still available?"

"Pill or shot?" the nurse replied.

"I'm thinking shot right now."

I was not hospitalized, but my feet had some pretty serious burns. I spent the night at Jeff Walker's place near Noblesville. Jeff and I are longtime friends, and I drove his sprint car many times. We held the wingless track record at Eldora for a long time, and we also had a couple of trips to New Zealand together.

After a couple of days I traveled back home, and began to fully appreciate what it is to suffer a burn injury. I had a sprint car school scheduled the following weekend at Skagit Speedway, and was a little nervous about healing up quickly enough to conduct the school. Right before I left for Skagit I had a follow-up appointment, and the doctor proceeded to pull all the dead skin off my feet. This exposed the raw skin underneath, and my feet looked like two pieces of fresh salmon under the lights at the meat counter.

I was definitely very, very tender as I walked around the Skagit infield all that weekend.

I did heal up okay, but I think that injury was Karma's way of saying that I should have had a lot more understanding for my friend and brother-in-law Tim Green when he was burned some years earlier. Today I have absolute sympathy and respect for Tim's ability to recover from very serious burns, as I respect anyone who has suffered that injury.

There were a couple other mishaps in my last couple of years with Gary Stanton, although they were—luckily—not nearly as serious.

I made a dumb mistake at Terre Haute in 1998 and spun all by myself right in front of Jack Hewitt. Jack had nowhere to go and t-boned me hard.

The impact broke the frame rail and the frame diagonals and pinned my leg to the torque tube.

Man, it hurt all over. My leg was hurting so badly that I wasn't even really sure it was still attached. But I did not like the feeling of being trapped in that race car. I finally managed to get my leg out and after a quick examination made sure the foot was still attached. Luckily, no broken bones.

Later that summer at DuQuoin we pushed our car to the qualifying line while I was standing in the seat. The steering wheel was sitting on top of the shaft but was not snapped in place. When we were getting close to the front of the line I slid in the seat and buckled up, then rolled out to qualify.

On my second lap I made the exciting discovery that I hadn't snapped the steering wheel in place. This revelation took place right in the center of the corner. I was able to diagnose the situation immediately because my hands were turning the wheel but nothing was happening.

The solution was simple: If I could, 1) remain calm, 2) line the splines up properly, and 3) push the steering wheel back in place, my troubles were over.

I could not do any of those things.

The car drove straight toward the ancient guardrail, and at that precise moment I did not feel like a confident, happy racer. I could see, however, that luckily they had stacked straw bales in front of the wall. I guess they had already figured out that things like this can happen!

Upon impact it was absolutely a straw bale explosion. By the time we got stopped and I climbed out of the car I was spitting straw out of my mouth.

Luckily the damage was light, and we only needed to replace a radius rod and the axle. Stanton had a good sense of humor about the whole thing.

"Hey, we'll have plenty of straw to soak up any leaks today!" he said.

ESPN was broadcasting the race, and I didn't think much about it. When I flew home later that night my mom picked me up at the airport and as I climbed into her car she looked at me with a curious expression.

"I saw you on TV today!" she said.

My heart jumped. "What was I doing?"

"You were trying to put your steering wheel back on!"

Boy…great. Just great.

"And you know what? Right before they ran the replay they were saying, 'Watch Jimmy Sills trying to put his steering wheel back in place!'"

It was almost embarrassing enough for me to change my name back to Luke Warmwater.

The USAC Silver Crown schedule leaves lots of gaps throughout the year, which allowed me to continue to race sprint cars and midgets well into the late 1990s.

By this time some things had changed in the way I approached racing. I was still intense about winning, but I made it a point to try and have fun in the process. I was still an avid motorcycle guy—that's a passion that I will carry on until I can't sit on a motorcycle—and I would often ride my motorcycle long distances to run somebody's race car.

In 1997 my friend Bob Miller joined me on a ride down to Perris, which is a 500-mile ride each way. I had arranged a one-off ride in a sprint car owned by Ed Ulyate, a guy who teamed with Ron Shuman to win the 1988 CRA championship.

A one-off appearance in a new car can be a challenging proposition with lots of uncertainty. They don't know you, and you don't know them. You need some time to develop some trust that the other knows what they're doing, and one race night doesn't provide much time to do that.

I had learned that when I got into somebody's car for the first time that it usually didn't go well if I immediately starting preaching to them about how they should set up their car. So I always followed the same process: Rather than telling them specifically what to do to the car, I just asked them to adjust the car in a way to address a certain condition.

If you've been teamed with this guy for 20 minutes and you're telling him, "Take a turn out of the left rear!" he is probably not going to like being told what to do. Instead, I'd say, "Can you make the car tighter?" Focus on the result, not the specifics on how to do it.

My experience was that people like that a lot better. However, sometimes the direct approach works better; this was one of those nights.

We drew three to qualify, and in hot laps the track was still pretty greasy. I asked our mechanic, Sal Acosta, to snug it up a little bit. It was still too loose in qualifying, so I asked Sal to tighten 'er up a little more.

We started on the pole of the heat and when I throttled it into the front straightaway the car stood straight up on the back wheels and I was staring at the hood. It was obvious that we had *way* too much forward bite in the car.

I got to the end of the straightaway and tried to lightly set the front wheels down. I turned in for the corner and the right rear didn't want to slip, so now I've discovered that we've got *way* too much side bite, too!

I ran a few laps, keeping the right rear in the slick. But then the car was freeing up, and to compensate I ran the right rear about a foot higher. I immediately discovered that this was *NOT GOOD*.

The car stood up on the right front tire and by all appearances I was preparing to exit this place and not through the normal gates. The car traveled quite a ways on the right front and after a few moments the car settled back on all four wheels and my heart rate finally began to slow.

When the heat race finished I got back to our pit and Ed's eyes were very wide.

"Thanks for saving my car, Sills," he said.

"Ed, I was saving my ass, not your car!"

We managed to race our way into the feature, but that was about it.

Bob and I rode our Harley's home, taking the scenic route along Hwy. 395 to Hwy. 88. We discovered some cool sights and vistas and within a few weeks ended up taking another ride to Southern Cal to run the Morales Bros. Tamale Wagon on the pavement at Irwindale.

The night before the race I woke up in the hotel room around 1 a.m. Everything was shaking and rattling, electrical transformers were cracking and popping, and every motion detector in the area was going crazy. I woke Bob up and informed him that we were having an earthquake. We walked out of our room and stood in the parking lot in our underwear with everybody else. After a while the shaking stopped and we went back inside and went back to sleep.

The Irwindale trip was a little more successful, as we ran second to Bud Kaeding.

On the way home we dropped over Ebbetts Pass into Yosemite; it was my first visit. Although I had bike trouble—the stator which generates power to the battery burned out—and was delayed for a few days (we actually left my bike there and I rode home on the back of Bob's bike), it was still a great trip.

Travels like that—and days spent with friends like Bob Miller—give me great feelings when I think back through the years.

Throughout my career the one constant was coming home to California to race. At various times I might have spent much of the year on the road with the Outlaws, or racing in one region such as central Pennsylvania or the Midwest, or following the USAC Silver Crown schedule. But I always managed to do some racing around home, usually early and late in the season.

Along the way I connected with some people from the Sacramento and northern California area and developed friendships that have lasted many years.

One of the prominent local families in Sacramento racing circles was the Tiner family from Rio Linda. It's an interesting group of people and they've been a huge influence on racing in our area. Johnny and Mack Tiner were the first two family members I remember as a kid; Johnny was the driver while Mackie was usually the mechanic, although on occasion Mack would get behind the wheel. Mack was also a very talented painter. The Tiner car was typically the best-looking car in the pit area.

When I was just getting started in 1974 Johnny Tiner had a terrific year driving a second car for Bob Davis. Bob usually fielded two cars, with the primary car carrying No. 00 and the second car was No. 000. Bob started the year with Jimmy Boyd in the primary car until Jimmy left to race in Pennsylvania. At the time Jimmy was holding a sizable lead in the point standings at West Capital.

Bob Davis tried several drivers to replace Jimmy, but nobody could match Jimmy's results. In the meantime Johnny Tiner began winning in the No. 000 car. So during the week Bob would switch numbers, and put the No. 00 on Johnny's car. But when Bob was sure he had a hot driver in his primary car he'd switch the numbers back. But Johnny just kept winning and in the end Bob outguessed his way out of the points championship.

Johnny Tiner's sons, Richard, Steven, and Randy, all drove sprint cars. Steven lived in the Midwest for a while and drove a lot of ASCS races, and recently moved to Chico, where he has partnered with Kyle Hirst to open a performance shop. Richard lives just around the corner from me.

Johnny's son Rod Tiner is one of the best chassis builders in the country and certainly one of the best welders. Rod repairs a lot of sprint car chassis each year. He's got a great mind for sprint cars and in the early 1990s Rod designed the angle-stack car which Karl Kinser utilized for a while. I drove Rod's car a few races and we won a couple. Rod's cars were not fancy but you could count on him fielding a strong race car that really worked. Rod also wrenched Clyde Lamars's Tri C Special. We won the Mini Gold Cup together in 1988, and also won a race at San Jose.

These days Rod works on a World of Outlaws team for Kasey Kahne, and continues to repair a lot of sprint cars.

Rod's son, Rod Jr., works on sprint cars for Justyn Cox. Rod Jr. is a fine sprint car mechanic in his own right.

I got along great with all of the Tiner family...with one exception. Randy, the youngest son, was also known as Boo. Randy and I just could not be on the same race track without having difficulties.

Randy was deaf at birth, and he got his nickname—Boo—because it was one of the first words he could pronounce. He learned how to communicate very well with his brothers, and Randy grew up to become one of the most talented drivers in our area. Rod recognized Randy's talent and worked hard to help take him as far as he could.

I'm not sure exactly where the trouble started between Randy and me. Most of the time when you have an incident on the race track with someone you both get it out of your system right away. You go down and talk to each other—or maybe you yell at each other—but you put it in the past and move on. But for Randy and me, we had an ongoing stress with each other that spanned many seasons.

Our trouble might have begun many years ago at Chico, where we raced each other very hard one night. After the race Randy apparently decided we both needed to finish off the night by crashing.

The next incident occurred a short time later at Calistoga, where Randy and I were racing for the lead. I passed Randy on the bottom in three and four, and Randy drove back by me on the inside of one and two. We raced side-by-side along the back straightaway when he turned into the side of my car, shooting me right into the board fence.

Man, what a hit. The front torsion tubes of my car were ripped from the frame and the front axle was thrown all the way to turn three. My car landed upright with everything forward of the radiator cleaned off. The crash was so violent and frightening that Brent Kaeding came to a stop nearby and ran over and hugged me when he saw that I was okay. I wasn't hurt but Dennis Johnson's race car was completely wiped out.

Next chapter of Tiner vs. Sills came at a NARC race at Santa Maria where I was driving Don Berry's car. Randy was driving for the Orth family, and I passed him for fifth and then passed a couple more cars when the yellow came out. As we circled around under caution Randy tried to squeeze his car in front of mine, claiming that he should get his spot back. But a full lap had been completed and the officials were waving him to fall in line several cars behind me.

Randy was obviously not pleased and he kept bumping into me as we circled around, refusing to fall back to his position. After several laps of this bullshit I had enough so I aimed my left front torsion bolt at his right rear tire and rammed him, all the while riding my brakes so I wouldn't climb over his tire and tip myself over.

Now Randy had a flat right rear tire and he floored the throttle to run to his pit to change the tire. At that point the officials informed him that he would be restarting at the tail. Randy was not pleased.

The following year I was driving Dennis Johnson's car at the Dirt Cup at Skagit. We were running the qualifying feature and Randy was driving for Rod Fauver. Rod's car had four coil-over shocks and Randy was starting on the pole. I started in the third row and caught Randy going into turn one and found myself to his outside, where I'd rather not be.

Just as I reached my turn-in point Randy hit me. Not enough to crash me, but enough to scare me. And, of course, completely piss me off. I'm thinking I owe him one the next time I see him, which happened to be a few laps later when he was struggling with Bob Walker (Tyler Walker's father) and another car from Arizona.

Those three guys are really going at it, trying to crash each other. When I arrived on the scene Randy was loose entering the corner and I tagged him in the rear bumper just enough to send him spinning. He collected the other two cars and the red flag came out and I could see that all three cars were upside down. This was much more than I expected to accomplish and I immediately felt some pangs of regret, but oh well.

We went on to win the race and were later celebrating our victory in the pits. I saw Bob Walker coming over, and I figured he was pissed at me. Just when I think he's going to punch me, Bob extends his hand and says, "Thanks…I was wanting to do that to him for the last five laps."

Now the feud carries on to Tulare. I'm leading the feature in Dennis Johnson's car and came up to lap Brad Furr, who is usually fast but tonight is having a problem. Brad appeared to be running the bottom but just as I got alongside him he came out to the top—where I am. I went over Brad's right rear tire entering turn one and flipped really hard.

I climbed out of the car and was having trouble getting my breath. Mike Andreetta was the lead official and he rushed over. I explained that it felt like somebody has hit me in the middle of the back with a baseball bat. Mike calmly says, "Sills, you've broken your back. Get into the ambulance."

As I'm lying in the ambulance trying to get my breath I hear the familiar sound of Randy Tiner's voice, also in the ambulance. Apparently Randy was right on my ass when I hit Brad's right rear and he couldn't avoid the crash. Randy is yelling at me that everything is my fault and he's wanting to fight but he has a broken wrist and they're trying to haul us both away in the same ambulance.

I mustered enough oxygen to politely tell the medical guys to get that son-of-a-bitch out of this ambulance, right now. They apparently agreed that this was a good idea and they put Randy in a different ambulance and took us both to the hospital.

A short while later I was lying on an examination table, thinking about my situation. I was leading the USAC Silver Crown points at the time and we had a race at Colorado Springs next weekend that was a must-do event for me.

A few minutes later the doctor came in and informed me that I've suffered a compression fracture of the T5 vertebra in my back and that it was okay for me to get up from the table. What a relief, I can get up!

The first words out of my mouth were, "Can I race next weekend?" The doctor was shaking his head but he did say, "You can do what you want but there will be some pain involved." I explained that it was a smooth pavement track and I'll be okay but he was still shaking his head and appeared to be skeptical. I ultimately raced the Silver Crown race but I did cancel a dirt sprint car race I had been planning on running that following weekend.

As I walked out of the hospital I saw my mom sitting in the waiting area. I said, "Hey, it's nice of you to come down and check on me!" But then she explained that she came in on the hook, too. As she was driving to the race track a few hours earlier somebody ran a stop sign and plowed into the side of her van. So there was a lot of bad energy for my entire family that night in Tulare.

But we looked at the bright side.

"Great," I said. "You need a ride and I need a driver!" So off we went.

20

Ziggy

Just when I thought life couldn't get any more interesting, George Snider asked me to drive his race car. George and I had some history from the 1994 USAC Silver Crown race at Sacramento—we tangled in a racing deal and George got the worse of it—but he was willing to set all that aside. We agreed to go racing together in 1999 and chase the Silver Crown title.

I ran George's car once before, at Springfield the previous August. Gary Stanton's car had some difficulty and we were done before hot laps, and I begged George to let me drive his car that day. We didn't do all that well and finished 19th.

But the 1999 season was filled with promise and we ran pretty well. We won at Indy in May, won again at the 4-Crown at Eldora in September, and closed out the season with a win at good 'ol Sacramento. We finished fourth in points—the third straight season that we finished fourth in the standings.

There were some down days, too. We crashed two pavement cars at Orlando and Nazareth, Pennsylvania.

The Orlando race was the season opener, held in January at Walt Disney World Speedway. We had a two-week break before the next race at Phoenix, and instead of taking the car back to George's shop in Indy we headed west to stay in Houston. That was a good midway point between Orlando and Phoenix, and George's longtime friend/sponsor/car owner A.J. Foyt let us use his shop near Houston. A.J. also graciously allowed us to stay in his home.

What a thrill it was to hang around my childhood hero! I have great respect for George and all of his accomplishments as well, and it was fun to watch the interactions between him and A.J. as we worked in the shop.

Although he can be intense in a racing setting, George is one of the most unique and funny personalities I've ever met. He's got this dry, dour way about him, and when he cracks a joke it's usually with some dark humor that's just funny as hell.

George is a classic old-school racer, a guy who endured his share of hard knocks. He's a throwback to a time when racing was a lot more dangerous, and racers of that era developed a way of joking about the situation. Maybe that helps them cope with tragedy.

George had one of the coolest nicknames: Ziggy. I have no idea where that came from but it's great. It fits George perfectly.

In 1975 George was leading the USAC sprint car standings when he flipped out of the park at Winchester, badly breaking both arms. His injuries were significant enough that his forearms were a little crooked from that point on.

George was old-school in a lot of ways. Food, for example. He was a meat-and-potatoes guy who had no interest in health food or anything resembling it. We were sitting at Union Jack restaurant in Indianapolis one day, and the late Dave Steele was at our table. We were ordering lunch and George ordered a sandwich.

"Do you want a salad?" the waitress asked.

"Hell, no," George insisted. "In fact, I don't want one green thing on my plate. Not even parsley. Okay?"

The waitress nodded and walked away, and Dave looked at George and shook his head.

"George, you ought to eat more healthy food," Dave said.

"Aw, bullshit," George replied.

"If you don't eat vegetables or greens, you might get gout," Dave continued.

"Gout? What's that?"

"It's like a disease...you don't want to get it."

"Well, how will I know if I get it? What are the symptoms?"

Dave was staring at George's crooked arms as they were perched on the table.

"Well...the first symptom is that your arms start bending until you can't straighten them out!"

I came back to race for George again in 2000 and ran the first half of the season with him.

Everything fell apart in June after a tough night at Knoxville Raceway. Our car was way too tight and it was hard to get turned on that big cushion with a ledge, but early in the race we still were running in the top five or six.

I was rounding turn two on lap 18 with a lot of left steering input in the car trying to get it turned when the front wheel bit and I spun the car, bringing out the caution. We went to the tail and on the restart everybody slowed down, and it felt like they came to a complete stop. I was trying to thread the needle to get through, and just when I thought I had 'em cleared somebody cut down across my right front wheel and spun me out again.

George was not at all happy at this series of events and I heard his voice come across our radio. I did not need to see his expression at that moment to gauge his mood.

"Just bring the fucker in," he barked.

In George's defense, his car has just spun twice and nothing good usually comes from continuing on. However, from my perspective I have just spun twice on the same lap and now I'm on a mission to redeem myself. It will turn out good, just wait and see! I decided to ignore the voice on the radio and prove to George what a hero I could be.

I'm now on the comeback trail, passing cars and looking good. The laps click away and we're getting to the late stages of the race and at that point I was feeling very good about the hero part.

Right about then that big cushion tore the Jacobs ladder out of the frame. This is the piece that holds the rear end in place. When you're running right out by the fence in that situation, you're probably not going to avoid climbing on the fence and taking a big ride.

We flipped hard, and really put the hurt on George's car. I crawled out of the car and realized I wasn't hurt, but I had already concluded that I was not going to receive a hero's welcome back at our pit.

It was a TV race, and as I'm slowly walking away Gary Lee came running over with lights, camera, and a microphone.

"You're walking pretty slowly there, Sills," Gary says. "That looked like a bad one. Are you hurt?"

"No Gary, I'm walking slowly because I'm pretty sure I'm fired when I get back to our trailer."

To George's credit, he didn't fire me on the spot. He waited until he had lined up another driver, and *then* he fired me. I got the call the following Monday afternoon.

A couple of months later I reconnected with Gary Stanton. Gary had been running modified star Brett Hearn in his seat, but Hearn couldn't make some of the Silver Crown races because of his schedule.

Gary and I ran Springfield, DuQuoin, and the Hoosier Hundred together, but didn't have much success. Then we went to Eldora's 4-Crown at the end of September and it was like the magic we enjoyed in earlier years had returned.

J.J. Yeley was leading in George Snider's car but we were right there, all over him. We could get up alongside him a couple of times but didn't have quite enough to make the pass. Our car was too tight in turns one and two where the cushion had a curb, but were faster in turns three and four where it was loose dirt and right up against the wall.

J.J. and I had pulled away from the field in the closing stages and I knew it was time to make a run. I started running past my comfort level in turns one and two in order to get a better run at my good end of the track.

How about that expression: Go for broke. That's exactly what we did… broke everything on the car.

Six laps from the finish I got over the cushion coming off turn two and hit the fence. The front end sucked into the wall and we flipped hard down the backstretch. When we finally stopped flipping the car was lying on its side, with the cage facing approaching traffic.

All I could think about at that instant was Page Jones; he had been terribly hurt in exactly this situation. Luckily we had a big enough gap that everybody was able to miss us.

The next week was Sacramento, and I knew Stanton wasn't going to take his car out west. So I tried to get in touch with Darryl Guiducci of Team 6R; Jack Hewitt normally drove their Silver Crown car but he was staying in the Midwest to run a late model.

Before I could contact Darryl, however, I got a call from Fred Ede asking if I'd like to run his M&L Plumbing car at Sacramento. I told Fred I was a little sore and was knocked kinda goofy in the crash; could I call him back tomorrow and let him know?

I figured that gave me a backup in case the Guiducci plan doesn't work out.

Long story short: I got home and called Darryl but they had already hired Bud Kaeding for Sacramento. I immediately called Fred back but he didn't want to wait for me and had already hired Russ Gamester. So I screwed myself in that round.

I landed a ride with Bob Hoerner for the season finale at Memphis in late October. We didn't qualify well and raced our way in through the last chance race, and ran from 27th to 17th and were running at the finish.

And that was the end of my Silver Crown career, right there at Memphis.

Things had changed in my life.

I had started a racing school in California, and it had taken off pretty well. From a business standpoint the school became very important, and

I had to devote more and more time to making it work. By the end of the week I was worn out from the school and needed a couple of days off, but instead I'd be jumping on an airplane to go racing somewhere.

Anybody who has ever done this can tell you how hard it is. After a while you face getting burned out and it really saps your enthusiasm.

Something else was happening, too. There were moments in the race car when I caught myself thinking about precisely what I was doing and how I could teach it to my students. This is not good; driving a race car should come naturally to the point where you don't think about what you're doing. I'm certain that my racing suffered because my mind had shifted from simply driving the car to *teaching people* how to drive a car.

When you've raced successfully—won races and championships—showing up and running 15th is not something you're satisfied with. It's just not in your genes.

You're the first one to realize when you're not getting the job done. Nobody needs to tell you. After the race when somebody is telling you the mistakes you made, you already *know* what mistakes you made. You know it very well.

Everything all came together to lead me to step away from racing and focus my attention on my school. It was a life-changing moment for a guy who had chased race cars all of his adult life.

It was a tough decision, I won't lie. In my heart I still wanted to win races. I still felt like I should be winning races.

The most fun you can ever have is being in a race car. But I had reached a point where racing was just a job. Instead of *getting* to go race—a privilege and a thrill—I *had* to go race. There's a big difference.

It almost felt like when people say, "I've got to go to work in the morning." When you feel that way about racing, it is not good.

I was the first three-time champion in USAC Silver Crown history; I'm very proud of that fact. That's something I can hold onto for a while.

I still follow Silver Crown racing as much as I can. They're still racing on those familiar tracks and I can relate to what they're doing.

I've seen video of the night racing at DuQuoin, and I would have loved to run there at night. It looks great.

The footage and pictures from Springfield look as exciting as ever. The tradition of those dirt miles is fabulous and I hope the series—and those tracks—live on forever.

My most cherished memories will always be on the mile at the CalExpo Fairgrounds at Sacramento. That's my home town, and winning there four times—1990, 1993, 1994, and 1999—was a big deal.

Somehow that track suited me, and I always ran as little stagger as I could and ran a very hard tire. You had to drive the car hard with that setup, but with the harder tire you could easily make 100 miles.

Sacramento had a sandy surface, and Gary Stanton's car was really fast on that type of surface. Sacramento, the Indy mile, Del Mar...the suspension Gary created really worked well on those tracks.

At every track I ever raced—in any kind of car—I had the attitude that I could win. Every successful racer will probably tell you they feel the same way. When you've already won at a particular track, it's a boost to your confidence. When you *know* you can win, you have a better shot at pulling it off.

When we showed up at Sacramento, I knew those other guys were looking at me as the guy they had to beat that day.

That's a great feeling. A special feeling.

As the years passed after I stepped away from driving, I experienced racing from the sidelines. Instead of driving the car, I was now a spectator.

I don't know about anybody else, but there is no comparison. You cannot be on the sidelines and experience the thrill like you do in the seat. No possible way.

When you've had that thrill for more than 25 years, you realize immediately what you're missing. It's never the same.

Jack Hewitt sums it up best as a former racer. "Watching a race is like watching porn," he says. "Sooner or later you'll find yourself wanting to participate."

That says it.

21

Mayhem. No, really.

I've never seen any scientific studies, but it's a safe assumption that successful racers are not normal people. When you race you subject your body to great risks, and normal people would look at this as making no sense.

But I can honestly say that my life has never been normal. Almost from day one there was mayhem and great physical risk happening all around me. In fact, it involved almost everyone in my family, because all of us had an inherent love for anything with wheels. My mom was a speed demon, and my sisters and I took after her in a big way. Our lives were centered around the rice farms in the Sacramento valley, but in between the long working hours we were always looking for a way to go fast.

When we made the two-hour drive toward El Sobrante to visit Uncle Bob and Aunt Pat, it was like traveling to a different world. Their terrain was dotted with steep hills, vastly different than the flat farmland that surrounded our place.

We often made that trip for Thanksgiving, and at the end of the day we were usually giving thanks that all of us had survived the Hills of Death.

Those steep hills saw us coasting down the streets on a wide variety of vehicles. On one particular day the transit of choice was bicycles, which is fortunate because overall they had the best brakes. There was a cul-de-sac at the bottom of the hill and at some point you were going to need to get stopped. We also had a choice of a tricycle and a red Radio wagon, both of which were pretty treacherous because your feet were the only braking mechanism.

I got to the top with the tricycle when I discovered that the wagon was available. I handed the tricycle to my sister Carleen and hopped into the wagon, using the usual traversing pattern to keep myself under control.

About halfway down I noticed from the corner of my eye the tricycle—Carleen still aboard—flying straight down the hill at an amazing speed.

While I admired her overall speed, I immediately had doubts on whether she could hang on for the full ride. I was right.

They were building a house nearby, and a stack of lumber was sitting at the edge of the street. Carleen's front wheel caught one of those boards, and the tricycle instantly stopped moving. Carleen, however, continued on. Up and over the handlebars she went at a high velocity.

I've seen many flips and crashes in my time, but I'm not sure anything could top the ride Carleen took that day. It was magnificent. Luckily she was not seriously hurt and she lived to ride again.

A couple of years later on another visit to the Hills of Death I was riding a Stingray bike belonging to my cousin Billy. I took off down the hill and right away was going faster than I had ever been in my life. I'm not kidding, the tears from my eyes were blowing straight back across my ears. A few moments later the tears were flowing for a different reason.

My front tire hit an uneven patch and it kicked the front wheel out from under me. After a couple of tank-slappers I was over the bars, sliding down the pavement as my exposed skin was being separated from my body. When I finally stopped I began doing an inventory to see if any important body parts had left me when I heard laughter coming from the yard adjacent from my landing area. Four kids were there playing basketball, and they seemed to be enjoying my misfortune.

This greatly diminished the amount of emotion I was able to show, so I had to suck it up and limp the bicycle back up the hill. I took a major hit right above where Mr. Happy lives and it stayed black-and-blue for almost six months. I felt lucky and hurt, all at the same time.

Then came the year when we arrived for Thanksgiving to discover that Uncle Bob had purchased a mini-bike. I seriously question the man's judgment; I mean, us kids came very close to killing ourselves on self-propelled vehicles, so why would he want to introduce a motor to the situation?

This unit was one of the early mini-bikes that had appeared in just about every neighborhood in America: Briggs & Stratton engine, built low to the ground, wheels attached directly to the frame with no active suspension.

Uncle Bob decided we should start out slowly in the cul-de-sac in front of their house. My cousin Dick was the first rider, and he took it slow, riding in a circle. He soon picked up a little more throttle, and the radius of the circle began to widen. It seemed that the more throttle he applied, the bigger the circle. Finally the radius reached a parked car that belonged to Uncle Bill and Aunt Charlotte.

Dick's contact began at the taillight and it continued all the way down the side of the car with the throttle still wide open.

I'm laughing at the story now but at the same time I feel very sad. We lost Dick as a teenager in a crash in a Chevrolet Corvair. Dick wasn't the only fatality in a Corvair, alas.

The tricycle episode did not deter Carleen from her need to go fast. When she was in her 50's she decided it was time to buy a Honda 500 crotch rocket. After riding for a while she figured it was time for a new rear tire. Since this was a high-performance bike, shouldn't she have a racing tire?

Racing tires—on any vehicle—need to be warmed up before they give you a high level of grip. Plus, a sticker—brand new—tire needs to be scuffed up before it provides much grip. The tire guy tried to explain this to Carleen, but she pulled out of the tire shop with a handful of throttle and after a couple of major tank-slappers she was pitched over the handlebars.

Yes, you're right. The Sills family has some issues.

Our farm included several small buildings along with above-ground gasoline and diesel fuel tanks. I made a small dirt oval encircling the tanks, and that became my local dirt track.

My imagination ran wild on that track. My bicycle was usually the ride of choice, but later there was a go-kart. I'd cut many laps on that track, and of course I won every race.

I spent a lot of time with my Grandpa Sills—my father's dad—during my younger years. While Grandpa was doing various chores I would follow him around. We had an old Army surplus Jeep, and we'd ride around to check the water levels in the rice fields.

One of the challenges was keeping mud hens from eating the rice seed, and Grandpa would fire an Army flare into the air to scare them away. One night the flare landed on a levee between the water and caught the grass on fire.

"Aren't we going to call the fire department?" I asked.

"Nah," said Grandpa. "The fire will keep the ducks out. Let's go watch *Gunsmoke*."

I guess he was right because no buildings or personal property was lost, and the fire burned itself out.

That Jeep got a lot of service. One day I noticed the keys were hanging in the ignition and I told my cousin Steve to jump in. We were having a great time (at least *I* was having a great time) hot lapping on my little dirt track. We got going fast enough that we had the Jeep up on two wheels in the corners.

As we're coming off turn four I saw my mother running at us at full-speed, in total panic mode. I had an idea that this wasn't going to be a pleasant conversation and my intuition was right on the money. She grabbed me with an iron grip and proceeded to give me an ass-chewing of epic proportions. I didn't get everything she was saying but she mentioned the fact that we were up on two wheels and also advised that if I was that hell-bent on killing myself I didn't need to take Steve with me.

One challenge to the dirt track was that if you ran it clockwise the first turn was slightly downhill. You could pedal your bike as fast as you could and slide sideways into turn one without using your brakes. Kind of like a power slide, but no power. I've wondered sometimes, if the track had turned to the right maybe I would have become a good road course or flat-track motorcycle racer.

One winter my step-father Dick Johnson was in North Carolina, getting his stock car ready for Daytona. Since he was gone that gave me the green light to create an indoor go-kart track inside our workshop. The building was 60 by 40 feet, which was plenty big enough for a small oval. I laid out some old tires to line the infield like I had seen them do it at the indoor midget races in Oakland.

My go-kart had to circle the track clockwise because the motor drove off the left rear tire. I tried running the conventional counter-clockwise direction, but the kart got such a strong drive with the left rear the thing had a tremendous push. (This was my first real experience with chassis dynamics.)

It was fun making laps, but then I spiced things up by spreading some sand on the racing surface. This simulated a dry-slick dirt track and you could drive in a full-lock power slide at full throttle, all the way around the track. After a few laps a blue groove about a foot wide would develop and it was very fast if you stayed in that narrow groove.

I had several 50-lappers with all the doors closed during the winter season, and it's a wonder I didn't die from carbon monoxide poisoning. The haze was so heavy you could barely see across the shop. It's probably a fair guess to say that I killed a few brain cells at the very least.

I learned right away the need to be precise and hit the dark groove. If you missed your line you pushed out of the rubber and were doing a slide for life. I bashed into the air compressor, the boiler, and took out several legs of the work bench that ran the length of the shop.

Every time I hit something it broke the motor mount loose from the frame. We had a welder in the shop, but I couldn't locate the helmet. But since this was an urgent situation—I was parked until I fixed the kart—I decided to proceed anyway. I had never actually welded anything, but I'd seen it done enough that I had the basic idea. I'd get the rod close to the engine mount and close my eyes, cobbling enough of a weld that it would hold until I hit something else.

Later I got an updated go-kart motor which apparently had issues with leaking fuel. This led to a very exciting and memorable moment when a fire flared up while I was welding the motor mount.

The kart was pretty much cobbled together at that point, and the throttle was wired wide open. It was also direct drive—no clutch—so starting the engine was an adventure unto itself. You had to run beside it until the wheels started turning, and when you felt it fire you'd better jump your ass in because it was leaving, with or without you.

One day the motor wouldn't fire. I pushed and pushed, using to perfection some of the words I'd heard my grandpa and step-father use. Right about that time my four-year-old sister Marcy wandered in, and I enlisted her help. Marcy would eventually become a motorhead herself—she later married fellow racer Tim Green and their son Nick Green is a good little racer—and she was glad to help. I sat her in the seat, explaining that I was going to tune on the carburetor while I pushed. The damned thing hadn't fired all day, so I figured there was no chance of it starting anyways.

Looking back today, I don't know if Marcy was big enough to even reach the brake pedal. Not that it mattered, because this thing isn't going to start anyways, right?

I gave the kart a push and that thing fired on the first stroke of the piston. It ran like never before as it shot across the floor of the shop—WFO!—and ran head-on into the boiler.

Poor Marcy slammed her chest right into the steering wheel. She would have cried if she could breathe, and she summoned the strength to go running for the house.

Let that be a lesson. All of my sisters eventually learned that whatever it was I was messing with, the best idea was, "Don't get involved."

My grandmother Johnson had a mint '47 Desoto blue four-door sedan with suicide doors in the rear. The car had a straight-six engine with a fluid-drive transmission, a really cool setup. You had to start with a clutch but then you had a choice of shifting manually or shift automatically by lifting momentarily off the throttle.

When it came time for Grandma to get a new car, she was hilarious on her test drive. She bought a used '66 Chevelle, and on the test drive she would let off the gas and wait on the car to shift by itself. It was great! On any day she was quite scary to ride with, and my step-brother Steve usually had the assignment of riding home with her after she spent the weekend with our family. Each time he described the experience as "the ride from Hell."

The Desoto had a good life with my grandmother, but it was eventually handed down to my sister Val when she was a senior in high school. Life at that point changed for the Desoto. The headliner was made of a felt material that left a mark when you touched it with your fingernail, so everyone signed their name across the headliner.

Some friends were at my house one day and we decided to take the Desoto for a cruise. We were all 14 years old, with one exception: Ron Harrison was 15. Close enough! He was our designated driver. We drove through Elverta and Rio Linda without being spotted by the police, and on our way home we decided to detour onto a gravel road to see if we could spin out.

Ron whipped the wheel back and forth until the rear wheels came around, and now four teenagers are sliding sideways. I can't imagine any car being more top-heavy than a '47 Desoto, and as we were sliding the bias-ply tires almost rolled off the rim. The rim was digging into the surface of the road, throwing dirt up on the side windows. The car should have rolled over, but it didn't.

We all jumped out of the car, rolling with laughter. It's a wonderful thing, being lost in teen-aged oblivion.

The Desoto lived on and was eventually passed down to my step-sister Elaine. She later had an accident that finally put the old Desoto out of its misery.

Living in North Carolina meant we saw some snow. We California flat-landers went crazy in the snow.

Our dog Bosco—named after late model racer Bosco Lowe—had all kinds of fun chasing us on our sleds. He'd bite at our arms and roll around in the snow, having lots of fun. Bosco later lost his eyesight (caused by riding too long with his head out the window, the wind blowing directly on his eyes) but he lived to a ripe old age. He was a great ol' dog.

One night all the kids in our neighborhood were sledding down a big hill. It was nice and steep which allowed people to gain a ton of speed before they crashed into each other. Pretty soon Phil Shoppe arrived, driving his family's 4-wheel-drive Dodge Power Wagon pickup.

Phil hooked up a car hood on the back and offered to pull us through the snow. This sounded like a great idea and we jumped right on. We headed out to the back road which led to the crest of Mount Royal.

We were holding on for dear life as Phil climbed Mount Royal. The tires were kicking up so much snow it was like a blizzard and we couldn't see a thing—not that you'd want to, as we were going really fast—plus the snow was piling into the back of your neck. We finally reached the summit and that's when we discovered something important; four of us had been riding on the hood but now there were only three.

We climbed into the cab of the truck and started riding back to look for our lost friend. On the way down we could see where the hood had been whipping around behind the truck just inches from the trees that lined the road.

Our lost rider was finally found, off the side of the road with a gash in his leg from the jagged edge of the hood. He was alive and well and we chalked it up to another bullet dodged.

Life was dangerous in North Carolina. Then again, life continued to be dangerous for me after I moved back to California, so maybe location didn't have anything to do with it.

My friends and I heard about a place called Bat Cave. That could only mean two things: there is a cave and there might be bats. We had this really cool image that there would be clouds of vicious bats swirling around and attacking anybody foolish enough to venture into the cave. Five or six of us rounded up some flashlights and decided we needed to check this out immediately. We were having a great time, very deep in the cave, when we realized we were lost.

Mike Emory was a little older than us and had actually served in the Navy. He noticed that we had passed the same place twice so he dropped off to wait for us to come back around again. Mike had a bad tooth from which he could suck blood, and a lower partial plate that he could reposition to look like he had fangs.

Sure enough our lost party came back around and Mike was waiting. He had sucked enough blood from his tooth that it was running down his chin. As we rounded the corner he turned his flashlight on to reveal his bloody chin and fangs while the rest of his face was shrouded in shadow.

My friends were screaming like little girls but of course I was poised and not at all frightened. The fact that I nearly squeezed my flashlight in half was just a coincidence.

We eventually found our way from the cave and saw only sleeping bats which was a major disappointment. However on the way back to the car we crossed a creek and that gave us inspiration for our next adventure.

The next weekend we loaded up with inner tubes and headed for the creek. We wore tennis shoes with our shorts because we figured we might have to scale some rocks along the way. This turned out to be a very rocky creek, with no calm straightaways where you could leisurely float along. I was passing through a gap and my shoe got wedged in between some big rocks. The shoe stayed and immediately the fast current was pulling me under. I'm thinking this might not end well, and just before I hit panic stage the shoe came loose and I floated along down the creek.

Bob Butler was probably the craziest of our group and he was out front. We saw him drop over a two-foot waterfall and disappear. He didn't surface until a good 20 yards down the creek, and his tube was gone. We were all scrambling for the side to avoid the waterfall when Bob explained that he had went under a big flat rock but the opening was too big for his tube to pass through.

So Bob jumped back over the waterfall and disappeared, going under the rock again so he could push his tube the rest of the way through. Luckily for Bob he didn't get trapped in the tunnel and a few moments later he popped out of the water at the other end with his tube.

You have probably realized at this point that many of my friends through the years did not always practice good judgment. It was a recurring theme but it's too late to do anything about it now.

Living on Mount Royal brought lots of opportunities for fun. My stepbrother Steve and I would ride our bicycles to the top and coast off, and this was a high-speed deal. The roads were paved but were no wider than a typical fire road.

I learned that when racing each other while coasting, your speed off the corner is relative to your speed entering the corner. It's all about momentum, and the faster you enter the corner, the better.

Your momentum pushed you to the edge of the road, and sometimes you'd push off and drop the rear wheel off the edge. This caused the bike to kick sideways for a short distance then toss you over the high side of the bike. We had no helmets, and we were very lucky that we never landed on our head. You incurred some pretty serious road rash, however.

The roads at the peak of the summit were extremely steep and treacherous. On one occasion I was wearing the usual t-shirt and jeans, and Steve had on a vest and jeans with huge holes in the knees. Steve took off first, with me trailing by about 20 yards.

The road was paved but with a strip of gravel in the center, making it ever more treacherous. We were coasting at about 60 mph when Steve started braking for a long-radius corner. His back wheel kicked out sideways and it pushed him into the unforgiving gravel in the middle. Not only is Steve now sliding through the gravel, he's tumbling as well.

This would have been a spectacular and dangerous crash in full leathers and a helmet, and Steve had none of that. When he finally stopped we loaded him into a truck and took him down to our house. As you might imagine he was a bloody mess, and my mom was shocked when we carried him inside. She was also more than a little bit pissed off at me for getting him into this predicament.

Steve spent a while in the hospital getting the gravel picked out of all his open wounds. If you've ever had anything cleaned out in a hospital you know how they over-scrub the hell out of things, so he had a tough night before being allowed to go home the next morning.

It wasn't just bicycles that had trouble on those steep roads, as my sister Peggy discovered.

One Saturday night my parents took us out to dinner in Asheville. Peggy had her friend Sherry Lane staying over, and they wanted to stay home. When we returned home from dinner we noticed that the Volkswagen Beetle belonging to my sister Val was missing.

As we opened the door and went inside we found Peggy and Sherry watching TV. When we asked what had happened to Val's car, they both had a surprised expression and said they had no idea. Police were called; there were no clues, and no car.

Three months went by, and the girls stuck to their story. However, we noticed that Sherry was having trouble eating and sleeping during this period.

One day somebody was hiking up the hill when they spotted the VW at the bottom of a steep hill, lying on its side. That's when the truth came out. After we left for dinner that night, the girls had found the keys to the VW and decided to take a cruise around the mountain. Neither had a driver's license and neither had ever driven a stick-shift. But they figured it out enough to get themselves going, and they were having a good ol' time.

They encountered a steep downhill section of maybe 40 yards which leads into a sharp left turn. When Peggy got to the turn she made the rookie mistake of pushing in the clutch pedal instead of the brake. Of course that caused an increase in speed and they missed the corner and went off the side of the mountain.

The car ricocheted off a few trees before rolling over and coming to a rest against a tree, upside down, wedged between a couple of trees. The doors were jammed and they managed to crawl out the back window. It was a miracle they weren't hurt.

They walked back up the hill to the house and went inside and turned on the TV, carefully forming their cover story.

Finally, mystery solved. Scratch one VW Beetle.

The introduction of a driver's license injected a significant amount of fun into the snowy roads in North Carolina. Steve and I had a blue '62 Chevy 4-door with a 6-cylinder and a three-on-the-tree tranny. This car was known as the Blue Blitz and it seemed to perform best when it was loaded down with our friends.

The friends came in very handy as the car's bald tires often led to us needing a push on any kind of sloped surface.

The Blue Blitz was very good for me socially because it led to the introduction of lots of new faces and names, most notably officers of the North Carolina Highway Patrol. During my family's stay in North Carolina we lived in two different houses, and much to my dismay both had NCHP officers living nearby.

At our first house in Mount Royal my parents left me alone one day, and we all know that is not a healthy arrangement. I was 15 years old and figured this was a prime opportunity to try out my dad's Honda 160 Twin for a cruise around the mountain neighborhood.

As I crested a nearby hill Officer Schuler—a neighbor with whom I would become well-acquainted—was outside getting his mail. He looked up to see this 15-year-old kid who is obviously unaware of the local laws because he's riding without a helmet.

He flagged me down and asked where my helmet was. He also asked about the registration and the inspection sticker, and also my driver's license. It was a clean sweep as I had none of the above.

Officer Schuler then asked where I lived and he insisted that it was time for me to ride directly home without passing "GO" and don't let him see me on the road again anytime soon.

On a later occasion I was practicing my feats of daring on my favorite dirt road, riding my 650 Yamaha. Kenny Roberts had been winning lots of AMA races on a similar bike, and I can understand why; this bike was absolutely the best at power sliding. I had removed the bike's mufflers to give it the full racing effect, and it was loud as hell. Little did I know that a NCHP officer had his garden along this road, and he was apparently working in his garden as I came racing past. A few minutes later I pulled into my driveway and was quite surprised to discover that a state trooper had followed me home, and was even more surprised to learn that he lived right next door.

He was quite vocal as he lectured me about wheelies and noise and the fact that I was going to kill myself and everybody else on the road (this guy didn't even know the difference between a wheelie and a power slide). And, by the way, get the mufflers back on that thing and what the hell's wrong with you. That was the gist of the conversation as I recall. Luckily he was off-duty and the lecture was the extent of my punishment.

That was my introduction to Officer Caudell. In the spirit of good neighbors he and I would have many interesting conversations like that first one.

One day we were cruising around on the snowy roads when Officer Caudell pulled me over. Once again he was quite animated and vocal. He said he tracked me down by following the "erratic" tracks left by my bald tires. He threatened to write me up for reckless driving but said he would give me a break and only cited me for the bald tires. Bald tires? Like that is a bad thing? Seriously, it would have been much less entertaining and challenging to drive the Blitz if we had snow tires. What was he thinking?

22

A new direction

Launching a racing school wasn't an overnight thing. It took a number of months to think through what I wanted to do and then begin putting the pieces together.

I wasn't going to race forever. That was just the reality. You can *think* you're going to, but that's not how it's going to be. Everybody who ever raced has an expiration date. *Everybody*.

When I launched the school I wasn't ready to quit driving race cars completely…but the end was in sight. I wanted to find a way to stay involved in racing, partly because—and I'm just being honest here—that's all I knew and all I ever wanted to do. I was approaching 50 years old and I was facing the truth that the end of my career was at hand.

So I hit upon the idea of a racing school and started putting things together. I'm no business guru but I knew it would take a few years for a business to be profitable. I wanted to lay the groundwork while I was still racing so that the school would be in the black when I quit driving.

I had the name right from the beginning: The Jimmy Sills School of Open Wheel Racing. The name was long but I wanted people to know that this was no fender or door place. I wanted to utilize sprint cars and midgets, with wings and without. If you had your own car—anything from a 600 Micro to a winged 410 sprint car—that's cool, bring it with you to class.

A successful racer has to know a lot more than just how to drive a car. So my idea was to teach you—and your crew—how to properly square your chassis, apply your set-up, and learn the adjustments that are possible to match your car to the track conditions and your style of driving. My advanced classes included the driver plus four crew members; the idea was to have everyone speaking the same language when they completed the school.

The classroom session covered suspension geometry, tire construction, tire stagger, cross weight, corner entrance on all shapes and track conditions, running the bottom, running the cushion with a curb, running a cushion with loose dirt, reading the track, and much more. I would come to discover that the classroom was just as important as the track time. Years after they had attended the school, I had many drivers tell me, "I wish I'd paid more attention in the classroom…I didn't realize how important that stuff was!"

I taught my students that racing is a puzzle, with three main pieces: Track, Car, and Driver. But within those pieces there are an endless number of smaller elements that, when put together properly, make it all work. All drivers have different personalities and preferences, and every car has different things it likes. At each corner of the car there are approximately 20 available adjustments. And the track will change with every lap of traffic. Other variables are the type of dirt or clay, how much water the prep guy applied, if the wind is blowing, are you near an ocean where tidal patterns affect moisture, etc. Track shape, the degree of banking, corner radius, corner-to-straightaway ratio, all are of concern and it's the driver's responsibility to read them correctly.

It's important to train your subconscious mind to drive a race car. Just like driving a car on the street, you don't want to have to think about turning, braking, etc.; you just automatically do it. Sometimes you can drive home without remembering the trip because your brain was acting on instinct. That's an important element in a race car because your conscious mind has plenty to think about: traffic, track conditions, and set-up. Every corner has three sections: Entrance, Apex, and Exit. Your car is doing something different at each section and maybe something different at the other three corners. If you have to actively think about what's happening—turning, braking, throttling—you're going to be way behind.

Inside the race car, your brain is on overload. The brain is handling so many things in a very condensed time that's it's difficult to process everything properly. I always taught my students that immediately following the race it is very important to get away from everyone for a minute or two to replay things in your mind before you communicate with your mechanic.

It was important to provide our students with lots of solo track time so they could concentrate on driving without traffic interrupting their thought process. I offered low-cost track time to people who had attended my school and later wanted track time to bring their car any day I was holding a class. Several people took advantage of this, and it was great experience. Every time I hosted a school session, John Golobic brought his son Shane and put in around eighty laps, and Shane progressed quickly with all that track time.

When I began hosting the school I immediately discovered the dynamic that exists within a father-and-son racing operation. A father and his son often don't agree, and as they sat in my class one might point to the other and say, "See, I told you that's how it worked!" I was often a buffer between the parties.

When I first started I had a car to use for my school, but no shop. Rod Tiner pitched in to store my car at his shop, and he would tow it to the track for each school session. Rod also helped with our chassis class, and helped with getting people in and out of the car and pushing them off. From the very beginning he was a great help and as the years went on he repaired a few frames that were crashed.

One morning we blew a motor during class and Rod hauled the car back to his shop for a quick motor change. I told all my students, "Let's be drivers today and go have lunch while they change the motor!" Rod was a huge help to me and is still a good friend today.

In the beginning I scheduled our track time during daytime hours, which allowed the students to see the track better. Plus, they didn't need a fast track, especially those who were driving for the first time. The daytime conditions brought two problems: One, it can get very hot during the California summer; and two, we were wearing the hell out of our tires.

That's when I became a tire scrounge. Every time there was a race in my area I filled my truck bed with take-offs (used tires). Everyone teased me about scrounging tires and said I was the Fred Sanford (or was it Lamont?) of sprint car racing.

During track time I placed cones on the track as reference points for shut-off and pick-up points for the throttle. Most new drivers tend to turn into the corner too early, so I used cones to help the driver open their entrance. I would stand next to the track and use arm signals for my student to move their line; raising my left leg meant more braking; and my right arm sticking straight out meant more throttle. Fortunately I never got ran over, but I did have to run like hell a few times.

Our host track was Marysville, which was called Twin Cities Speedway at the time. I came to Marysville because it was privately owned. Most tracks in our area are located on a public fairgrounds, which means any activity on the track is done with the approval of the State of California and the local fair board. This presented a problem because fairgrounds tracks are limited to a certain number of days of activity, and it was a big hassle to negotiate open days for my school and then get state approval.

My friend John Padjen, who promoted several tracks in the area, helped guide me to Marysville. Richard Sinnott was the owner and we made arrangements to host my school there.

I didn't have a lot of money to invest at the start, and the only way the school came to life was the support from others.

Don Berry and Jack Elam from J&J Racing worked out a deal so I could utilize J&J chassis, the best sprint cars on the market. Donny Schatz is today the dominant driver of his generation in a J&J chassis.

Don Berry would also load me up with old parts each time I went to his house and drove his race car. Don gave me a deal on a truck as well.

Another choice of Donny Schatz is Shaver Racing Engines. Ron Shaver built engines for many of the best car owners I have had the pleasure to drive for, and Ron was more than generous in helping me out. Ron had a genuine desire to promote interest in sprint car racing.

Richard Farmer of RPM Engines had a shop in Grass Valley, and Richard helped me with motor rebuilds and loaned me a motor for at least a half-season. Richard is a good friend and we once had a great time when we rode motorcycles to Sturgis. Richard has a diverse background as he also built the engine that holds the land speed record for motorcycles, ridden by Chris Carr and owned by Bub Industries in Grass Valley.

Steve Lewis of Performance Racing Industry helped me in many ways, with promotional material, contacts, and advice. Steve was very generous, and he even gave me a booth space at the PRI trade show when he had a late cancellation. We also had a booth at Steve's west coast trade shows at San Jose and Sacramento and Reno.

I was driving Steve's midget at an ESPN race in Ventura when we had a TV camera mounted on our roll cage. The camera provided a view of my helmet, so I took a strip of racer tape and wrote, "Racing school" and my phone number. Larry Rice pointed it out on TV and even read the phone number. My phone rang off the hook for a while after that race. That was a huge shot in the arm for my new business.

Dave Calderwood supplied me with a midget and two different motors, wheels, and plenty of parts. I bought a trailer from Gene Jacobson, and Dave's paint shop painted the trailer for me.

Daryl Saucier at DSR and later Sid Waterman helped on fuel pumps. Lots of manufacturers helped: Carrera Shocks, Red Line Oil, MPD (John Bickford), KSE Steering (Dave Moyes), and more. Robert Bass of Ultra Shield supplied me with safe seats for my school cars as well as my personal racing seats and belts. Larry Brown at TCR built me a great midget that I later used to win a race!

Randy Frank is a brilliant artist, and he did all my painting, lettering, and artwork. Randy now works for James and Katie Standley at DESIGN 500, and he's still a great artist! Bill Simpson helped me when he still owned Simpson Race Products, as did Bell Helmets.

Pat "Porky" Hughes is another guy who was a huge help. Porky flagged and timed at the track and helped organize things when I had track time. Pork was an old racer who won a lot of races in his time, but like many racers is remembered more for his career-ending crash. Porky was qualifying at the treacherous Calistoga and like many before him, hooked a first turn rut that sent him into a horrific series of flips up and out of the place. Pat broke both arms and didn't wake up until the second hospital he was in. He made a comeback but it was short lived.

Pat was in the hot rod business for a while. He would buy really nice hot rods from the Midwest and drive them to California to sell, because the value out west would jump a grand or two. About every three weeks Pat traveled to the Midwest and brought back another new rod. This all worked perfectly until the DMV informed Pat that he would have to become a licensed car dealer if he continued buying and selling that volume of cars, so he slowed down on his hot rod business. Pat recently passed away, and it was a sad day when I got the news. He was a neat guy and a good friend.

Chuck Stovall was from Arkansas, and I hired him fresh out of the University of Arkansas to help me at the school. Chuck wanted to be a race driver but didn't know anyone with a car or the knowledge to help him, so he took a job with me and learned to work on race cars.

Chuck and Porky hit it off immediately. They both loved big-time wrestling and knew all the players and their women. They would debate constantly about who was the baddest guy in the wrestling ring.

All those people who helped…the thought of them just really makes me feel good. It still feels good today, knowing that so many good people had faith in me to help me get my school off the ground. I can't thank them enough.

Our school hosted many young racers who would go on to a terrific professional career. One of the best was Kasey Kahne. Kasey's dad Kelly had been around Skagit Speedway for many years, mostly by sponsoring cars through his company, Kelly Kahne Logging. Kelly got a car and brought Kasey to the school. When it came time to get in the race car Kasey adapted quickly to a different track. There wasn't much instruction needed.

Dave Playle was helping me at that time, and we started putting different settings on the car—cross weight, wheel offset, stagger—so that Kasey could tell what each change felt like. Kasey adapted so quickly that we decided to have him go out for three laps, come in, and stay in the car while we made changes. Then he'd go out for another three laps. We didn't immediately tell him what the change was, but as far as feeling what the change did, he hit it dead on every time.

Right along that time Steve Lewis asked me, "Have you seen any special talent lately?" I immediately told him about Kasey; I don't know if I had anything to do with Steve hiring him, but he did and Kasey's career took off from there.

Janet Larson is a promoter/hustler who won't take no for an answer, and I really appreciate her for that quality. Janet and her husband Mike are well-known personalities in the Sacramento area, and Janet took an interest in helping organize events at Cycleland, an eighth-mile track near Chico that features Outlaw go-karts.

I've known Mike and Janet for a long time. Along with Rick Hirst, Tim Green, and several other racers, each week we met at Mike and Janet's house to race slot cars. Mike was an ace at building slot cars, which he hand-painted to look exactly like the race cars we were driving. The slot cars actually had torsion bar suspension! Mike built the slot car track to have the inside lane flat and bumpy then the next two lanes had more banking and were smoother. We had some great battles on that track. Janet always made the best tortilla chips and bean dip for intermission.

Their son, Kyle—yes, *that* Kyle Larson—was too small to see over the table so he would play on his oval rug with his toy sprint cars.

Janet wanted to help me advertise my school at Cycleland, so she made up some stickers for each of the races. Most of the students were too young to drive a 410-in sprint car, but it helped plant some seeds that would be important in the future. In return, as a sponsor I promised a free driving class for the winner of the open division at Cycleland.

Guess who happened to be one of the first champions? That's right, Kyle Larson.

The day arrived for Kyle's school and we got him in the car. I showed Kyle the fuel shut-off, the mag switch, and the gear handle, and he pretty much took it from there. We pushed him off and he rolled around a lap to read the track conditions, and off he went. He made some laps around the bottom, then went to where we would become accustomed to watching him race: right up next to the wall.

Afterwards I wrote a letter of recommendation for Kyle, and soon after he was allowed to race a sprint car for Dave Vertullo. He would go on to win the King of the West title in Brent Kaeding's car, and twice won the Gold Cup at Chico (at the second win Kyle started from the rear!).

Kyle has also done very well in NASCAR, and there is no doubt in my mind that he will someday win a NASCAR Cup championship. If Kyle landed a ride in Formula One, he would figure it out and win races. He's a rare talent that only comes along every great many years.

Cheryl and I recently traveled to Charlotte to attend Kyle's wedding. He and Katelyn really did it up right and it was a beautiful ceremony. We were honored to be invited, and it was great to see some people there we hadn't seen for a long time. It was just a great day all around.

Rod Fauver was a big help in the later years at the school. Rod is another guy who knows how to do virtually anything when it comes to race cars. He could build motors (he built a few for me) and he knows how to fix cars.

One night a driver poked my car into the wall, bending the right front torsion tube. Rod hammered the torsion bar out of the tube, then butt-welded the torsion tube together and reamed the bushing to true the alignment. Rod put the same bar back in (it sprung back straight) and we finished the night. He saved the day, really.

Rod knows fuel systems really well. We ran into overheating problems with one of our cars and Rod cleared up the problem by tuning the fuel system. I joked to Rod that I appreciated him making my engines run cool but now that my fuel bill was going up I had no profit left to pay him! Rod was a true friend and we had a lot of great times together.

Rod was more than just hands-on with the race car; he was also good at helping drivers adjust their line to improve their lap times. Rod was especially helpful because when I finished the classroom session he could take over and teach set-up while I watered the track and prepared for our track time.

A typical one-day advanced class started with watering the track at 8 a.m. and at two-hour intervals throughout the day. My classroom session started at 11 a.m. and went until three when Rod would take over while I grabbed a bite of lunch and jumped on the water truck. I would dig up the top groove and water it pretty heavily so it would hold a cushion.

Once we got everyone suited up I would fire the car and wheel pack and hot lap, usually one lane in the center so that the groove would gradually move up the track but leave some moisture on the bottom.

Some sessions had two sprint cars available, or maybe a midget. Some classes included experienced people, racers with their own cars, or people renting track time to fill in between my cars on track. It made for a busy day (or night) trying to keep a car on track at all times utilizing track rental while fueling, changing tires, setup, scraping mud, coaching, and changing drivers. All the while we watched the track conditions and coached the drivers on what line to drive.

We had an 11 p.m. curfew and usually finished well before. One night we had crashes and breakdowns and at midnight the sheriff showed up but he allowed me to run one more 10-lap session after I explained that one driver was from Canada and wouldn't be able to come back.

After we put everything away and shut the track lights off we opened some beers. Sometimes my students stuck around and we told racing stories, or we laughed about something that happened that night. There were usually plenty of things to entertain us throughout the night.

Even though it was enjoyable, I always felt stressed. I was constantly worried about someone getting hurt and suing me. My other worry was making sure that everyone who paid had a good time. I tried to let them drive fast but stay within the parameters of safety. The problem was that, like real racers, you couldn't predict when somebody might do something stupid and out of character.

I learned that it was very difficult to read people based on your initial impression. The guy who showed up and wanted to make sure I had a "full 410" and then asked about the track record; that guy usually turned out to be a putter. On the flip side, the mild-mannered guy who seemed intimidated by the whole thing would go out and putt-putt during the first two sessions and then feel confident and try to take three seconds off his lap times.

One of the greatest hurdles for almost every first-timer was to understand the importance of getting the car rotated at the entrance of the corner. Proper rotation allows you to apply throttle as the car is already turning. Beginners usually drove in too straight, and when they added throttle the car went straight toward the wall. By the time they got it turned the second time it had reached the area where dirt was loose and the wall was close. This led to the demise of a lot of right rear wheels and Jacob's ladders. We also abused a lot of torque tube studs because drivers often turned on the ignition too early and then drove too slowly, chattering the drive train.

I took my school to a few other venues through the years, including a couple of sessions at Skagit Speedway in Washington.

Our track sessions took place during the day at Skagit, because the climate is nice and cool there in the summer and we avoided the cost of running the track lights at night.

One day we rained out early (rain at Skagit...gee, what a surprise) so we scheduled everyone for the next day. Dave Lemley was the track promoter at the time, and we were hanging around the track early in the afternoon with nothing to do. Dave's son Brock was there as well. Brock later became an accomplished racer, winning the Dirt Cup in 2014.

I don't know if Brock was old enough to drink beer with us that day, but his dad sure was. I've been going to Skagit since the early years of the Dirt Cup, and had met a lot of people up there. A couple of guys I knew were camped near the pit sign-in shack, and they had a big wood stove in their campground (even in the summer a stove is a good idea at Skagit) with a big exhaust pipe out the top. They would toss a bit of methanol into the stove and a humongous flame would erupt out of the pipe. Just another example of good clean fun at the race track after a rain-out.

When it finally got dark (around 10 p.m. in Washington) we realized we were hungry. The concession stands were all locked up, so everyone went across the street to Dave's house, where there was leftover spaghetti in the fridge. We were a little short on spaghetti sauce but with the addition of a bottle of ketchup nobody seemed to know the difference.

Great memories!

23

The Professor

For the first 10 years of the Jimmy Sills School of Open Wheel Racing I continued to race at various events around the country. It was right about that time when—while racing here in California—I was tagged with a new nickname: "The Professor."

The nickname came from Bobby Gerould, one of the top announcers in the country. Bobby announces at the King of the West series along with his sidekick Troy Henning, and Bobby also emcees a very nice banquet at Calistoga in September.

Bobby is a second-generation announcer, following in the footsteps of his father, Gary Gerould. Gary, aka the G-Man, has a long and great history in northern California racing, dating back to the 1970s—or maybe even earlier. You probably recognize Gary's name, because he has been one of the top racing reporters on national television for many years, covering a wide variety of racing. Gary is also the longtime radio voice of the Sacramento Kings in the NBA.

The locals from the Sacramento area will always remember Gary from his days as a local television sportscaster. He was also the track announcer at West Capital, creating many frantic commutes after the races in order for Gary to make the 11 p.m. news broadcast. He had to race across town to make it in time, praying that the drawbridge wasn't up across the river!

G-Man also wrote articles for *National Speed Sport News* and the west coast newspaper *Racing Wheels*. One of the things I really appreciated about Gary was that if you were leading a race and dropped out, he would come down to your pit after the race and ask you what happened instead of writing what he *thought* happened. This involved extra effort on his part and I really respected that.

Gary and Bobby Gerould are icons in northern California, the type of people whom everybody likes and respects.

I got a call one day in the late 1990s from Indianapolis Motor Speedway and was asked to hold for Tony George. My first thought was, "Wow! He's calling to tell me I have a ride in an IRL Indy car!" However…that was not why he was calling.

Tony said he wanted to bring his stepson, Ed Carpenter, to my school to drive a midget. Tony also wanted to come along and take some laps in a sprint car.

Ed did great at our school, and went on to win the pole for the Indianapolis 500 and have his own very successful Indy car team. When Tony jumped into the sprint car you could tell he had the blood of his father—USAC champion Elmer George—in his veins, as Tony was scary fast.

Our school also had a program where I could come to your track and help your race team on-site. Two brothers—Bradley and Alfred Galedrige—raced midgets with BCRA, and I worked one of these programs with their team. I immediately liked this family when on the first night at a race they were short push trucks and their mom, Molly, brought out her Tahoe with a push bumper and pushed-off midgets. Their father, Big Al, is a Paving contractor in the San Jose area. Al and Molly didn't have a racing background but they really supported the boys and their racing efforts. I went with the team to Manzanita, Hanford, Belleville, Indiana Midget Week, and Las Vegas. Finally it was time for college and both boys attended top schools in the Midwest.

Ryan Kaplan attended one of our schools, and later I did some on-site work with Ryan at several tracks. Ryan raced locally in midgets until the time came to take on the best wingless sprint car racers in the country in the Midwest. Ryan spent a summer with Tim Clauson, driving Tim's sprint cars in USAC.

Tim's son Bryan Clauson was bad fast and tried to help as much as he could, but drivers don't always like the same set ups. I traveled to Indiana Sprintweek to coach Ryan and we had some good runs until Ryan was punted by another car at Kokomo and dinged his head and his back. Ryan returned home to California and Rod Fauver helped him win a few midget races there. Unfortunately Ryan later flipped a midget at Calistoga and sustained another head injury. Ryan then made the decision to save his head for better things, and today he is a successful farmer in Chico and Triathlon competitor.

Justin Grant lived in Ione, California and brought his midget to our school. Justin raced BCRA on pavement with his own car, and drove

Dave and Wendy Thurston's car on dirt. I went to some of Justin's dirt races, and if he didn't have a mechanical issue he would consistently win. Justin struggled with his pavement car, and would call and talk about chassis theory and setups. My help was limited; I wasn't much of a pavement guy myself. Justin later won the BCRA championship in 2007 and then moved to Indiana, where he began his successful sprint car career.

Justin is a very dedicated guy, and he made the long drive from Ione to Marysville to help me whenever I had track time at our school. He was always looking to learn something, and maybe hot lap a car or two.

Justin has had some hard luck with non-racing injuries over the past few years. He was at a chassis dyno with a midget he was going to drive, and was standing next to the race car when an oil line came off. The hot oil sprayed onto the headers and ignited a huge fire, and Justin received second- and third-degree burns on his arm. He was bandaged up and raced a couple of days later at Lawrenceburg.

On a night when he wasn't racing, Justin and his friend Travis Hery drove from Indianapolis to Eldora to watch the World 100 late model race. On the way home Justin was sleeping, resting up to race the next day. Along the way they made contact with a concrete culvert that gave them a big launch into a cornfield. Given the distance from the launch site to first hit, they had plenty of air time. The debris field was scattered for hundreds of feet with plastic pieces hanging in corn stalks. Justin was thrown clear but suffered a broken neck. Travis had some minor injuries but both were lucky to survive the wreck. Justin recovered and was racing late that following season.

Cheryl and I went to Terre Haute, Indiana to watch Justin run a USAC sprint car race. We were sitting in the grandstand and would lose sight of the cars in the dust as they entered turn one. I lost Justin as he went into the corner, and then saw something go flying out over the first turn wall. The red flag came out and we counted cars; no Justin. He had lost a right front torsion arm and flipped clear out to the parking lot (about 60 yards and across two fences).

Justin had no idea where he had landed, but he immediately realized that it was very dark. As he put one foot outside the sprint car and tried to stand up, it was crunchy with some give to it. This was really puzzling, until his eyes adjusted to the light and he realized he was on the hood of a car and the crunch was glass from the car's windshield.

In January 2017 Justin's wife Ashley gave birth to twins. Just a few hours after their birth Justin's phone rang while he was napping, and it was Tim Clauson on the line. Justin had been up all night with Ashley, and he was groggy as he answered the phone. Tim asked Justin if he'd like to drive his midget at next weekend's Chili Bowl.

Justin thought somebody was messing with him but after a couple of minutes he was convinced that it really *was* Tim Clauson on the phone, and he really did want Justin to drive his midget at the Chili Bowl.

Justin won his Friday night qualifying race, and then won the pole shuffle that put him on the pole for the big race on Saturday night.

Tony Stewart and his crew reworked the track right before the feature, and Justin jumped out to a big lead. He knew the top groove would eventually come in, and that sooner or later somebody would be coming up to challenge. He focused on hitting his marks, trying to watch the big TV screen to see if anybody was getting close. He was right; eventually they came. Christopher Bell and Daryn Pittman managed to slip past Justin on the outside before he could move up to the faster line.

Justin has built some very nice USAC Silver Crown cars for owner Chris Carley and is doing very well with them, and is also doing well with his sprint car and midget racing. Justin puts his all into racing and he is the kind of guy you want to see become a success.

The school led to me helping a few racers on an extended basis. I guess this was natural; you might call this "graduate training." People would hire me to come to their shop and help prepare their cars, and travel with them to the races. I would provide everything from setup help to driver coaching.

And of course this also involves what you might call, "mental health counseling." Racing is a demanding gig and it beats you up pretty regularly, both physically and mentally. When you are early in your career it's good to have someone in your ear that helps you stay upbeat and positive, reminding you that everybody makes mistakes and everybody gets down now and then.

(The idea of me providing mental health support to anyone is, obviously, highly ironic.)

A good example of a long-term teaching relationship was Murray Erickson of Odessa, Texas. Murray made the decision to dedicate himself to becoming a race driver, and along with his very capable mechanic James Hicks bought two midgets and came out to our school. I later made several trips to work with Murray in Odessa, where they had a nice three-eighths-mile track. The track had longer corners, which made it easier to drive than at Marysville. Murray started to get the hang of it and wanted to have more races in his home town, so he bought the track and promoted a two day midget race.

Murray called and asked me to bring my two-seater sprint car to his race, looking for some extra promotion. He also asked if I had any additional room in the trailer for the midget we used at my school; he was paying $300 to start at his race.

I hadn't raced anything for three years, but I wanted to help Murray out with his car count. I got Pat "Porky" Hughes and a kid named Tim (with a CDL) to help drive and away we went. I brought my own fuel, so we loaded up a full drum and filled both cars to the top.

On the opening day we did some rides that afternoon for media people, and the racing that night consisted of three classes of local stock cars. We did well on selling rides, and some of the West Texas people had never before seen a sprint car. I thought it was really cool that the first time they ever saw one, they were riding in one!

We arranged to sell rides in between the races on the final night. It came time to hot lap the midget, so we aired up the tires, which were old take-off tires we had been using at the school. I came in from giving a sprint car ride and had to immediately hop into the midget, which I noticed was really tight.

I jumped back into the two-seater, and when I finished they told me I was in the next heat, and would have to hurry. I managed to put a smaller left rear tire on so the car would turn, and we raced. I told Porky and Tim that I'd probably just putt around the bottom; they should have the two-seater ready when my heat had finished.

I guess I still had some racing left in me; when the green flag dropped I went from third to first in the first corner (one of the cars I passed was Dave Stricklin, Jr., who is definitely no slouch). We won the heat which put us on the front row of the feature.

After a couple more two-seater rides we prepped the midget for the feature, putting on a bigger left rear tire. As I aired it up I realized why the car had pushed so badly earlier; I had forgotten that the fuel tank was filled to the brim. We had burned off enough fuel that it was just right for the feature.

Just prior to the race Murray came to my pit. "Don't you stink up my race! Make it look close."

I ran the top and allowed Stricklin and Ryan Durst to dive under me a couple of times, but went on to win. The midget grossed $3,300, and we grossed $4,100 with two-seater rides. It was a good night.

I definitely celebrated too much at Murray's after-race party, and I was glad we brought Tim along to help us drive home.

Murray is a native of Canada, and got his start there in the oil business. He later moved to Texas because of the warmer climate. If you've spend any time in Canada you will quickly discover that those folks can hold their liquor; if you spend time in Texas you'll find that those folks can hold theirs as well. It is a potent combination for Murray, who can totally drink you under the table.

Murray is a self-made businessman, focusing on the oil industry. He invented some type of process and tools that aid in capping off an oil well, and received residuals for his invention. Murray spent his money like most guys would if they got the chance: he owned a warehouse full of hot rods, muscle cars, sports cars, and a few motorcycles.

The throttle of every vehicle Murray purchased was immediately pegged to the floor. Warmed up, cold, sober, not sober, it didn't matter. One day Murray was in his Lotus and he drove 'er in too deep and slid through a neighbor's yard, taking out a shrub that was native to west Texas and costing him $3,500. Unfortunately they had a hard time getting another shrub to grow in its place, and I had to laugh every time I came to town and passed that poor old bush.

Murray let me take a ride on his Boss Hogg three-wheel motorcycle, which featured a 502-inch Chevy motor. In the desert you can really get some speed on that bike; my sunglasses blew off my face and were never seen again.

Murray also bought an airplane and learned to fly. That adventure, however, was a little too much for me. I would ride with Murray in his cars, but not the airplane. His friend and mechanic, James Hicks, felt the same way. We had seen some of Murray's antics on the ground and figured it might be pushing it to experience those things at 10,000 feet.

We loaded up Murray's midgets a couple of times and hauled to Tulsa for the Chili Bowl. This race is one of the toughest events of the year, and you have to really be on your game from the moment you unload the car. Murray struggled on our first trip there, and spun out several times. Each time he spun out, one of my favorite announcers, Jack Miller, eagerly told everyone, "Murray is a student from the Jimmy Sills Racing School, and Jimmy is here coaching him!"

I was a little concerned about the potential for negative advertising, so I told Murray that I would sub for him on Saturday and get his car moved up from the J Main. I dressed in his uniform and put his helmet on in the trailer and kept it on as I got into the car. The cars in our race were a little sketchy and I got caught up in a pile-up three laps into the race.

A couple of years ago somebody was kicked out of the building for doing that very thing. I hope the statute of limitations has run out…I'd sure hate to get kicked out of my favorite race!

24

The ride of a lifetime

I mentioned our two-seater sprint car earlier, and that was a good addition to our school program. Not everybody wanted to go to the trouble of attending a school, but lots of people want to experience the thrill of a sprint car. The two-seater was a great way to provide that, and through the years we gave a lot of people a ride they will never forget.

The origin of our two-seater car was interesting. The World of Outlaws were racing at Las Vegas, where Brad Furr crashed backwards into the wall. The rear of the car was destroyed, and Brad and his crew had no time to repair the car as they were heading down the road to the next race. So they stripped everything from the car and left the frame in the pit area.

Rod Tiner brought the frame home and called me. "I've got the perfect candidate for a two-seat sprint car," he explained.

Rod cut the car in half and built a new rear section that added 20 inches behind the driver's seat to accommodate another seat. Rod figured everything out and delivered the car to me with the frame, body panels, and hood.

One of the challenges of a long sprint car is the length of the driveline and torque tube. Glen Sander of Sander Engineering built a steel torque tube with a solid titanium driveshaft with a bearing for support. This system worked perfectly; however, on a tacky track the driveshaft would sometimes wrap up and shake a little.

I could have gone with a 360-inch engine, but I installed a 410-inch because I wanted people to get the full sprint car experience. In later years I actually had a 430-inch engine in the car and it was snappy.

The two-seater was one of the most fun adventures I've ever been a part of. People were enthusiastic and it is a great feeling to provide excitement and happiness to others, the type of experience that helps them feel more connected with racing.

Jack Hewitt was the first to build a two-seater that was done right, and my idea was to bring the idea of a cool car like Jack's to the west coast. He gave me a lot of input and guidance and was a huge help. Our two-seater programs were a little different; some things that worked for Jack didn't work for us, and vice-versa.

One thing for sure: when you climbed into Jack's two-seater or our two-seater, you were going to get your money's worth.

My first outing was on the mile at Cal Expo, giving a TV reporter a ride to promote the upcoming race there. The track was dry, but we had enough straight-line speed that the wing was burying the left side. So I reversed all the bars and that made the car perfect. We raffled tickets for a ride and it was a big hit.

Many of the track promoters out west saw the value of allowing people in the grandstands to experience firsthand the sensation of sprint car racing, so they were supportive of our program. When we visited a track I tried to maximize the number of rides we could provide. I didn't want to hold up the show, so when the track was open for us I was ready to push off. This meant we had to be efficient in getting riders in and out of the car, and Johnny "Chewy" Medina and Pat "Porky" Hughes were a tremendous help to us at various times.

Calistoga was probably the most exciting track we visited. The track is a full half-mile with long straightaways, which produced top speeds of well over 100 mph. Early in the program, when the surface was still tacky, I could run wide open all the way around the track.

Andy Forsberg's wife Candace rode with me at Calistoga one night when the track had a big cushion. Candace insisted that she wanted me to flip during her ride so that she could experience what happens to Andy when he crashes. I laughed and told her that, no, she doesn't really want that experience, especially at this track. We rolled out and had a beautiful lap going until I caught the curb and tossed the front wheels toward the fence. With the car's long wheelbase it took some doing to get it to turn left again, and the fence was coming closer and closer. I was full on the gas to avoid contact. Luckily it worked out and when we finished the ride I informed Candace that she was awfully close to getting her wish.

One night a lady rode with me early in the program when the track was bad fast. We had a wide-open ride and when she climbed from the car she gave me a look that was equal parts sheer terror, amazement, and anger. She looked directly at me and said, "There is no reason to drive people around like that! You could kill somebody going that fast!"

One of the best two-seater experiences came in Jack Hewitt's car at the Chili Bowl. Jack would bring his car to Tulsa and raffle a few rides. One year Jack was healing up from a racing injury and needed guest drivers to help give rides. I gave a couple of rides, and Jack asked Kevin Olson to take an older gentleman for a ride.

Kevin is one of the most quirky, outrageous personalities in racing, and he has a real knack for being wacky and weird.

The rider was waiting by the car when Kevin walked up with a beer can in his hand. Kevin casually told the guy, "I just blew a .12 a few minutes ago!" and climbed right into the car. The passenger said nothing, probably thinking, "Well, this is how we do things here." Kevin put the car in gear and pushed off, and Jack's big V8 with open exhaust commanded the attention of everybody in the building. Right at that moment Kevin tossed the beer can from the car and hit the gas.

The two-seater is 31 inches longer than a midget, so it's important to really bend the car sideways to make the corner. This was Kevin's first time in this big car, and he immediately got into a push that he couldn't get out of. The car ran the right front up the wall and gently lay on its side.

Up and over at the Chili Bowl! Now that's getting your money's worth on a two-seater ride.

Fred Brownfield was the hardest working person I've ever known, by a long way. Fred was one of those guys who had such a capacity for work and success that there was almost nothing he couldn't do. He crammed about 200 years of accomplishment and living into his 50-some years here on earth.

Fred was a very successful racer from Snohomish, Washington. We raced against each other for many years, and Fred eventually transitioned into the role of track owner and series promoter. Fred also launched a manufacturing business that created electrical and structural parts for highway use. He could take on just about any type of project, especially if it was a challenge.

We raced many times together at the old Elma fairgrounds track in Grays Harbor, Washington, and when Fred took the place over he completely reconfigured it. In the summer it doesn't get dark in Elma until around 9:30, so drivers raced with the sun in their eyes in the early stages of a racing program. Fred redesigned and repositioned the track to avoid that, and built a nice grandstand so that the evening sun was behind the spectators. It was great.

Fred felt like something needed to be done to attract racers and give them a place to race, so he created the Northern Sprint Tour (NST). He built it, and they came.

With the help of his hard-working wife Debbie, Fred promoted a Speedweek tour through the Northwest at Medford, Lebanon, Cottage Grove, and Wenatchee, finishing after a day off with a big event at Elma. Fred invited us to bring the two-seater to his Speedweek and it grew into something we looked forward to every year.

On the day before the Elma finale Fred organized a big parade to promote the final race. I hopped in the two-seater and we fired the motor, then Porky pushed me with a quad through the parade. The truck in front of me was throwing candy out for the kids, and as they rushed into the street to grab the candy I would rap the throttle and startle the hell out of them. That night Fred had a big barn dance and you could feel excitement building for the race. It was a wonderful promotion.

One of things I liked about the Speedweek concept was visiting a different track each night. I liked it as a racer and I liked it with the two-seater.

One night at Lebanon, Porky strapped in a nice woman passenger and away we went. The track was fast, and I could run into turn three flat. As I got into turn four I heard a sound—BANG!—and immediately thought, "This isn't good." That's not the sound you want to hear at that moment. The steering box had broken and things quickly went from bad to worse.

The car wouldn't turn and we plowed into the wall as we exited the corner, right in front of the grandstands. To add insult to injury, without steering or brakes we ricocheted into another wall in the infield. My first worry was our passenger, but she was fine and was very understanding as we helped her from the car. The grandstand gave her a huge ovation, and right about then Porky showed up on the quad. We put the lady on the back of the quad and Porky drove her along the grandstand, letting everyone see that she was okay. The car wasn't hurt too badly and after some repairs we were able to continue with the rides later that night.

While sitting in a bar one night, Johnny "Chewy" Medina and I came up with a great idea. We decided to start a rider program where any woman willing to donate an undergarment would see her garment displayed on the ceiling of our trailer. This was a great program but we would have liked to have seen a little more participation.

We were at Cottage Grove one night and Chewy was supposed to be loading a nice-looking woman into the car while I checked track conditions. I came back to the car and no Chewy, and no rider in the car. I shouted, "C'mon Chewy, we gotta go!" I looked up to see him at the back of the trailer, waving at me. I ran to the trailer just in time to see our next rider proudly displaying her new breast implants and leaving us with some very nice items to display on the ceiling.

One year Chewy's daughter Sarah was in trouble so as punishment she had to travel with us to Speedweek. Sarah had the time of her life, and as the cutest girl in the pits she had the attention of every driver as well as their crew guys. This created more than a little bit of stress for her dad. One of the hot dogs at the track was Roger Crockett, and he started hanging around a bit too much for Chewy's comfort. Sarah and Roger were talking one night and Chewy shouted, "You better keep that rocket in your pocket, Crockett!"

Each year when Speedweek ended it was almost like I was still racing, remembering some of those long stretches back in the Midwest. It brought back a lot of memories, and the emotions were the same. When you've raced—or ran the two-seater—for a long stretch without a break, you're kind of glad when it's over and you're glad nobody got hurt.

We got paid in cash from all our riders, so that was a little bit like the old days too. When we got back to the motel and counted the money to see how we did it was almost like the feeling you get when you've won the feature.

On the final night Porky would usually start the celebration a little bit early and get into the cooler while we were still giving rides. After several at the track and several more back at the motel Porky decided he'd take a shower while I was taking care of the books. All of a sudden there was a huge crash in the bathroom and Porky was yelling for help. He had fallen backwards through the shower curtain and was lying on his back on the floor, unable to turn himself over to get up. So being a true friend I went in and helped him up. He looked like a turtle lying there and that almost became his new nickname, but how could you improve on a nickname like Porky?

Speedweek had finished and Chewy and I were driving home, pulling the trailer behind us. We were just south of Medford when my left front tire exploded, causing the truck to make an immediate left turn. I was assessing the situation as my truck and trailer were headed for the northbound lane of Interstate 5 and my actions were having no effect on their trajectory! There are lots of vehicles in the northbound lane for us to collide with when we get there.

My immediate assessment was that we're about to die, this is how it ends, me and Chewy wiped out on I-5. Suddenly the left front rim left the pavement and dug in, and at the same time I used a little brake and the right front still had a say in what direction we're going to go. We abruptly turned right, back into the I-5 southbound lanes.

We got to the side of the road and got stopped, stepping out to assess the damage. A driver behind us stopped to offer help and when he walked up to the truck he said, "Do you need any toilet paper after that maneuver?" He said it looked like the trailer was definitely going over and only a miracle kept us in one piece.

After a few minutes the tire was changed and the truck looked like a modified with no fender on the left front. We then discovered that the truck would start but wouldn't run, and after a long process of elimination discovered that part of the tire knocked a fuel filter loose and it was sucking air.

Whether you're racing or running a two-seater, the highway experience can be the same. Interesting, adventurous, and dangerous as hell.

Fred Brownfield still had a controlling interest in Skagit Speedway, and I took the two-seater up for Dirt Cup in June. Neither Chewy nor Porky could come along, but other people pitched in to help make everything work. As in many of our trips, Deanna McGinnis helped organize the riders, and Shawna Willsky allowed me to drop our trailer at her speed shop.

I remember this trip especially for the fun I had away from the track. The area is absolutely beautiful, and I brought my Harley and my mountain bike along. I rode the Harley to Anacortes and took a ferry to Orcas Island, camping overnight and riding the entire island. Another day I rode through Sedro Woolley on Hwy. 20 and over the Cascade Range to Wenatchee, coming back via Hwy. 2 through Everett. It was one of the most magnificent rides I've ever done.

Skagit is a really fun track because it usually develops a narrow but deep cushion next to the fence, making for some great rides. After qualifying I was able to squeeze in four rides while the officials put together the heat race lineups. I blasted around the track with my first rider with a time that would have put me on the front of a heat race. At the end of the run I felt the brake pedal go to the floor. My left front brake mount had broken, tearing the caliper loose.

This was not an immediate problem as I turned the wheel back and forth to scrub off speed. When I got back to my staging area three young Asian girls were waiting; they were our next three riders. To add to the ambiance of the moment, the brake fluid that had squirted onto the headers caught fire.

I turned and looked at the girls and said, "I have no brakes, but as soon as we get the fire out we'll go for a ride!"

A quick-thinking racer saw the problem and ran over with a pair of vise grips and folded the braided line and clamped it off. The girls, who could speak very little English, had no idea what these crazy Americans were doing. But they had just the right amount of trust, allowing them to climb in and go for the ride of their life.

They all felt that this was the most danger and excitement they had ever experienced, crammed into just a few special minutes. They loved it! And seeing the excitement in their eyes when they climbed from the car, it was great. So much fun.

Fred also invited us to bring the two-seater to his World of Outlaws show at Elma. At the end of the night Fred agreed to allow us one full hour after the racing program had completed to give as many rides as we could squeeze in.

We had 14 people suited up and in line. I was going back out as fast as Porky could get the passengers aboard and buckled in. I don't know what sort of alcohol Fred had been serving at his concession stands, but our riders had enjoyed plenty of it.

One of our riders was a woman who was big but not very tall. As she got into the car she told us that she was very claustrophobic. To give riders something to hold on to we installed a dummy steering wheel that attached with a KSE quick-release mechanism. Some of our riders were too big to attach the wheel but in this case Porky snapped the wheel in place after the woman was buckled in.

Porky told the woman to leave her visor up until we got on the track and were up to speed. As soon as the push truck touched our bumper it was enough for her to click the visor down and before we were pushed it was already fogging up. She was obviously already breathing hard.

Many times at the end of a run I could hear people shouting with pleasure in their excitement. But this woman's shriek had a very different sound and tone. As I rolled to a stop one of the Outlaws officials who was hanging with us gave me a thumbs-up, but I shook my head. No, this sound is not good!

She was in complete hysterics. Porky figured if he could get her helmet off she might not feel so closed-in, but her husband had pulled the strap through the D-rings and tied it in a tight knot. In a slight panic Porky popped the seat belt to relieve some pressure—which it did—but her belly blew out into the dummy steering wheel.

All the while she was screaming at the top of her lungs that she is dying.

After several attempts to remove the steering wheel Porky resorted to his old cowboy days, remembering how you get a horse to suck in a little more girth so you can cinch your saddle tightly. So he elbowed her in the gut and she exhaled for an instant and he pulled the steering wheel off.

We all reached in and grabbed her and pulled her up and out of the seat. Like a cork coming out of a bottle of wine she came out all at once and landed on top of us, everybody in one big pile. After some rolling around in the dirt we managed to get her helmet untied and off.

I'm proud to report that she lived. And, as far as I know, is still going strong. Somewhere.

Fred was a very understanding and supportive guy, and I really appreciated that he was a reasonable businessman. After seeing my success at the after-hours Outlaws event Fred invited me up the following year.

This time, however, Fred told me we'd have to work out a revenue-sharing plan. I agreed that was fair, and Fred said he'd assess how we did and decide afterwards what a fair split would look like.

After about six rides my motor blew up and we were done for the night. Fred knew that I was looking at a significant expense, much more than I made that night. So he let me off the hook and said I didn't have to pay him anything.

Good ol' Fred.

Unfortunately Fred left us in 2007. He was promoting the races at Elma when he was struck and killed while lining up cars for a restart. It was an absolute tragedy for everybody: his family, his friends, and all of racing.

Obviously I worried about crashing the two-seater and injuring my passenger. But also, lurking in the back of my mind, was that the experience could be so intense that somebody might have a heart attack.

A guy from my area had a 94-year-old great-grandmother who lived near Elma, and he thought it would be a good idea to have her take a ride and then interview her on the front straightaway immediately after.

My thought was that nothing would kill business quite as effectively as stopping on the front straightaway and pulling a 94-year-old corpse from the car, dead from heart failure. So this was a ride where I was very conservative and careful. I gave her the grandma ride, full throttle only partway on the straightaway and half-throttle in the corners. I really took it easy.

When we finished and she climbed out of the car for her interview they asked her how she liked that ride. She kind of rolled her eyes and said, "Is that all it had?"

(To this day, I'm still a little suspicious that she had been coached to offer that observation.)

There are a couple of two-seater memories that really stand out.

Danny "McGoo" Chandler was a well-known motorcycle racer who suffered a spinal injury in France while riding for Kawasaki. Danny's injuries were significant; he lost the use of his legs, and could move his arms but not so much his hands. My friend Jerry Ponzo built a Honda Odyssey for Danny, incorporating some special control mechanisms. Danny could ride that thing wide open, and one day Joe McTernan and I went riding with him. Joe and I, going full-tilt on our motorcycles, couldn't keep up.

Chris Edgbert, a pilot with Southwest Airlines and a friend of Danny's, brought Danny over one night for a two-seater ride. We got Danny strapped in and I gave him all the ride I could. He loved it, but was unable to hold his head up very well. He said after the ride that his head was hanging out right over the right rear tire.

Another great memory is the ride we gave Shawn McDonald. Shawn, a huge racing fan, was a bodybuilder who went to the hospital for a heart operation. While hospitalized he contracted a Staph infection that attacked his body so severely that he was left unable to walk or speak. He had to communicate through a keyboard, and his hands were so twisted that it's a very challenging process. He was also forced to use a wheelchair to get around.

Shawn was a fixture at the Gold Cup in Chico. Someone suggested that we get Shawn in for a ride in the two-seater. Lots of people were excited about the idea, so I approached Shawn's dad to see if that would be okay. I was especially concerned about how the g-forces might affect Shawn.

Mr. McDonald looked me in the eye and said, "Jimmy, he'll be fine. It doesn't matter to Shawn. He would rather die in your sprint car tonight than live another day in that wheelchair."

It took six of us to lift Shawn's 180 pounds out of his chair and into our seat. We taped his hands to the cross bar behind the front seat and taped his head to the back of his seat. We discovered that Shawn wears only his boxer shorts under the blanket while in his wheelchair.

Chico was its usual tacky, sticky surface and we were blasting around the track in the low 13-second range. Ted Johnson, founder and president of the World of Outlaws, was standing in the infield talking to someone when he looked up at our car and said, "That fucking Sills has somebody riding in his car wearing nothing but his underwear!" Ted wasn't sure what the implications might be for his insurance but we finished before anything could be said or done.

When the ride finished we had to undo the back of the wing so that we could lift Shawn straight out of the car and place him back in his chair. Once in his chair Shawn had his keyboard and somebody said, "Shawn wants to tell you something."

As I leaned down close to him he typed on his keyboard and pushed the voice button. A mechanical voice said, "Thank you so much." I saw tears in Shawn's eyes and as I hugged Shawn I had tears of my own.

As I stood up and turned around, tears streaming down my cheeks, it felt a little odd to cry in front of all those big, tough crew guys standing around. But then I realized there wasn't a dry eye among any of them.

Lots of people were curious if I ever crashed the two-seater, other than at Oregon when the steering broke.

In fact, I flipped the car once at Marysville while giving my neighbor, Mike Cull, a ride. Mike had loaned me equipment to build my MX track and I felt like he deserved a fun ride. It was early in the year, at one of our first schools of the season on a Saturday. Mike came up to participate in the school and I decided to fire up the two-seater to get heat in the motor and iron out the track a bit. We were waiting for our first two-seater rider to show up so I asked Mike to hop in.

I hadn't checked the tires yet, and didn't realize that the right rear only had about four pounds of air pressure. We hauled it down into three wide open, and the car stuck great. So I hauled it into one, where the track had a couple of swells—uneven humps that made the car bounce pretty hard. It was just enough to get the car bouncing twice and then the right rear dug in and we were cleared for takeoff.

We did two nose-to-tail endo's and landed flat on the bottom frame rails. It killed a set of wings and pushed the rear bumper a little but other than that was surprisingly okay. It took just a few minutes to fix and we were able to give rides later that day. Mike was fine and it provided an excellent baseline for our school session that day: Always check the tires before you stand on the gas.

25

Students

Operating a racing school means that you will spend a lot of time watching people with absolutely no experience driving your expensive race car. This was scary to me at times; of course I was worried about somebody getting hurt, but I also worried about tearing up our stuff.

It isn't easy to teach people to drive a race car that is, by nature, out of control at times. Steering with the right rear tire instead of the right front, and getting everything working together—steering, brake, and throttle—isn't easy. If you're running the right line but not using the throttle and brake to steer the car, that isn't going to work out very well.

Just starting a sprint car is a class by itself; put the car in gear, turn on the fuel, wave the push truck, wait for the rear tires to start to turn over, watch the oil pressure, then turn on the ignition. Then give it a little throttle, and as you feel it begin to pull away signal the truck to stop pushing.

Some of my very first classes included some time outlining exactly how a sprint car works, but I soon realized that this was too much information for my students to digest. I learned that it was better to focus on the essentials: how to start it, how to stop it, and how to avoid crashing in between.

After all my years of racing, putting somebody else in a car I owned brought a new and interesting reality to me. I asked my former car owner, Don Berry, how he could watch a driver do something stupid and crash his equipment (not that I ever did that), yet still speak to him afterwards.

"It's the car owner's responsibility to ask if the driver is all right after a crash, even if you don't really care," Don explained. "Actually, you might even hope that the dumbass is hurting just a little."

I told Don that I would remember that bit of advice.

Cory Kruseman operates a driving school in Ventura, California, and

Cory will rent a car to somebody to race in the weekly program at Ventura Speedway. Cory had one guy who was particularly hard-headed and was tearing up the car every week. So what did Cory do? He sent him to me.

Getting Larry to drive aggressively wasn't a problem. I placed cones at the proper shutoff point for turn one, but Larry kept driving it in deeper and deeper just to prove to me that he could. The only thing saving him was that he was really pitching the car sideways. But he kept drifting up the track and I knew this was going to lead to disaster.

I did everything I could to get Larry's attention and slow him down, and I was standing on the fence waving the orange cone at him when he drove it in so deep that he flipped the car backwards onto the cage.

Now I was more than a little bit pissed.

We ran over to the car and rolled it back over on its wheels so that Larry wouldn't have to climb out when it was upside down. As the car landed on all four wheels Larry called out, "I'm all right!"

"Oh, okay…I forgot to ask that," I said.

Cory and I still laugh about that one. I always notice that Cory laughs harder than I do.

Kevin Cullen has a show on MAV TV called *The Motorhead Traveler*. The premise of the show is that Kevin travels to an area and selects a couple of motorsports-related activities to participate in. Some, like mine, are schools with some kind of water crafts, or snow machines, or motorcycles. Kevin is pretty skilled at operating whatever he drives or rides.

Kevin brought his show to our school and drove my non-wing sprint car and my winged 410-inch sprint car. Cheryl and I had fun doing the show, and Kevin did a fantastic job of driving both cars and produced a very fine program for MAV TV.

One of our most fun schools was when two stunt women attended. Laura Lee Connery and Shauna Duggins came on a Saturday in December, a season that is sometimes difficult to find enough dry weather to get track time. We had to work their schedules as one lived in Los Angeles and the other lived in Vancouver, British Columbia, and both were in high demand by the movie industry.

It was interesting to learn about the way vehicle stunts are performed for movies. The director would describe to the girls what he wanted, and where the car needs to be at the end of the stunt. The girls would then modify the car for the specific stunt, such as rigging the parking brake so that the car would rotate when applied. If the car had to go over a jump or perform a rollover, they had to devise a ramp of some sort and a driver containment setup.

Laura Lee and Shauna also did falls from as high as four stories, falling down stairs, and fight scenes. Basically, all of the things you wouldn't want to happen to you.

Both girls had drifter cars, so a sprint car on a dirt track was right down their line. On the day of their school they were our only students, so we pitted the car on the back straightaway. At the end of each on-track session they would pull the car out of gear and lock up the brakes and slide to a stop. You could hear screams, laughs, rebel yells, and they would jump up and down, high-fiving each other and laughing like crazy. They were very good on the track as well as understanding how to rotate on entrance and straighten out for exit. They were so much fun I let them run till the fuel was all gone.

Another interesting combination at our school was Lisa Caceres and Joey Hand, two young kart racers. They were brought to the school by Joe McTernan, a great friend of mine who builds engines for motorcycles and karts. Joe was a tough kid who had diabetes as a boy and later underwent a kidney, pancreas, and liver transplant all at once. The operation gave Joe another twenty-plus years of life, but his poor body finally said it had enough and we lost him. Joe lived life to the max while he was here and he helped a lot of young racers along the way.

Joey Hand was looking at midgets as his next career step from karts, so that's what we utilized during the school session for him and Lisa. They were very different drivers; Joey drove too hard and spun out a couple of times, while Lisa was very precise and never let the car go out of control. If we could have blended their styles it probably would have created the perfect race driver.

In later years I didn't keep up with Lisa's career, but Joey did some midget racing with Terry Caves. It was soon evident that Joey's real talent was road racing, and he spent some time driving for the BMW factory team. Most recently Joey won the 24 Hours of Daytona driving in the Chip Ganassi Ford GT car.

Among all the great people I met through the years at the school, probably none were more interesting or memorable than Fred "The Ace" Alexander of Las Vegas.

Fred was a "flying Ace" with the U.S. Army in World War II, and on our shop wall we had a picture of Fred alongside his P-51 Mustang, with a smaller picture of him standing alongside my sprint car. Fred signed the photo, "From one Ace to another!" Man, I loved that photo.

Fred attended our school several times, and even pitched in to drive the water truck a few times. We became good friends, and Fred later invited me to stay at his home in Las Vegas when I was helping Willie Hernandez (a racer from Montana) with his sprint car.

The personalized license plate on Fred's Corvette read "Corwet," and one day I asked Fred what that meant. He explained that his wife is Asian, and that's how she pronounced the name of the car.

Fred celebrated his 80th birthday by coming to our school and driving our sprint car. It was an interesting coincidence that day, as we also had Jim Paniagua (Paul and Bobby McMahon's grandfather) celebrating his 80th birthday in the same fashion. You could sense a little competition between them, as each wanted to be the fastest old guy. However, Carol McMahon (Paul and Bobby's mother) applied her long-ago quarter-midget skills and was fastest of the day.

Fred had done some racing on his own, and brought his Hinchman driving uniform. On his fourth visit to our school things became especially memorable.

On the night before Fred's visit I had two drivers in a session; one from England and the other from Canada. Both were struggling to get into turn one correctly. So I had them stand in the infield in turn one, and I climbed into the car to demonstrate how and where they should lift, rotate the car, and pick up the throttle.

I made a couple of fast laps and was going down the backstretch when the universal joint broke and swung around, taking the fuel and steering pumps off the motor plate. It continued to rotate around to the top of my foot, breaking the metatarsal bone—right about where you tie your shoe. It then went on to the bend the floor pan before making a final round to finish off my foot.

We pushed the car back to the shop, and my foot was turning purple as I held it in the ice chest. I watched my foot continue to swell up and show all sorts of Technicolor hues and finally decided that a trip to the emergency room might be a good idea.

They gave me a temporary splint and told me that when the swelling went down I should have a more permanent cast placed on my foot. I was genuinely grateful that the U-joint broke while *I* was in the car, because it was uncomfortable to imagine someone else getting hurt in my car.

The next day my helper Josh and I had to repair the car with me hobbling around the shop. We had to work quickly because we had another class scheduled for that night.

We got the car repaired, and everything was going well until Fred the Ace climbed in for his first run. There was a flat area off of turn one which is where we pushed the car, and I was standing in the infield as Fred got underway. The instant Fred hit the switch the car leaped wide open onto the track, and the stagger turned the car into a retaining wall in the infield. The car hit hard on the left front, spun around in the air, and hit the opposite end, tearing the rear end out.

The throttle was still wide open and the engine was free-winding (it was good that we had a Shaver engine). I was on crutches and couldn't get there, but Josh and Randy Frank quickly reached in to shut off the engine.

I got to the car and asked Fred if he was okay. I was sick with worry that my throttle had stuck on poor Fred. I reached in and worked the bell crank and could feel weight pulling against it. Fred's foot was on top of the pedal stirrup; when he climbed into the car it was dark and he sensed that the top strap was the bottom of the pedal, because the fuel line across the top of his foot felt like the top of the stirrup.

Fred climbed out of the car and walked to the shop and didn't want any medical attention. I explained to Fred that he had just hit a wall at about 80 mph and we should have him checked out. He was still reluctant but finally agreed when I explained that they have some good-looking nurses at that particular emergency room, and he should leave his uniform on to impress them.

When Fred's x-rays were developed the doctor came into the room and said, "You have nothing broken but there is some internal bleeding I want to monitor for a day." And then the doctor said with a little bit of amazement, "I see you've been shot before."

"Oh, that's just some shrapnel," Fred explained, like it was no big deal. He then explained that they were on a bombing raid over Germany when he was hit by anti-aircraft fire that ricocheted around the cockpit armor and lodged in his shoulder. Although seriously wounded, Fred managed to fly back across the English Channel and land at his base.

While we were waiting for Fred to be transferred to a room I pried a couple more stories out of him. We were sitting there talking when a couple of nurses walked past and I heard one of them say, "Who is the older man in the racing suit?"

"Oh, he was attending a racing school at Marysville Raceway tonight."

"Well, then who is the guy on crutches?"

"That's the instructor…he was in here last night."

Fred was discharged the next day and got into his truck and drove himself back to Las Vegas.

In all the years of conducting schools I only had three people injured; two of them were in two days and one of them was me.

After 15 years of running the school, by 2015 I was ready to step away from the adventure.

One of the key reasons was the nagging fear of somebody getting hurt and suing me. Racing is a dangerous endeavor and if you do it long enough it's going to bite you (I can point out several scars to back up that statement). I knew that eventually we would have something bad happen—seriously bad—and as time went on that thought bothered me more and more.

Running the school was a lot of work, too. Each school session involved three days of hard work: day one to prep the track, prep the cars, get the administrative stuff in place, field the phone calls, etc. Day two involved the classroom and track time, which was a long day. Day three involved cleaning up the cars, maintenance, and all that.

Through the years I tried hiring people to help me, but that was challenging because if you paid your help properly there wasn't much profit left. In later years I hired someone to do the marketing with the hopes of attracting more students, but that still left me with all of the work in the shop.

I guess the root cause for closing the school was money. When you counted the money and paid all your expenses, there wasn't much left over. So it was hard to justify all that work—and enormous worry—when you weren't really making any money.

I was ready to move on, too. Cheryl and I had gotten married, and we were ready to spend our time traveling and doing different things. Cheryl was a very enthusiastic helper at the school—she was the flagger and kept the lap times—and she enjoyed connecting with everyone. Cheryl is a natural "people" person and she liked being around everybody and having fun.

But we were both kinda done with the whole thing. So, with some bittersweet feelings, we closed the school at the end of 2015.

Over the 15 years we ran nearly 1,000 people through our school, and I'm proud of that number. I like to think that those people had a great time and came away with a better knowledge of sprint car racing. And I hope the serious guys became better racers because of the things we tried to teach them.

One thing I believe is that you can't teach someone to be a racer. You can coach a racer and give them techniques to make them better, but if a person doesn't have the basic tools no amount of schooling will make them a racer.

I had one guy come through the school who was utterly lacking in driving skills. I tried to teach the guy a few basics but he just didn't have a grasp. In fact, the guy was so bad that when the class was over, I asked which route he was taking on his drive home because I was going to make sure to not go that way.

Many people who have operated a business will tell you that it is tough to deal with the public, because people can be very demanding and unreasonable. I guess racing people are different, because I had almost zero bad interactions with people.

Overall, I'm happy to report that racing people are some of the best human beings in the world.

I did run into a few exceptions, of course.

After his two-seater ride at Elma, a guy from Marysville, Washington decided to quietly walk off with one of my uniforms. I'm never amused by people who steal, and this guy was definitely a thief.

Another guy crashed my school car twice when he did the exact opposite of what I told him to do. He made a partial payment to cover the damage and asked if I could wait a couple of weeks for the rest of the money when his sponsor paid him. That never happened, and I confronted him at Cottage Grove. The idiot said he didn't have the money, and…well, let's just fight! I'm getting too old for that stuff, but I did notice that his driving hadn't improved any.

The closing of the school wouldn't be complete without a good story.

In December 2017 I was still renting the shop on Simpson Lane to store race cars and parts from the school. I had been procrastinating on dealing with all my stuff, I guess because there wasn't any urgency. So everything was still in the shop and was basically in the same condition as when we had our final school session.

I got a call from the county asking if I still operated a business there; I told him that I didn't, other than the equipment that was stored in the shop. The guy then explained that the weather people had issued a warning of significant rainfall in the area in a few days, and there would likely be flooding in the area. His call was to alert me because they didn't want any oil or chemicals seeping into the water.

This forecast was not a complete shock, as my shop had flooded a couple of times before. So I immediately called for a 40-foot container to be dropped at my house. My nephew, Scott Hall, provided a trailer and we began the 30-minute drive to Simpson Lane to figure out how to load all this stuff and get it to the container in just two days. When we arrived at the shop my first stroke of good luck was sitting there. Channel 13 had just interviewed my neighbor, Reese, about evacuating his used tire and battery store because of the approaching flood. Reese is from Pakistan, and the reporter hadn't understood a word he said.

When I pulled up and spoke English the reporter had a look of relief. When she learned that I had a business there she asked if I would do an interview. I agreed, but we'd have to make it quick because we had a lot of work to do. She was a very nice lady who actually had done some racing and she enjoyed seeing the race cars in the shop.

Several people saw the segment on the news that night and offered to help out. Charley Mars was already on board, and Rick Hirst and my nephew Jimmy Wristen immediately pitched in. The move was finished on Friday and the rain came in as predicted. On Sunday Cheryl and I left for our favorite race of the year, the Chili Bowl.

In a great piece of irony, there was no flooding at the empty shop—but water was soon threatening my house, steadily creeping up the driveway. Luckily, the flood subsided before we had any damage. There was some worry about a nearby dam bursting which would have flooded the whole valley, but the dam hung in there and the water eventually subsided.

A flood is never good news, but that's what it took for me to move my stuff and begin the process of finally dealing with the things I no longer needed. Rod Fauver bought most of my stuff, and he hopes to resume the school at some point. I will be glad to help out when I can; Rod was a great help to me through the years and I'm all about returning the favor.

It would be cool if Rod resurrects the school. Although the name would be different, it will have the roots of the Jimmy Sills School of Open Wheel Racing and that would be pretty neat.

In the college world, when a professor retires they refer to him as "professor emeritus." So that's me. Jimmy Sills, Professor Emeritus. Sounds pretty fancy, doesn't it?

26

An amazing new world

There is a place on the other side of the world where beer flows freely, the people laugh easily, and the racing is exciting and intense: Australia. And, I will certainly add to the discussion the island nation of New Zealand, located to the southeast.

My experience with trips Down Under followed the same philosophy as voting in Chicago: Early and often. I made my first trip to Australia when I literally had just a few weeks of experience as a racer, and I would return there many times throughout my career.

I could probably write a book on my Australian experience alone. That would be a little much but I wanted to share some of my adventures here. And these stories are not in perfect chronological order; some go back a long ways and I honestly can't pinpoint the exact date things happened.

The idea of bringing Americans down to race in Australia dates back quite a few years. Many times the local promoters organized the Yanks into a "team" that competed against the local racers in "test matches."

That was the setup on my first trip during our winter of 1974-75. Because of their location in the southern hemisphere, Australia and New Zealand summertime is our winter. Larry Burton was the captain of the American team on my first trip, and he was looking for three other racers who could bring their sprint car to Australia and be part of the team. Larry recommended that I grow my curly hair as long as possible so that he could bill me as "The 16-year-old American racing sensation."

I was actually 21, and I was far from a sensation. I had won a few races locally—after all, it was my absolute rookie season—but I was learning that the idea of promotion sometimes means exaggerating things in order to put people in the seats. It was a good experience early in my career, because American drivers were at the center of a lot of interviews and media attention.

This was good for me. It helped me learn how to speak in front of a group, and learn how to stay poised during interviews. It gave me a chance to critique myself, learning not to say, "Uh" and to speak a little faster with more confidence and sound like I was enjoying myself.

I faced an immediate challenge to joining Larry's team: I didn't own a sprint car. I had only driven Ed Watson's super modified cars, so I had a little experience but no car of my own. Don Tognotti, who operated the most prominent performance shop in our area, had just purchased a sprint car team from Rebel Jackson. One of the cars in the deal was a beautiful Edmunds four-bar car that Mike Andreetta was taking to Australia. The other car in the Jackson stable was an older Ram chassis (built by my friend Jerry Day) with a cross-spring front suspension. This car had recently won a race at Elma, Washington, so it was a capable car.

All I had to do was talk my mom into a loan to buy the sprint car from Tognotti. This was a slam dunk, right? Giving a 21-year-old kid money to buy a sprint car which he would take halfway around the world with just 10 races under his belt…good investment, right? Luckily Mom was supportive and we made the deal happen.

My plan was to return home after the Australian season and drive a sprint car for Bob Davis. Bob was very helpful in preparing my new car for shipment and racing. We got everything in order and took our car to Kenny Woodruff's shop where we would prepare all the cars for shipment overseas.

Instead of a shipping container everything was going to be rolled directly into the storage hold on the ship. The shipping cost was based not on weight but by overall size, so we compressed our tires into bundles and tied them all over the car. We also bolted very narrow tires and wheels on the car as well. When we were finished these were the most god-awful looking sprint cars in history.

The ship sailed and a few days later we headed for the airport to make the 17-hour flight to Sydney. We arrived to discover that we had no idea where we were supposed to be racing, and which promoter we would be working with.

Our team was Larry Burton, Gary Patterson, Mike Andreetta, and me. We also had a reserve driver from New Zealand, Willie Kaye. This was the beginning of my lifelong friendship with Willie, who went on to become a top promoter in New Zealand at tracks such as Western Springs and Bay Park. Willie would play a big role in many of my later tours in New

Zealand. And I might add, Willie has helped a great many racers make the trip down, and he's also brought many Kiwi racing fans on various American racing tours.

Captain Larry quickly made arrangements for us to do an exhibition at Liverpool, a track located in West Sydney. Liverpool was promoted by Mike Raymond and his partner Frank Oliveri. Frank had a reputation as a tough, no-bullshit guy who could be very intimidating. Liverpool had just been converted from dirt to pavement, and they wanted to showcase sprint cars on the new surface.

It seems that most things in racing end up in a huge thrash, and this was no exception. We got the cars off the ship and hauled everything to Sid Moore's shop, about 20 miles west of Sydney. We barely had time to get the bundled tires off the car, mount pavement tires and get them on the cars before heading for Liverpool.

We got to the track and found over 10,000 enthusiastic fans in the stands, eager to hear these big Yankee V-8 engines come to life and race around the track at amazing speeds. We rolled the cars out onto the track and we were totally excited and pumped.

What a disappointment...none of the cars would start except Larry's, and he ran just a quarter of a lap before he had to pull off with a badly bent axle, probably from being dropped off a fork lift during shipping. All of the cars had plugged fuel lines, caused from sitting in the hull of the ship for two weeks and the fuel turning to gel from the high humidity.

Everybody was completely deflated. Us, the fans, the promoters, everybody.

Later that night we were herded into the promoter's office, where Larry insisted that we still should be paid for the exhibition. It turned into a heated discussion complete with threats, which worried me. Frank Oliveri had a badass reputation and he was a powerful man. He even owned the local bus company; for days after that confrontation we kept a sharp eye out for local buses which might be trying to run us down.

We worked it out without coming to blows but we were most certainly fired from racing at Liverpool. At least for the time being.

We eventually got our cars running and made our real debut at the Sydney Showground. A crowd of 22,000 people filled the stands on our opening night. It was an amazing introduction to the great passion Aussies have for racing, which they call "speedway."

All of the American teams would hang out at the Texas Tavern in the Kings Cross section of Sydney. This neighborhood was Sydney's answer to North Beach in San Francisco. During the war in Vietnam, Kings Cross was where the American soldiers on R&R would end up. "The Cross" had casinos, strip clubs, nightclubs, hos, pimps, drag queens, just about every wild thing you could imagine.

One of my earliest discoveries was this: Australian beer is much stronger than American beer. This point was made absolutely clear one day when Andreetta—aka "The Rat"—and I decided to go out to Sid Moore's shop to work on our race cars. We didn't have a car, so Rat and I somehow managed to steal the Liverpool Ute ("Ute" is a small utility or pickup truck) from Gary Patterson. Yes, this was the same Liverpool we had already been fired from. This was used as a pace car and had Liverpool Speedway lettering and graphics on the sides and a revolving light on the roof that would prove very useful.

After a day of hard work it is customary to have a beer with all your new mates. So off to the pub we go for "schooners of piss"—(really big glasses of beer). After a few games of snooker (a form of billiards on a huge table and with smaller balls) we heard them call out "closing time!"

We hopped into the Liverpool Ute and headed for our next party stop. With the Rat driving on the left side of the road we were headed down Parramatta Road, normally one of the busiest streets in the area. We were rolling along at 100 kph and found that the revolving light on our roof came in really handy as people pulled over to the side and let us pass.

Everything was working out very well when I heard the Rat say, "Uh-oh..." I looked back and could see flashing blue lights, three hills back. Then they were two hills back, then one hill, and then you could hear the siren.

The Rat turned the Ute into a side street when an unmarked Valiant Charger came skidding around in front of us, blocking any further progress. Two cops jumped from the car, and when I saw that they had their guns drawn I realized they were taking the situation quite seriously.

Some days your luck is against you; on this day it was definitely with us. The first cop walked up and asked our names, and immediately said, "Are you blokes racing at Liverpool or at Sydney for that bloody Owen Bateman?"

Since we were sitting in the Liverpool pace vehicle we figured we should say Liverpool.

The cop happened to be a midget racer and he elected to let us go. Which, considering we went from being target practice to being set free within the span of a minute or so, was a good outcome.

We went on down the road and the Rat only had to stop once for me to spew or "chunder" as they say locally, on our way back to the Cross.

Overall my first tour of Australia went pretty well. We kept our car in one piece and managed to sell it for a good price at the end of the tour to help Mom recoup her investment. Garry Wright of Brisbane bought the car, and it raced for many years after that.

The important thing was that we had raced fast enough to be invited back. My Australian adventures were just beginning.

Australia—like racing—can be hard on a marriage.

At the beginning of our first Australia tour, Larry Burton and Mike Andreetta were both newlyweds. Each brought their new wife along for the first part of the trip before sending her home, because they weren't able to be away for the full three months.

After our tour had finished and we were headed home, Mike and I stopped in Hawaii for a couple of days and connected with another American racer, Larry Rice. Larry Burton met us there and we all flew home together.

Upon our return to the U.S., Larry Burton and Mike each discovered that their wife had left them. I guess a three-month separation isn't always a good thing.

Larry would remarry right away, and the following year brought his new wife, Barbara, along on our tour. This created an interesting scenario as Larry introduced her as his new wife, and everyone said, "Oh, yeah, we met her last year!"

The following year we organized another trip, this time with my American sprint car owner, Bob Davis. We raced at Brisbane Exhibition Ground, and like all races Down Under the night's competition was followed by a big party.

The party began at the track, and when the fairgrounds ran us off the party moved to Johnny Bell's BP station just up the road. The station was located next to a three-story brick building, slightly uphill from the station. Johnny had a standing challenge for anyone at his party to throw a beer bottle high enough to clear the top of the brick building. If your bottle fell short it would break on the bricks and fall harmlessly to the bottom of the wall. Everybody got caught up in the contest—there is a good supply of empty beer bottles at any Australian racing party—and the next morning there was literally a foot of glass on the ground along the wall. Only two people could clear the wall: Bob Davis and Ron Wanless, a champion Australian midget and supermodified racer. Ron was also a boxer in his youth and had a lot of success as an owner of trotting horses.

After such a party and throwing so many beer bottles you tend to work up a terrific hunger. The only place open at that time of night happened to be across the street from a police station. We towed the race car with our panel van to the "milk bar" and while we were eating one of the racers managed to get into a fight with another diner. In moments the place was crawling with cops.

Bob and I finished our food and waited until everything settled down before we tried to leave. It looked like the coast was clear but Bob walked over to the yard in front of the police station, looking up and down the street. He waved me on so I moved forward to pick him up. As soon as I turned the corner a police car came out of the driveway with the lights on.

I had already been counseled by the locals: "If you get stopped and don't have the keys in your possession, you don't have intent to drive!" This was the apparently the local strategy of getting out of a DUI or speeding ticket. So I quickly reached down and tossed the keys under our van.

The cop approached my window and his first question was, "Where are the keys?"

I'm thinking, "We've got 'em now!" So I explained that I didn't have the keys.

This officer was apparently well versed on the "losing the keys" trick and he just looked at me with a very serious expression. "Mate, if you don't come up with the keys we're going to beat the shit out of you, and then we'll take you to jail."

So in the interests of being reasonable I crawled under the van and retrieved the keys and handed them over.

I realize that drunk driving is a serious deal and you shouldn't do it, and I also realize that the penalties are much stricter today. My penalty was spending the night in the "watch house" and I was prohibited from driving in the state of Queensland for 30 days. A day or so later we left for Sydney and as soon as we reached the New South Wales state line I was back behind the wheel.

I ultimately made 14 trips to Australia—as of today—and I've always seen lots of dead kangaroos along the road. On this particular drive Bob and I were headed for Sydney when a herd of live kangaroos came bounding across the road in front of us.

I came to a skidding halt and Bob and I both jumped out of the car, yelling and hollering in our excitement. We were even unconsciously jumping up and down ourselves!

In all the excitement I forgot that my camera was back in the van, so I have no pictures of the only kangaroos I've ever seen in the wild.

On our second tour we were again teamed with Gary Patterson, Mike Andreetta, and Larry Burton and his new wife Barbara, not to be confused with last year's new wife Dianne. Mike Raymond, the promoter at Liverpool, invited us to dinner at the home of Dave Booth. Dave was the track announcer at the Sydney Showground and a writer who operated his own racing newspaper.

We drove out to the suburbs to Dave's house and had the typical Australian dinner of chops, sausages, and I'm sure there was a red beet in there somewhere. Along with a large quantity of red wine.

Sometime during the evening Gary talked everyone into going back to the Texas Tavern to smoke some pot. Some of us had certainly tried it, but several guys had not, including Larry, the Rat, and Mike Raymond. So it was decided that we would head back to Sydney.

Mike was driving us, and he found himself behind a cop. He doesn't want to pass the cop—for obvious reasons. But the cop catches on to this and he keeps slowing down until we're only going about 20 mph. Mike finally turned onto a side street and the cop immediately turned around and pulled us over.

Mike explained that we have had a drink or two—strictly in the name of international diplomacy—and he needed to get these Yanks back to Kings Cross and out of harm's way. The cop agreed to let us go, and insisted on following us—almost all the way to the tavern.

This led to an unusual moment when we were nearly back home. A traffic light was red and Mike stopped. We sat there for a very long time and began to wonder if maybe the light was malfunctioning. We had our police escort—well, sort of—and Mike looked both ways to make sure nobody was coming and drove through the red light. We looked back to see the cop just hit the palm of his hand to his forehead before he gave up and turned the other way.

Our third tour of Australia came in 1977 when I teamed up with car owner Bill Shadle. Bill and I arrived in Australia and were informed that our car and equipment were delayed.

The ship carrying our stuff left Oakland and sailed to Seattle, where they ran into a bridge. Then they had a fire in the engine room. Luckily it was only a two-week delay but in the meantime we had to line up some borrowed cars so we'd have something to race.

I scored my first Aussie midget win in a car Gary Patterson had driven, with a Chevy II motor. I also raced a Walt Reiff-built sprint car that was brought over by LeRoy Van Conett. It was fun to drive LeRoy's old car but it had been in mothballs for a while.

Rowley Park Speedway in Adelaide was owned and promoted by the Racing Drivers Association (RDA), and the president of the club was a gentleman named Selwyn "Sel" Harley. Sel was heading out of town with his family and he graciously offered to let Bill and I stay in his home while they were away.

We accepted his invitation and that allowed us to explore some genuine Australian food such as peanut paste (peanut butter) and a jar of stuff that looked like dark almond butter and said "Vegemite." A peanut paste and Vegemite sandwich sounded nice, but it only took one bite to say that this is NOT RECOMMENDED.

The RDA provided us with a Ford Falcon station wagon for our tow car. They even lettered the vehicle, "Jimmy Sills USA Sprint Car Team" in bright letters.

Kevin Fischer of Murray Bridge invited me to drive a Stock Rod at their little track. On the way to Murray Bridge we ran into a swarm of beetles so thick that it clogged our wipers and forced us to pull off the road. We got some water out of the ice chest and spent several minutes trying to clear all the yellow matter and bug parts from our windshield.

A Stock Rod is basically a modern American modified with mud-and-snow tires and no stagger. You really had to back them into the corner to make them work. They race clockwise on the track—backwards to us in America—and braking is controlled by a hand lever, allowing your left foot to operate the clutch. (I have no idea why anyone would set up a race car in this way.)

This was all no problem until we took the green flag and drove into turn one (turn four, actually). As we headed down the backstretch there was a huge pile-up right in front of me. Naturally, I jumped down with my left foot and it took an instant for me to realize that all I was doing was disengaging the clutch. By the time I reached for the hand brake I drove right into the pile of cars.

However, my car was built for just this type of contact, and the big bumper just knocked everyone out of the way and I kept going. It was actually really fun.

When Sel and his family returned home Bill and I relocated to a flat near the beach. Our race car still hadn't arrived, so we had plenty of time for recreation.

One of my good friends from a previous trip was Peter Tucker, who owned several florist shops in Adelaide named Tucker the Florist. Gary Patterson had given him the nickname, "Tucker the Fucker" and that really stuck. Tucker also had a really cool vintage double-decker London bus that advertised Tucker the Florist.

The bus was a rolling party, complete with Tucker's posse of Fitzey, Finch, Pizza Tommy, and Jimbo. Everyone would pile into the bus and go on a pub crawl, wine tasting, or to the speedway meetings (races). Tuck always had the bus fully stocked and everyone would get pissed—not "mad" pissed but "drunk" pissed.

In our free time Bill and I went to the drag races at Adelaide Intl. Speedway. They were hosting a couple of visiting Yanks with their wheel-standing specialty cars, L.A. Dart and Hell on Wheels. They would travel the entire quarter-mile in a wheel-stand, with sparks flying off their wheelie bars. We connected with the guys and they later went joined us on the bus for a wine tasting tour.

Adelaide also hosted a Formula 5000 race at that time, and we spent an afternoon on the patio drinking beer with Alan Jones and Teddy Yip. Alan would go on to become the Formula One World Champion in 1980 and Teddy and his Theodore Racing became legendary as well.

Our race car finally arrived, so Bill and I busied ourselves getting it ready to race. We immediately ran into a complication; Bill was bringing a round of drinks to our table when he tripped on a rise in the floor and fell. The drinks went flying all over everyone, and Bill fell right into our table. His ankle was severely sprained (when we returned home weeks later it was discovered that it was broken) so he was hobbled.

My buddy Bill wasn't all that into working on cars anyway. He figured his job as car owner was arranging financing, making sure we were having a good time, and help push the car to the staging area. Bill was superb at the first two but he fell notably short on the third area. We had no small pit vehicles at that time so we had a lot of work trying to push our car around the pit area.

Everything was going well on opening night at Rowley Park Speedway until I lost a left rear wheel. We were running a Halibrand speedway wheel that was built for Indy car racing, and discovered that you had to safety wire the wing nut on to keep it snug. Well, we discovered this *after* it came off at Rowley Park.

As I spun coming off turn two and was sliding down the back straightaway I could see my wheel bouncing off the wall and soaring to a high altitude. It looked like it was headed straight for the center of my hood, and I could hear the huge crowd cheering for that very outcome. I'm not sure if it was my strong will, a gust of wind, or just the racing gods looking down on us, but the wheel narrowly missed the hood and glanced off the side nerf and rolled into the infield. No harm done.

Rowley Park ran just another year or two before it disappeared, replaced by Speedway City.

Next we were off to Warrnambool, Victoria, a great old whaling port on the southern coast. Our little Falcon wagon was loaded with tools, spares, wheels, and tires. It was squatting rather precariously in the rear, and it handled very badly. We began to think that this wasn't a very good setup for the uneven and narrow rural roads. Many times the road was so narrow that if you passed a big rig you had to drop your left-side wheels off the shoulder, which would send you into a bad whip trying to get back to the center of the road.

We were figuring that this trip was likely to end with a double-fatality on the highway, and the breaking point came when the car didn't have enough piss to get to the top of a hill and was overheated by the time we got to Murray Bridge. We stopped at Kevin Fischer's shop there and Bill arranged the use of a Ford F100 pickup.

We raced the Grand Annual Classic at Warrnambool, probably the largest sprint car race in Australia and one of the most prestigious races in the world. I don't remember where we finished but I certainly remember the celebration after the race. The party after the Classic is without a doubt the biggest racing party you could ever experience. It is fun and amazing and truly a memorable thing.

Australia has many poisonous and harmful creatures that can kill you, both on land and sea. One such creature is the Funnel Web spider that bores a hole into the ground and makes a web shaped like a funnel. While we were in the Sydney area we saw a news story where a small boy died after being bitten by a Funnel Web spider. A few days later we saw one of the spiders on display at a museum in Adelaide and made a mental note to keep a sharp eye out for these lethal things.

Bill and I were on a long trip across the Australian Outback, where petrol stations are scarce. We set aside two of our fuel cans for petrol so that we could make it to the next station. We were traveling at night, using a safari light that attracted every insect within five miles. The bugs were so thick that you didn't dare open your mouth.

We were rolling along when our fuel tank finally went dry and we pulled off the side of the road. Bill and I hopped out to pour the two cans of petrol in the tank. We finished the chore and as I was climbing into the truck I looked down to see what looked like a gigantic Funnel Web spider right next to my foot, ready to pounce.

I jumped so hard into the truck that I slammed my head into the A-pillar, screaming, "FUNNEL WEB! FUNNEL WEB! FUNNEL WEB!" like a hysterical child.

After our 10 gallons were gone we ran out again, and we were so far out in the bush that you literally couldn't see a dot of light on any horizon. It was absolutely silent, except for the wind. There is very little traffic out there—very little meaning literally almost zero—and we were getting a bit anxious when far, far off in the distance we could see the tiny headlights of a semi-truck.

A big rig in Australia is a very different proposition than an American big rig. The trucks are equipped with gigantic bars in the front to knock kangaroos—or anything else—out of the way as they roll along at high speed. They yield not an inch to cars, and when you see one coming it's in your best interest to get the hell out of the way.

The truck drew closer, and we heard his air brakes come on as he slowed to see if we needed help. He was towing a flatbed trailer, and luckily was going our direction. I asked if he could give me a ride so that I could get some gas to bring back to the truck.

"Mate, I've got a chain, I'll just give you a tow," he said.

That sounded like a helluva deal. What's the worst that could happen? My new best mate backed his trailer up and hooked up the chain. His only request was that I keep the slack out of the chain while he works up through the gears.

"No problem, let's go!" I replied.

We took off and I was doing well at keeping the slack out of the chain until we were almost up to speed and he reached for another gear. I coasted up almost to his trailer—it's a short chain, so it wasn't very far—and he found the gear and surged forward. It just about yanked the front end off of our Ford, with the race car and trailer hanging on for dear life behind us.

I looked at the dash to see that we were traveling 110 kph (about 70 to 75 mph). We had no power steering because our engine was off, and no power brakes. I figured I should stay off the brakes to save whatever power assist was left until we really needed them. I also turned off our headlights to save our battery. So there is nothing in the blackness but the trailer taillights just a few yards in front of us.

We were rolling right along and everything was okay until we ran into a storm. It was absolutely pouring rain and now his taillights were just a dim, distant glow. The road had several low spots that quickly filled with water, which caused our pickup to hydroplane toward the edge of the road. That allowed us to drift along a couple of yards out of line when the chain would jerk our truck back to the center of the road.

Is our trucker friend slowing down for the difficult conditions? *NO FREAKING WAY.*

We finally arrived at a petrol stop and Bill almost had to pry my fingers off the steering wheel. The trucker came back to help us unhook the chain, and I thanked him for the tow.

"No worries, mate," he grinned.

As we were filling the tank of our pickup we could see the trucker standing at the window of the coffee shop, with an audience of fellow truckers around him. He was pointing outside at our truck and they were all laughing at those dumb Yanks that he pulled back to civilization.

My most successful racing season in Australia came in 1978 when I drove the same car Bill Shadle and I had raced the previous year. Kevin Fischer bought it and put together a good tour that brought us many feature wins.

The biggest was the Grand Annual Classic at Warrnambool. All these years later I'm extremely proud that my name is on the list of winners of that great race.

We also should have won the National Title race. We were leading with two laps to go, with Garry Rush running second. When we went into turn three for the restart the yellow light was still on, which means we aren't going to restart on this lap. Right?

Wrong. We came off turn four and Rushie was on the gas and the flagger threw the green flag. By the time I got up to speed we ran out of laps and finished second. Bummer.

27

Tormenting Trostle

Ron Wanless is what Bob Davis would refer to as, "A fucker, a fighter, a buckin' horse rider!" Ron had an extremely colorful and successful life including a boxing championship in his younger days, an Australian National Speedcar (Midget) Title, and stint as owner of a huge scrap steel yard and auto salvage operation. He would also become one of the top racing promoters in Australia.

In 1979 Ron brought Steve Kinser, Doug Wolfgang, Larry Burton, and me over with the biggest racing budget, the most aggressive schedule, and the most rental car damage ever seen in one season. We moved down the street from the Texas Tavern to the 15-story Chevron Hotel.

Larry Burton wasn't widely known in American sprint car circles because he was primarily a west coast supermodified driver. However, Larry had built quite a following among Australian speedway fans. He hired Duke McMillen and Butch Bahr to assemble enough cars, tires, and parts to run our entire tour. Duke and Butch managed to stuff a 40-foot container completely full from floor to roof.

The cars were not assembled, allowing them to enter the country under a smaller duty. They shipped five cars, nine engines, and enough parts to fill a Speedway Motors warehouse.

We opened at the Sydney Showground. One of our cars was fitted with an enormous 6-by-7 foot wing built by a guy named Steve Stribling, better known as Buffalo. Actually, Steve's wife Carla built most of the wings. We only had one of the giant wings so it was decided that we would rotate the wing among us from night to night.

All of the tracks we raced—except Parramatta—were dry and slick. The car using the Buffalo wing had a huge advantage on those tracks, and almost always won. If your motor blew up or something else happened and you didn't win with the wing, you really felt cheated because the wing rotated to the next driver the following night. You felt like you had missed your prime chance at winning.

Our second race was at Parramatta, where we went out on a Tuesday afternoon for a practice session for the TV cameras. The Aussie promoters got a lot of coverage and hype from local television stations, which helped fill the huge grandstands on race night.

Wolfgang's motor was down, so the rest of us—Steve, Larry, and me—got set to drive some hot laps for the cameras. Wolfie and his wife Jeri, along with their two girls, Niki and Cori, were hungry and decided to take the rental car to McDonalds for some lunch (McDonalds was the only food the Wolfgang family found to their liking in Australia).

As the three of us were following the camera car around the track in our race cars, here came Doug around the outside, gassing it up in the rental car. Niki and Cori were in the back seat, hanging on to their McDonalds lunch for dear life. Just as Doug reached the camera car a hubcap went flying off the Holden Commodore rental car, sailing through the air. It was spectacular!

One day we got an invitation to ride Honda Odyssey off-road vehicles on somebody's dirt road course. We spent all day on those things; it was more fun than I could ever explain. We were covered with dirt from head to toe by the end of the day, just laughing like crazy. What a great day.

We later went swimming where the water faced a huge drop from a cliff. There was a rope swing at the top, and Steve swung way out on the rope. It was a helluva drop, and you could see that he was debating whether he wanted to let go. He finally released his grip but by then he was swinging back toward the rocks.

It looked for sure that he was going to smash into the rocks and move everybody in America up one spot on the race track. Steve made it safely in the water but he was really close to the rocks. Even just watching him was a scary, scary moment.

Our trip was a long one, and toward the end Steve and Doug hopped on a plane to return home for the World of Outlaws season opener in Florida. Sleepy Tripp and Charlie Swartz—the craziest man alive—subbed for them for the final race of our tour.

Charlie was full of outrageous ideas. Australia still featured sidecar motorcycle racing—yes, a guy rode in the sidecar—and Charlie decided we should give that a try. Charlie worked on lining us up with a ride, but none of the bike owners wanted to trust their stuff to these strange Yanks. So in retaliation Charlie waited until after the races and went streaking around the track buck naked while carrying an American flag.

You just don't see stuff like that anymore.

Here's a great story about Ron Wanless. Ron made his money in wrecking yards, and often would work the front counter of his business. One day a guy came in asking for a hub cap for the right front of a '62 FJ Holden. Ron tells him, "Sorry, mate, but I'm fresh out of them."

The bloke gets a little angry, insisting that a salvage yard this large surely must have a part as common as that. The guy is getting more and more agitated and finally Ron said, "Okay mate, I will look again for you." He went to the back and grabbed a tire iron, then slipped out the back door. He found the guy's '62 FJ Holden in the parking lot and popped the hub cap off the left front and brought it back inside. "You were right the whole time, mate, I had one out back!" The guy was ecstatic and he paid Ron the $40 and drove off a happy customer.

At the end of the 1980 racing season my wife Karen and I bought a house at the northern edge of Sacramento. I promised Karen that, no matter what, I was going to stay home that winter and sit with her by the fire, and maybe even read a book. No Australia trip for this boy and I'm serious!

Right around the first of December it was a cold winter night and we are all snug in our house. Karen was on the couch reading, the Christmas tree was twinkling, and life was good.

Then the phone rang.

It was Con Migro, the promoter from Perth. Con explained that he was in dire straits. Little Al Unser was scheduled to race with Bob Trostle's three-car team with Jac Haudenschild and Mike Brooks, but Al's sprint car owner in the states—Gary Stanton—said Al couldn't go because he would miss Florida Speed Weeks and El Centro.

Karen's nose was still in her book, but I could tell that she was listening carefully to every word I said to Con.

"I feel bad for you, Con, and I'd love to help you…but I promised to stay home this winter and I am a man of my word. You'll have to get somebody else."

I hung up the phone, but he called right back. Same answer.

On the third call he was downright desperate and he kept telling me how important this tour was for the well-being of racing in Australia. Plus, Con was getting much more generous with financial incentives.

My mind was working…the tour was only for one month, and then

Rich Vogler would arrive and take my place. And besides, the very future of racing in Australia was at stake and it had fallen on my shoulders to help save it!

I mean, I'm only going to be gone for a month, I'd be bringing home a nice paycheck, I'd be getting Con off the hook, and Australian racing would be saved. That's a win-win-win any way you look at it.

Karen was still listening very closely and she heard me say, "Okay Con, send me a ticket."

She leaped to her feet and threw the book across the room at me. "You lying mother-fucker!" she screamed. "I knew you wouldn't stay home!"

I was new to marriage and I'm not a counselor or anything but I could sense that our relationship could be described as being a little strained at that moment.

It was a fun trip, starting in Perth and Bunbury and working out of Jeff Murphy's shop. We hired an up-and-coming driver, Ian "Bonds" Bradford, to travel with us and help. When we got to Warrnambool we met another young Aussie driver, Max Dumesny, who worked for John Sidney—where we kept our cars in Melbourne.

John was a car owner who kept this stuff in meticulous condition. He operated a repair shop that serviced Ferrari and Maserati cars, so he was accustomed to very high standards of work.

My engine blew up at Mount Gambier and Trostle told me to pick out one of our spare motors and put it in my car. I couldn't get the motor past the hole in the motor plate and Trostle came over to have a look.

"Oh, that's a cast iron crankshaft," he observed. First off, John Sidney would never run a cast iron crankshaft, and what Trostle did next just about stopped John's heart. Trostle grabbed a cutting torch and cut the flange off the crankshaft. The motor bolted right in place and actually didn't vibrate all that much.

Poor Trostle. We gave that guy so much of a hard time, even when we weren't trying. One day we finished working on the cars and headed back to our hotel. We stopped at McDonalds for burgers and of course Haud had to special order because he wouldn't eat pickles. Because if a pickle has touched the burger at any time in the cooking and assembly process, that burger will not touch Jac's lips. Under any circumstances.

Haud's special order always slowed us down at McDonalds, and it pissed Trostle off every time. He was getting highly annoyed. You could see on his face that he was not in a good mood in any way, shape or form.

We got our burgers and continued on. I was driving, with Haud riding shotgun (in the left seat) and Bonds and Trostle in the back seat. We were driving through a really busy section of the shopping area when I missed the turnoff to our hotel. I was carrying a lot of speed and as I pulled across to a side street Jac reached down and yanked the parking brake and we spun out in the middle of the busy street.

The sound of all four tires spinning to a stop was deafening. As the sound fell quiet and we were enveloped in tire smoke Bob's voice erupted from the back seat.

"You sons-a-bitches!" he screamed. "You're going to get us all killed or arrested and I don't want to be in a foreign jail!"

That was a really fun tour. Incidentally, Max Dumesny went on to became one of the all-time greats in Australian racing, and later relocated for a while to Knoxville. His wife Malinda was also a very good sprint car driver, and her dad Sid Moore owned the shop we raced out of on my first trip there in 1974.

28

The Preacher

Right about now would be a good time to share some Gary Patterson stories. Gary was also known as the Preacher, the Dancing Phantom, the Hostile Hippie, and The Great GP. Whenever he was in Australia, Gary was the undisputed king of the Texas Tavern. He had spent a lot of time in Australia and had a way of finding the best party hangouts.

When we were on tour there we would often cross paths with the U.S.A. stock car team which usually consisted of Gene Welch, Ed Wilbur, Wayne Sue, and Mike Kline (aka Hash Brown). There was also a U.S.A. midget team, consisting of Patterson and Larry Rice.

Larry was an elementary school teacher at the time, and when they were on tour together they were promoted as, "The Preacher and The Teacher."

One day Larry and Gary had just come in from Perth when we met up at the Texas Tavern. Noel Bradford had flown them to the Hutt River Province where Prince Leonard owned several thousand acres which he designated as his own country. When Prince Leonard first announced his plans to secede from Australia, the government didn't take him seriously. But when he started printing his own money and his own postage stamps it kinda got their attention. It started a political and legal scuffle that still goes on to this day. But on their visit 30-some years ago Prince Leonard saw fit to knight Sir Larry and Sir Gary and they had the papers to prove it.

One evening Sir Larry and Sir Gary and I went to dinner at Doyle's On The Bay, a restaurant with an iconic view of Sydney Harbor including the Harbor Bridge, the Opera House, and the skyline. The fattest dog I have ever seen lived there, prowling around the place begging for table scraps.

When dinner had finished we grabbed a bottle of red wine and walked across the street and down a trail to the South Head, which features a steep cliff that drops to the Pacific Ocean. On the other side of the opening to Sydney Harbor lies the North Head.

As we were walking down the trail we heard voices coming from a hole in the rock. It was a guy and his girl sitting in a tiny cave, and they invited us inside. The cave was just big enough for the five of us, and we passed around the bottle of wine and watched the waves crashing onto the rocks below us. It was magnificent.

Gary had a nose for interesting and unique stuff. One day he took me to a graveyard in Sydney just down the coast road and showed me the coolest gravestone in the history of racing—maybe in the history of the world! Phil Garlick was killed in 1927 at Maroubra Speedway and is honored with a headstone featuring Phil sitting in the cockpit wearing a leather helmet, holding the steering wheel, chiseled in stone. It's just cool as hell.

GP also had a knack for finding the best saloons and pubs, anywhere in the world. One of Gary's requirements was that there had to be some kind of game to play. Coming home from Baylands Raceway one night he took me to Cordelia Junction, one of those bars which encouraged you to staple something on the wall or ceiling. There was a pinball machine that actually paid money, and that's where GP spent a lot of his time.

Gary was working at the plating company owned by Duke McMillen and Bill Shadle and one day I stopped in around lunchtime. We decided to grab a bite to eat at The Outpost, just down the street. After lunch and a beer we started playing the pinball machine, and the more we drank the more we felt like the ball was rolling too fast on the table. So we stacked ashtrays under the table legs to lessen the slope. That seemed to help for a while and somehow Gary discovered that if you kick the machine straight up under the front it would give you free points. The kicking resulted in some broken ash trays and sore legs the next day, but we never had to pay for another game.

We had a day off on one of our Australian tours to hang out at the Texas Tavern and found ourselves bored. We went downstairs to the pub and began playing Pub Pong. It was GP and me against the machine; I played front court and Gary played backcourt. We played for two solid hours and didn't lose one game, finally deciding to go outside to rest and stretch our legs. After a few minutes we went back inside and that machine kicked our ass for the next two hours.

One evening they arranged a nice dinner for our team along with promoters Owen Bateman from the Sydney Showground and Garry

Hoffman from Adelaide Intl. Speedway. This was a nice affair, and the team sat together at a table. Our group consisted of Larry Burton and his wife (the newer one), Mike Andreetta and his wife, Larry Rice, Gary Patterson, and myself. The restaurant was called, "Dirty Dick's" but it's not what you think. It was actually a very nice restaurant, complete with an Elizabethan play during dinner. The actors in the play were also our servers.

The food had a medieval theme, like a Henry VIII feast. There were turkey legs and a huge, complete fish—eyes and all—that took up almost the entire platter and was covered in sauce.

This was not Patterson's kind of deal, and he was looking for a way to exit the proceedings. When the giant fish arrived at our table GP seized the opportunity. He grabbed the fish off the platter, shouted "Hey, Hoffman!" and tossed the fish down to the other end of the table, where it landed right in Garry Hoffman's lap.

SECURITY TO TABLE SEVEN…

Of course GP was ejected and he took a cab back to the Tavern.

As you might have noticed, it is common in Australia to spell "Garry" with two R's. Phil Christensen was a friend and a writer for several racing publications along with the *Sydney Herald*. After a race one night Phil called the race report in to the paper and said, "Gary (one R) Patterson won the race tonight." The next morning the newspaper carried a headline that said, "RACE WON BY AMERICAN DRIVER GARRY "ONE ARM" PATTERSON."

We called GP "One Arm" for a while but unfortunately that nickname didn't catch on.

The Sydney Showground was a huge stadium that featured speedway racing throughout the summer. They attracted enormous crowds, and Owen Bateman was especially good at pitting the Australian racers—and fans—against the visiting Americans. They scheduled a series of "test matches" that fired up everyone's sense of patriotism.

One night the teams were called to the front straightaway for special introductions. The American team, consisting of Patterson, Larry Rice, Larry Burton, and me, proudly stood on one side, each of us holding an American flag. On the opposite side stood the Australian team—Garry Rush, Steve Brazier, Bob Tunks, and Garry Winterbottom—each proudly holding an Australian flag.

During the introduction Patterson decided to stir things up a bit. He walked over and snatched the Australian flag from Tunks, then walked out front where he knew he was in full view of the entire packed grandstand. He bent over a little and acted like he was wiping his ass with their flag, and then threw it on the track.

I immediately sensed that I was about to be in a huge fight with the Australian team, along with 18,000 outraged Aussie fans who also wanted a piece of us. The Australian team just laughed it off as GP firing up the fans, and the fans saw it as an excuse to bombard our team with beer cans.

(I have heard reports in situations like this of *full* beer cans being thrown. I dispute this, because in my experience no self-respecting Australian would waste one ounce of good beer, not even on a miserable, bloody Yank.)

On one of my early trips Down Under I discovered that GP and Larry Rice were leaving the USA several days before I was scheduled to go. I had nothing going on so I changed my flight and tagged along.

We were flying with Air New Zealand, on a DC-10 with the entire back row to ourselves. The flight stopped in Hawaii for fuel and we were allowed to get off for one hour while the plane was serviced. When Gary bent down to get his bag he hit his head on the seat in front of him and the oxygen masks in the entire row dropped down.

We headed for the bar in the terminal for a few drinks. The Wiki Wiki buses—shuttles that take you out to the airplanes—had finished running for the day, so after a few drinks we headed back on foot toward the departure gate. We came to a fork in the path and Larry and I agreed on one fork while GP insisted on taking the other. Our path took us back to the plane, and we were sitting in our seats watching the crew getting ready to push back from the gate, figuring GP had missed the flight. Just as they are closing the door GP came walking onto the plane, both elbows and forearms skinned up and bleeding. He explained that a security man chased him down for being in a restricted area and tackled him.

We arrived in New Zealand and The Preacher and The Teacher got me together with a midget racer, Trevor Morris, who owned a radiator shop in Auckland. Trevor and his wife were very nice and I had a great time spending a few days with them. Trevor's wife was very pretty and owned a hair salon where they served wine while you got a haircut. The salon was doing very well.

After a couple of days I needed a paycheck, so race promoter George Tervitt agreed to hire me to drive a supermodified. The car was a Tipke roadster pavement car from Washington and I have no idea how it ended up in New Zealand. We got the car running and took it to Western Springs Speedway on Saturday night. The speedway had a paved bicycle track on the outside of the race track, with a steep banking that was very tempting to drive on. However it was very loose with crumbs from the dirt track. I gave it a try and gave George and the fans their money's worth by executing the most perfect 360-degree spins you have ever seen.

Gary and Larry were in New Zealand when the promoters brought A.J. Foyt and Mel Kenyon down to race midgets. At the end of their tour A.J. gave his uniform to Patterson. Gary got back into Sydney early in the morning. His first stop was my room at the Texas Tavern, where he knocked on my door at 7:30 a.m. I stumbled to the door about half awake, and there was Gary standing there in A.J. Foyt's racing uniform and an A.J. Foyt Chevrolet hat.

"Is Bob Davis here?" Gary said, totally serious, referring to my car owner. "I heard he was looking for a driver!"

John Padjen was the promoter at West Capital Raceway in Sacramento, and later Silver Dollar Speedway in Chico. In 1975 John was promoting a USAC midget race and felt GP and I would add something to the event. I was still very much in the early stages of my career and I appreciated John giving me a chance to drive a midget. John lined up a ride for me in a beautiful Edmunds car with an Offy engine.

We soon realized that USAC would not allow me us to race without a physical exam. John came to the rescue, as he knew a doctor who could do the "exam" at his house. GP needed a physical as well, so we piled into Duke McMillen's '57 Ford Ranchero and headed for the doctor's house. John was there, and we all had cocktails as GP and I checked each other's blood pressure while the doctor filled out the medical forms. John took the forms and we were good to go, and GP and I left the doctor's house and found a bar in Fair Oaks for a few more drinks.

I suddenly remembered that I had a date with a girl I was meeting at the movie theater. GP was also late for an engagement, but he must have forgotten about it. As we were driving down Marconi Avenue GP's girlfriend Shirley spotted us and did a textbook police move, turning around in heavy traffic and then forcing us to the curb so that we couldn't escape.

Shirley marched up to the car's open window and began to bawl out GP without mercy, and amongst all the ranting I could kinda make out, "Where have you been…" Finally Shirley wrapped up the yelling and, with a rousing finish, hauled off and punched GP right in the side of the head.

She then stomped back to her car and burned out, throwing gravel at the Ranchero. GP looked over at me with a big red mark on the side of his face and calmly said, "Okay Sills, what do you want to do now?"

I reminded him of my date at the movie theater and off we went. My date had waited long enough and was just leaving when we got there. Luck was in my corner and she got held up at the light, but as it turns out she was not very happy, either. That sort of thing can really put the chill on a nice date, you know?

29

Down Under, again

In 1988 I traveled to Perth with an American team that included Kramer Williamson, Danny Lasoski, Randy Smith, Rocky Hodges, and a young Jeff Gordon.

We discovered that Lasoski is very jumpy if somebody goosed him. As you might guess, that was not a good secret to get out because every time Danny started to do an interview somebody made sure to goose him. We traveled to a local radio station and as we were getting on the elevator somebody goosed Danny. The doors were already closing but he somehow managed to get out through an opening about six inches wide. It was both amazing and impressive.

Jeff Kendrick is an engine builder from Perth, and he invited all the Yanks to his place for a party. At any Aussie pool party there is a time in the night when somebody is going in the pool against their will. That night I went in early and was then signed up for the "hunt for more victims" committee.

Jeff Gordon and Todd Osborne were too fast to catch, so the group turned their attention to Eric Slack, the largest man to ever fit into a sprint car. Eric easily scaled out at about 400 pounds. In Australia they would call this amount, "20 stone," which might not sound as heavy. But when you are trying to lift a 100-pound arm that is trying to beat you up, that's a no-win situation. Eric suffered a broken toe in the mess but to his credit managed to stay dry.

We later heard about a nearby nude beach, and of course we had to check it out. Lasoski and Randy Smith and I headed over for a look. Danny's dad, George Lasoski, decided he wasn't going to drop his gear so he waited for us at the entrance.

It didn't take long for us to discover that most people at the beach probably should have stayed dressed, and after a few minutes we headed back. George was waiting, and he couldn't resist taking a photo of the three of us walking toward him, buck naked.

That picture used to make the rounds at Knoxville, and of course today it would have gone viral on the Internet. Every time somebody mentions that picture I am quick to point out that it was a very cold day.

On one of our trips to Australia we stayed at Steve Brazier's house in Sydney and raced out of his shop. Steve is a multi-time national champion in Australia, as is his son Garry.

Steve lost an older son, Steven, in a highway accident a number of years ago. Steven and his mechanic were towing home from a race in Adelaide when they were killed. It was a terrible tragedy for the Brazier family as well as for racing in Australia.

After Steven's death Steve turned his energy toward his business, maybe to help him find a way to continue on after such an awful experience. Steve built a large drum reconditioning plant, building and setting up the operation himself. The business recycled industrial drums from various industries and put them back into use.

As Steve built up his business he visited all sorts of industrial sites, chasing down drums to recycle. I went on one such run with Steve, along with his son Garry who was about five years old.

We were standing out front of a business and the man Steve was negotiating with was nervous because he was apparently slipping the drums out the back door of the plant. As Steve talked with the guy, five-year-old Garry stuck his head out of the truck and yelled, "Hey Dad, just bash him on the head and we'll take all his drums!"

It was funny at first but he kept yelling louder and finally to shut the kid up the guy gave Steve a good load of drums.

Steve and his wife Kay had an 8-by-10 walk-in cage filled with birds. Among the species of birds were three young sulphur-crested cockatoos. The TV show *Baretta* was popular at the time, and the character in the show had such a bird. The birds were suddenly the rage back home, and they are very common in the wild in Australia. But they are protected birds and very hard to export.

Steve and Kay set aside one of the birds—named GP—for Gary Patterson, but they had no way to get the bird to him. The other two birds were named Henrietta and Herbie, and Kay said we could have those two birds if we agreed to take all three birds to the states and deliver Gary's bird to him.

We went to downtown Sydney, where we applied for an export license and a permit from the Fish and Wildlife department. Kay had written us a receipt dated one year earlier, proving that we had owned the birds for the appropriate time. Next an inspector visited the Brazier home to check on the birds and he gave us permission to take them home with us.

One of the requirements was that we had to get cages of a certain size for their transport. When we landed in Honolulu a guy had to walk past the cage and stamp our papers, for which we were charged $800.

When we arrived in San Francisco we went downstairs to get the birds and took them with us through Customs. By this time the birds were pretty agitated, squawking like hell, and the agents waved us right through. After 30 days the birds had to be inspected again—yes, we were charged another fee—and after that they were ours. Bill kept Henrietta and I was the proud parent of Herbie.

I never thought birds would have a personality, but they do. One of the downsides of a cockatoo is that they can—and sometimes will—bite the hell out of you. But overall Herbie was pretty cool and it was fun to watch him flying around the house. He was definitely the life of the party when we had people over.

When my daughter Stephanie was born I ended up giving Herbie away because he wasn't compatible with our new baby. Herbie woke up at the first glimmer of light in the morning, and as soon as he was awake he would start screaming like hell until everybody in the house was up. This would scare Stephanie awake and get her day started off on the wrong foot and it just wasn't a good situation.

My friend Dale Carter had just lost his bird in a divorce, so he was glad to take Herbie off our hands.

Very early in my adventures Down Under I discovered that many items easy to obtain in the U.S. are hard to find in Australia, and people there were eager to purchase them. No, I'm not talking illegal drugs or anything like that.

In those early years the idea of global marketing was nowhere near as developed as it is today. In fact, the idea of shipping basic consumer items that far away had hardly been explored. American consumers and Australian consumers, for example, shared very little products. If an American product was superior or just more cool, the Aussies would hear about it and want to buy it from visiting Yanks.

But there was a catch: the market was quickly changing, and something that was highly sought-after when you left Australia in February might be in wide supply when you returned that following December. That's because American companies were starting to expand their reach into Australia, which was slowly beginning to open up their markets.

Larry Burton was already well-versed with this scenario when I joined him on my first trip. Larry taught me how to bring stuff into the country to sell, but he always cautioned me to be careful because of changing demand. For example, one year Marshall Sargent advised Larry to bring a big supply of American razor blades on his next trip down. "They can't get 'em and you'll sell all you can carry," Marshall told him. So Larry bought a bunch of razor blades and put them in his shipping container. But when he arrived in Australia he discovered that the manufacturer—probably Gillette or Schick—had opened up the market there and their stuff was in every store in Australia. Larry was stuck with his big inventory of razor blades.

"I had enough blades to shave with a new one every day for years," Larry told me.

I was pretty ambitious on my second trip to Australia and brought a bunch of racing parts to sell. I purchased a big trunk at K-mart and filled it with rear-end center sections, two sets of quick-change gears, three weight-checkers, a Schroeder steering box, and assorted racing t-shirts. The trunk was so crammed with stuff that I had a leftover Goodyear tire that wouldn't fit so I tied a handle on it and checked it as luggage.

When we entered Australia I checked the box that said "Nothing" on my customs form, meaning that I declared no property coming in. I was pretty naïve, hoping they wouldn't look inside the trunk. As I lifted the trunk off the turnstile I tried not to look like I was straining, but the handle pulled off under the weight. I managed to lift it onto the inspection belt, trying my hardest not to look like a smuggler.

Amazingly enough the trunk made it through okay, but the Customs agent looked at me and said, "Is that a new tire? What's it worth?"

I told him that it was in fact new and was worth $120, American.

"Would you sell it to me for that?" he asked.

I told him to come see me in a fortnight and I would give him this tire absolutely free. He kind of smiled and said, "Okay, move along."

A year or two later I was at the plating shop, planning my next Australia trip. Bill showed me a nickel diode that is put into a tank for plating metal pieces. They were about the diameter of a quarter and looked similar to a crater. We hit upon the idea that we could make some cool-looking items to sell to the Aussies.

We polished a bunch of diodes to a really high gloss, then drilled a hole along the edge. Bill got some chains from a jeweler friend and we made necklaces and called them, "Moon Stones."

They were a big hit and we had a lot of fun with them. Some we sold and some we gave away, but the best part was inventing really wild stories on the origins of the "Moon Stones." I don't think we told the same story twice throughout the entire trip.

The commercial idea of selling stuff could work the other way, too. On my first trip I packed a bunch of authentic Australian items—kangaroo skins, wine, boomerangs, you name it—to bring back home. When we arrived at the U.S. Customs desk I claimed a small portion of the items at a reduced amount, and as I was negotiating with an agent another agent walked up and said, "Be careful with what you're declaring…sometimes we confiscate everything you have, price it out, and charge you that amount for a fine."

I said, "Well, since you put it like that, I do have a couple of opals in my back pocket." The duty turned out to be just $50, and paying the duty looked a lot better than going to the back room for the rubber glove search.

On one of my early trips I was standing at the Immigration desk in Australia and the agent kept looking at my passport and then looked very carefully at me. Then another nearby agent walked over—a little unusual—and he studied my passport carefully before staring at me.

I was starting to wonder if I was about to be escorted to the back room, and I pointed to the second agent and asked, "What's up with him?"

The first agent replied, "He thinks you're Leo Sayer, and so do I."

Leo was a popular British singer at the time, with a couple of major hit songs such as, "Long Tall Glasses" and "You Make Me Feel Like Dancing." My hair was really long and bushy, and Leo had obviously been inspired by my look because he had the same haircut.

They finally agreed that I was not Leo Sayer but the one and only Jimmy Sills. Leo got the song royalties and I got to race. There you go.

In the early 1990s I was racing in Indiana when I ran into Willie Kaye at the race track. Willie, a native of New Zealand, was one of the first people I met when I made my initial trip to Australia many years earlier.

Willie had taken the job of promoting Western Springs Speedway near Auckland, New Zealand. Willie also organized tours that brought New Zealand racing fans to the U.S. during our racing season.

Willie asked if I would be interested in coming back to New Zealand to race a midget. I hadn't been south of the equator in several years so this sounded like a great idea. I asked Dave Calderwood if he would consider sending his midget down for me to race, and Dave jumped at the chance. We loaded a car and plenty of parts and spares into a container that was bound for the South Pacific and we were all set to go racing.

Dave is unable to sit on an airplane for 16 hours without working on something, so he didn't make the trip personally. Instead he sent a great mechanic who is also a New Zealand native, Dave Playle. I had already worked with Dave, and we got along well and raced pretty well, too. We also had Pete Benson, who is primarily a motorcycle mechanic. Pete was crew chief with Nicky Hayden when he won the world championship. Warwick McKenzie provided a shop and we were all set.

The biggest draw at Western Springs Speedway is an international contest between New Zealand, Australia, and the United States that is known as a Test Match. The program consists of six-car heat races with two cars from each nation. It was very competitive and the racers are handpicked from each country.

The opening night ceremony included a group of traditional Maori tribesmen who perform a war dance known as the Haka. At the end of the dance they place a spear on the ground and if you pick it up that means you have accepted the challenge and the race (or game or match or war, whatever) will begin.

I was the new guy so I was invited to represent the U.S. at the ceremony. I was honored to be asked and just as I walked out toward the ceremony Sleepy Tripp took me aside and said, "Hey Sills, don't laugh during the ceremony. They get pissed."

Immediately I thought, "Why would I laugh?"

The Maori warriors painted their faces and wore traditional outfits. They danced and jumped, waving their spears, and then the head guy ran directly toward me, screaming a war call and sticking his tongue way out. That's when I knew what Sleepy was talking about, and if he hadn't said anything if would have been a lot easier not to laugh.

We raced every Tuesday and Saturday, which was a nice setup if you needed time to repair your cars. It also allowed you a day or two to recover from the Car Park Feature which follows every race at Western Springs.

The Car Park (parking lot) feature is a gigantic party in which the last person standing—literally—is declared the winner. I never actually won this feature but I was on the podium a few times.

The first few nights of racing the track was typically sticky, rough, and one-groove on the bottom. The infield featured a curb around the inside of the track, with a layer of sand installed just inside the curb. If you went too low on the track and got your tire into the sand that was enough to earn you a trip to the official's tower for an ass chewing. I felt like if I didn't get at least one of those each night I wasn't trying hard enough. Actually what

I was trying to do was use my left front tire to pull sand across the track to kill the bottom groove and make the top more competitive. The track conditions and the one-groove racing made it easy to crash, which I did on a couple of occasions. It usually took me a couple of races to figure out the track and get settled down.

Sleepy Tripp was fast at Western Springs, and he raced there for many years. In fact Sleepy married a nice Kiwi girl, Erin, and brought her home to southern California, where they raised their daughter Shay.

Sleepy had a reputation as a contact driver, but I never saw him put a wheel or bumper to anyone who didn't have it coming. He was also very skilled at not getting himself involved in anybody else's crash.

One night I slid up in front of Sleepy and felt that tug you get when another car hits your right rear tire. I immediately had a bad feeling and as I came back around my suspicions were confirmed as Sleepy as upside down against the fence. When he and his car got to the pits I went over to express my apology and offer my help in fixing the car. Sleepy declined my help and said with a smile, "We were racing and sometimes shit happens… sometime it might happen to you."

It did.

Western Springs had a clown who entertained the crowd during lulls in the competition. There was apparently a famous clown in New Zealand named Round Tree, so the track named their clown Square Bush.

I didn't pay much attention to him until they rolled us out onto the track in preparation for being pushed off for the feature. I saw Square Bush walking toward my car with a chainsaw that looked like a toy. I mean, it *looked* like a toy. Square Bush walked toward my car, and I started to perk up a little bit, wondering what was happening. He fired up the chain saw and put the bar against the downtube on my car. Sparks immediately flew from the chainsaw and it absolutely looked like he was cutting through the frame.

That's when I just about shit myself.

It took a moment but I realized it was a trick chainsaw and it wasn't really cutting anything. I was the new guy and they pulled this gag on everybody when they first arrived. The crowd got a big kick out of it and I guess it really was pretty funny. Kind of. A little.

Square Bush was engaging with all the fans, throwing candy and tossing a Frisbee with the kids. He rode around in a small midget with the engine mounted in the back, allowing him to ride long wheelies. He also had a motorcycle sidecar that he rode in, falling off and hopping up to dust himself off while the motorcycle went around in circles until he could hop back on.

Square Bush was a cool guy but a bit of a clown.

Speaking of motorcycles, in the mid-1990s some of the Australian tracks still raced speedway motorcycles on the same program with race cars. Bikes need a very hard and slick track, or they crash big. Some of those riders never had the experience of what too much grip feels like.

One such guy was Michael Figliomeni, who was a four-time Australian Champion and seven-time Western Australia champ. Michael began the transition to race cars and on his very first outing got to turn one and flipped his ass off. The very next race he got through turn one okay, but in turn two busted his ass again.

All week we teased Michael, "Hey, wait until you get to turn three…it's *really* a bitch down there."

The bar at our motel in Auckland wanted to bring in more people, so they highlighted the race teams that were staying there and invited people to come party with us. One night they rented a Karaoke machine but nobody wanted to sing, so the manager announced that anybody who sang a song would receive a free drink.

Warrenne Ekins, who was on the Australian team, and I each volunteered and went up and belted out a few songs and downed a few more drinks. Somehow the offer suddenly changed to offer us a free drink for every song we *didn't* sing, which was also okay with us.

Warrenne was a fun-loving guy, the kind of person you instantly like and enjoy being around. He loves to laugh and have fun.

We were informed that Robby Flock had skydived into the race track the previous year and it had been a spectacular entrance. Not to be outdone, Warrenne and I decided we'd try that same stunt. This was all sponsored by the company that promoted sky diving, and it sounded like lots of fun.

We were on our way to the take-off area at Parakai, 30 kilometers north. That's when we were informed that it was too windy to jump that day and the idea was scrapped. However, I later went over and did a couple of tandem jumps, where you're strapped to an expert jumper. Still scary but really fun.

The following year I again talked Warrenne into trying a jump. We got suited up and boarded the plane, which was very tight with four of us in the back. The plane climbed to 10,000 feet and Warren and his guy were first out of the plane.

We were next, and the girl I was strapped to allowed me to use my hands and feet to spin us around as we were free-falling. She finally pulled the chute and we were floating along and I asked her if she could see Warrenne. She turned us in a circle and I heard her say, "Uh-oh, a malfunction."

"Oh, shit, a *what*?"

"A malfunction. Not us, them."

We looked off in the distance to see a chute floating along by itself, and a little ways below we could see another chute floating down with Warrenne and his expert attached underneath.

When we reached the ground I got undone from our chute and hurried over to where Warrenne had landed. He was visibly shaken and rightfully so. He looked up at me, eyes wide, and shook his head.

"When they first pulled the ripcord the chute opened and jerked on me balls and I thought I was going to injure me self. Then I asked, 'What is that flapping sound?' the bloke says, 'Hang on, we've got to get rid of this one!' And then we were falling again until another chute came out and 'bout killed me balls again."

That was Warrenne's last jump, by the way.

I eventually did three midget tours in New Zealand, followed by three more tours with sprint cars. My last trip was in 2006, and I hadn't been racing much at that point. By this time the Springs was promoted by Bill Buckley, and given the fact that I had almost retired from driving it was nice of him to invite me.

I drove a car owned by Ron Salter, who owned a trucking company and raced big-rig tractors on road courses. Ron purchased cars from Craig Dollansky at the end of the World of Outlaws season, and Craig stayed on and raced with me in a second car Ron provided.

The first week the track at Western Springs was very rough. By this time I had lots of experience running my driving school—and preparing a track—so I agreed to join Danny Lindich in trying to get the track straightened out. We headed to the track on Wednesday to get to work.

Danny owns a construction company and was able to supply the equipment we needed. Danny also owned the car Sleepy Tripp usually drove.

As we graded the track we discovered that much of the base consisted of sand, which shifts around too much and allows the surface to get rough. We hauled more than 25 loads of sand out of there, which we had to store on the premises behind a nearby Quonset hut to avoid getting a permit and encountering tons of red tape.

If you had seen the track on that Wednesday you would say there was no way it would be ready to race by Saturday. We stayed with it and as we put everything back together we installed a much-needed progressive banking in the turns.

All ended well, as the track was ready by Saturday night and the new surface was well-received by the racers.

The most fun I had on a New Zealand tour was the year Tony Elliott, Dave Darland, Mike Drake, Jay Drake, and Jeff Walker were there.

We had endless fun on that one. Of course when you think about that lineup of personalities it isn't hard to guess that fun was very much a priority.

Someone heard of a luge ride in Rotorua, a couple of hours from Auckland. Along with our mechanics, Dave Playle and Peter Benson, we drove up to try it out.

The luge sleds were like sitting on a shop creeper with a joystick that controls steering and brakes. It traveled downhill along a paved path that was wide enough for three sleds. Of course this isn't going to be just a ride down the hill; it's going to be a *race*.

We lined up and somebody said, "Go!" and we were off. My sled seemed to have less resistance so I was leading down the first straightaway. I started braking in anticipation for an approaching right turn, and four sleds went flying by me and crashed in a spectacular pile-up. We didn't know it, but this was actually the most mellow portion of the course.

A couple of turns later we encountered a steep downhill drop with a jump at the bottom. You have to be dead straight when you left the ground, otherwise you would really bust your ass when you landed. Which we did.

From there the trail went to another high-speed section, where Mike Drake crashed big. Mike—father of famous American racer Jay Drake—went sliding one way, the little helmet they give him went another way, and the sled went yet another way. When we got to the bottom of the run we were all laughing and looking at everyone's skinned-up arms. We immediately headed for the chair lift for another run.

By our third run Mike had no skin on one arm and very little on the other, along with a few scrapes on his head. One really cool thing about New Zealand is that their legal and financial system is structured to allow very few lawsuits, so they allow people to do many things you could never do in the U.S. However, even they have limits, and Mike found the limit. They refused to allow him to ride again, and sent him over to the infirmary to get bandaged up.

You can understand how Jay Drake was one of the bravest drivers on four wheels, as it's in his blood.

One night at the race track they had a bunch of vintage cars on hand,

and the owners of the cars invited us to come over to a nearby small track to drive some vintage midgets. Some of the cars had roll cages, some had just a rollover bar, and some had nothing. Whatever your danger level and time period, they had a car for you. Warrenne Ekins even went as far as to wear coveralls and a skullcap helmet.

They also featured speedway bikes with sidecars mounted on the side. They asked the Yanks if we wanted to try riding on a sidecar, and of course everybody was eager to give it a try.

We quickly discovered that the leathers they wore were very heavy and hot and sweaty. Your job as rider is to help keep the bike balanced, so you're stretching yourself out as far as you can on the sidecar at times, and other times you're tucked up behind the driver as close as you can. There was a tiny platform for your right knee and a bar in front of the driver's boot, and you grabbed the bar with your right hand.

If you are positioned correctly your right shoulder will be close to touching the race track, running along at more than 60 mph. What a rush!

30

The greatest thing

In 1982 my life changed in the most dramatic way possible when my daughter, Stephanie, arrived on October 2. Every father out there would agree that bringing a child into the world really is a powerful change in your life.

I am happy to report that Stephanie has been a wonderful kid, from that first moment right up until today. We have enjoyed a very close and loving relationship and I wouldn't trade one minute of the time we've spent together.

She was considerate from the very beginning. As we prepared for the Gold Cup in late September, 1982, Stephanie's dramatic entrance was imminent. She was already a week overdue, in fact, and I was sweating through the previous weekend's World of Outlaws races at Baylands, hoping I wouldn't have to make a choice between racing or being present for Stephanie's birth.

I know that sounds ridiculous; what could possibly be more important that the birth of your child? But in reality the racing world waits for no one, and it's very difficult to tell your car owner you're taking a week off, no matter how valid the reason. They could easily put somebody else in the seat, win a couple of races, and as you're experiencing the warm glow of fatherhood you get a phone call that, oh by the way, you're fired. Remember, I took Milan Garrett's ride in 1986 when he took off for a few days for the birth of his child (sorry Milan…I still feel badly about that).

When you make your living as a racer, you face some extremely difficult decisions. My hope was that Stephanie would hold off until the middle of the week and I wouldn't have to miss any races, especially high-profile races like the Gold Cup.

We won the Friday preliminary at the Gold Cup, putting us on the front row of the Saturday main event. We ended up running fourth to Doug Wolfgang, Jac Haudenschild, and Jeff Swindell.

The following Tuesday we went to the hospital and the greatest kid in the world arrived.

Stephanie was very active and she began playing soccer at four years old, and later tried softball. In fourth grade she really stepped up her involvement in sports and added volleyball to the mix.

Stephanie was very athletic and you could easily see her skills on the volleyball court. She played with a group of girls that stayed together all through elementary, junior high, and high school, and they really progressed as a team. Watching them grow from that first experience as small kids practicing with a beach ball to spiking a volleyball at lightning speed was something to behold.

Throughout the years Stephanie traveled great distances with me as I raced, and as she grew up I returned the favor and traveled to watch her play volleyball. We traveled to Colorado, Oregon, throughout California, and even played for the high school state championship at ARCO Arena in Sacramento.

I remember one episode at a volleyball game when Stephanie was in junior high. In her PE class Stephanie ran to the net for a spike. She jumped up and slammed the ball right into the face of some poor young boy who didn't expect such power and speed to come from a girl. The ball hit him in the face with enough force to knock him backwards onto the floor, from which he slowly got up crying. It was not a good day on the social ladder for that kid. Stephanie felt terrible but she couldn't stop her competitive reflex action.

Stephanie loved to climb on the bars at school and developed forearms of steel, which helped her in gymnastics class. In second grade she fell off the bars and broke her arm but that didn't seem to slow her down much.

She and I had a couple of adventures getting her to school in the morning. It would occasionally snow in Placerville, and getting out of our driveway could be a challenge. Our driveway had a curve halfway up a steep grade with very little room to get a run at it. One morning following a fairly heavy snow Stephanie was excited about the prospect of a snow day but I took the situation as a personal challenge. Stephanie was skeptical enough that she wouldn't ride with me; she watched from the top of the driveway. I let some air out of the rear tires of my '75 Datsun pickup, and loaded some firewood in the back for weight (of course you have to put the proper setup on your ride!). Then I gassed it up and after two good runs impressed my daughter by getting to the top. Her enthusiasm was tempered by the fact that my success meant she had to go to school after all.

Stephanie's early years saw her spend a lot of time at race tracks. As early as two weeks old, she began a seemingly endless experience of watching cars go in circles and traveling in an RV. There were few kids her age, aside from Brad Doty's daughter Brandy.

When Karen and I divorced I missed a lot of quality time with Stephanie, and I didn't enjoy that at all. I arranged for her to travel with me as much as possible, but she wasn't really a racing fan. She did, however, like hanging out with her dad, and that was my good fortune.

At age seven Stephanie took her first trip with me to Australia. Although the 17-hour flight was challenging for a young kid, she travelled like a champ. We had a lot of fun Down Under and I'm sure she would tell you that it was a memorable experience.

Her next trip came at age 15 when I traveled to New Zealand. It was a sensitive age for a girl and I realized immediately that those Kiwi boys were checking her out at every turn. I kept a sharp eye on them, to be sure. We were at a fun New Year's Eve party at our hotel when I walked around the corner and caught her drinking a beer. Of course nobody knew where she got it.

One thing I'm proud of is that as Stephanie grew up she wasn't afraid to challenge herself and overcome her fears. As a small girl she was frightened of roller coasters and things like that, but by the time she was 15 she went skydiving with me. It was great to watch her savor the moment, and when we got to the ground she was so excited, high-fiving everyone and enjoying the experience.

Stephanie has grown up to become a successful adult and I couldn't be more proud of her. She and husband Carlos live in Long Beach, California, about eight hours drive from our home.

We make it a point to get down to see them at least once per year, and they'll come our way once a year as well.

I've always had a very close and strong relationship with Stephanie and I'm grateful for that. When I think about all the traveling we did when she was little, and the great amount of time we spent apart, I'm thankful we maintained such a good level of closeness.

It's an amazing thing to look around one day and realize that your kid is now an adult. The relationship changes, and it's better in so many ways. We can have discussions about serious life topics and I'm genuinely interested in her opinion. She's been one of my best friends, for sure.

Obviously you love your kid, whether they're little or all grown up. But it's really a bonus when you like your kid and enjoy being around them. That's been the case with Stephanie and it's a very good thing.

What's great is knowing that Stephanie truly wants her dad to be happy. That means a lot to me and I appreciate it very much.

Stephanie and Carlos have blessed us with an amazing granddaughter, Sophia. Sophia is eight years old and is pursuing her acting career in several dramatic productions around Long Beach. She also just maxed out her report card with a 4.0 gpa! She got great marks for being a very well-behaved student as well (obviously she has not taken after her grandpa in this respect).

She is also the cutest kid in the school. No, really. She is.

I was in Long Beach recently to attend one of her plays and when we went to lunch the next day people were calling out her name, praising the great job she did in the play. She is already a celebrity!

My life has taken a lot of twists and turns and there were times when I wasn't sure what my future years would look like. As things evolved I can honestly say that Stephanie has been a constant source of joy in my life and I wouldn't trade one minute of the time we've spent together.

Although racing wasn't her thing, Stephanie always cheered for me and was my greatest, most supportive fan. Well, she might not realize it, but that's exactly how I feel about her today. When I watch her as a mother, and see what a successful, happy person she has become, I'm Stephanie's greatest fan.

And I always will be.

Just about every racer I've ever known had a good mom behind them, keeping them going and pushing and prodding when they needed it. My mom was the absolute best, and as a bonus she loved racing and did everything she could to support the sport.

My dad had a Piper Cub airplane that was used to monitor the water level in the rice fields. Before they were married, Dad would take Mom flying. Dad would hop in the airplane and buzz my mom's house, and there weren't many regulations back then so he could do some really *low* fly-bys. It would scare my grandma but the moment Mom heard his airplane she'd rush outside to kick-start her 650 Triumph and hurry to the airstrip.

My mother was the most amazing and loving and caring person I have ever known. She raised three girls and me on her own until I was six. My father was busy along with my grandpa, making a career in farming and racing and also building us a home. Any one of those jobs would be a full time event, but he did them all at once and did a great job at all of them.

Mom also had an exciting streak. She loved fast cars, fast motorcycles, and even airplanes. She was in her mid-60s when her insurance company put her on probation for having too many speeding tickets.

A few years ago when my race car retirement and my motocross careers were intersecting, I had a bad spill and broke my collarbone. Mom told me, "That's going to hurt for a while."

I was amazed at the comment. "Really, Mom? Have you experienced this?"

She explained that yes, she had. She hit a dog once while riding a motorcycle, and high-sided it and broke her collarbone. It was certainly interesting to learn all these interesting things about my mother.

As a kid I would beg my mom to put the gas pedal on the floor of the car, and she'd happily do so. She'd lift after just a second and I'd plead with her to do it again, only longer. She always had a station wagon (the SUV of the day) and it didn't have much punch anyways.

Mom was supportive of anything I did, starting with Little League baseball. I wasn't a stellar baseball player but she would drive twenty miles to take me to East Nicholas for practice and games. After a couple years of not getting enough playing time (plus the long drive both ways) we put an end to the baseball career. It was more me than her, because Mom didn't mind taking the time to get me to the games. Throughout her life she continued to attend sporting events for all her grandkids and great-grandkids. If she ran out of kids to watch she would find someone else's kids who were playing somewhere. She later would attend lots of softball games for my wife Cheryl's daughter Ronee.

Mom proved to be my greatest fan, and throughout my career she went to a lot of effort to get to the track and watch me race. As the years went on I was doing more traveling, so Mom needed an RV. She got a new Linde, not really all that special but a nice and functional 25-foot unit on a Dodge chassis with the bare necessities. That RV made countless trips to the Northwest for Dirt Cup at Skagit, and across Interstate 80 to Knoxville, Iowa. The Linde would be packed with my sisters and their kids, or anybody who wanted to tag along. They would camp at the Marion County Campground, and one year in Utah they got caught in a big storm that nearly blew the little RV over.

One summer I was heading to the Midwest for some midget racing, starting at Denver and then running Eagle, Nebraska. and the Belleville Nationals. I was driving an old BMW 633 with a 5-speed transmission, and Mom had a mini-van. I talked her into trading cars with me so I could sleep in the van, just like old times. When I got back home she explained that she really wasn't all that impressed having to shift gears all the time. She also didn't feel that the car fit her image very well.

That old BMW was kinda fancy and it didn't fit *my* image very well, either. One day I was sitting at a stoplight when a carload of Hispanic guys pulled up next to me in an old beater with smoke rising from underneath. One of the guys looked over at me and yelled, "Hey, man, got any Grey Poupon?" We all cracked up at that one.

One night at the races Mom was sitting behind two girls who didn't know Mom. The girls were looking through binoculars and one said, "That Sills guy has bedroom eyes!" Mom wasn't sure what that meant but I did, and I figured at that point I had it made!

When I moved to Pennsylvania in the summer of 1988 to go racing, Mom drove all the way from California—by herself—to watch me race. She never wanted to be in the way, so I barely knew she was there.

What a great lady. Truly, what a great lady.

The year 2000 marked the first time in quite a while that I wasn't racing a midget at the Turkey Night Grand Prix, allowing me to celebrate the holiday at home with my natural family. After our Thanksgiving dinner I suggested that Mom and several other family members go with me up to the Marysville track where I could give them a ride in our two-seater sprint car.

It was a perfect day for high-speed rides. It had rained earlier in the week, so the track had plenty of moisture. We didn't have to iron the track out much at all, so I told Mom to climb in.

I explained the setup: she could tap my right shoulder to go faster, and tap my left shoulder to slow down. We rode around slowly while I worked the track in, building heat in the motor. After a while Mom was getting tired of putting around and she reached up to tap my right shoulder.

Just as her hand reached up I hit the throttle and it threw her hand back. The track was beautiful, and I could flat-foot it around three and four, just barely lifting in turn one. Mom knew right then that if life was going to continue on as she knew it, a hand must reach that left shoulder—and fast. However, the g-forces were preventing that from happening.

After another lap she was finally able to get to my left shoulder, and I slowed down. After I putted around another lap I thought, "Maybe she meant to tap my right shoulder, and wanted me to go faster." So I gassed it up again.

Uh-uh. As soon as my foot got on the throttle I felt another tap on my left shoulder. This one was a little more urgent, the "slow your ass down" tap.

The rest of my family didn't get the shoulder tapping option, and it was flat-out, balls-to-the-wall laps for everybody else. They all said their neck was sore the next day from holding their head up through the corners. As it should be! It was a really fun day, the kind of day you remember for a long time.

31

Reflections

Throughout the middle stages of my life I spent a lot of my time alone. Sure, I was surrounded by people—racing mechanics, friends, people on an airplane, that kind of thing—but when it came time to turn out the lights at night I was usually in a room by myself.

After my divorce in 1987 I kind of bounced around a little bit in terms of a relationship. I had a couple of longtime girlfriends, but after a few years things always seemed to run their course and didn't work out. I dated Charlene for quite some time, but she eventually took up with a fire chief in Chico and we went our separate ways. I met some nice ladies through match.com, but nothing long-term came of any of the people I met.

I can't hide the fact that one of the biggest things to sabotage a potential relationship was racing. Unless you meet a woman with roots in the sport, it's highly unlikely they will embrace the racing lifestyle. I mean, who can blame them? It's a lot of late nights, hard travel, low pay, crappy hotels and food, and the conditions can be challenging. Unless you're into it, the allure eventually wears off.

I enjoyed the bachelor life at times, I have to admit. It's nice to have the freedom to do what you want without having to consult somebody else. My house in Elverta was very much a guy's house; it was combination mountain home and bachelor pad. I set the place up exactly like I wanted it and life was good.

But as the years passed I wondered if maybe I could meet somebody fun and enjoy our life together.

Everything changed one day in 2007 when my phone rang. I was amazed to hear from Cheryl Simmons, a long-ago friend from over 30 years prior. Cheryl was married to my friend Ron Simmons, and along with my former wife Karen we socialized quite a bit all those years ago, including lots of time riding dirt bikes together. In fact, when Karen and I were married, Ron and Cheryl were in the wedding party. But I lost track of them until receiving her phone call out of the blue.

Cheryl and Ron had been living in Carmichael, California, and she had some sad news to share. Ron had passed away from mesothelioma, a form of lung cancer caused from exposure to asbestos.

When we wrapped up the call I took down Cheryl's number. As the next few weeks passed I realized I was thinking about her a lot, so I called her back. This was few weeks after the memorial service. That began a steady series of phone calls, and in the process we discovered a lot of chemistry. We could talk not just about the "good old days" of our 20s but also about current things. I found myself confiding things in Cheryl that I had never before been able to talk about with anyone. It was amazing and exciting at the same time.

That December I was at the PRI show in Orlando and every spare minute we were calling each other.

My mind was flooded with mixed feelings. I was really connecting with this person but at the same time, this is my friend's widow. As far as I know there is no published guideline on the statute of limitations on something like this. So we continued to talk on the phone until a few more months passed and I finally invited her to come see my racing school and take a ride in the two-seater sprint car.

I realized that this lady was special. Special enough, in fact, to make me consider ending my run of 21 years as a single man. I called my daughter Stephanie to share my situation and tell her what was happening with this great lady who had come into my life. She said, "Dad, you'd better get a new truck and buy yourself some clothes. You better not screw this one up."

Cheryl and I began riding my Harley with another couple we had both known all those years ago, Mike and Sherry Zine, along with Jimmy Boyd and his wife Betty. We dated for several years, spending more and more time together, steadily growing closer.

I was still traveling for racing purposes—mostly related to my school, and helping former students with their racing program—and Cheryl traveled for her work as well. She worked for a company providing software to the medical industry, and she attended a lot of trade shows and medical conventions. We figured out how to coordinate our travel and we enjoyed a bunch of really fun trips together.

We connected at cool locations like the Outer Banks of the Carolinas;

Butte, Montana; and Seattle. I drove the RV to Indy and helped the Galedrige brothers and she met me there before traveling to Georgia.

There were so many great trips…we traveled to South Carolina and connected with Chris Browning, President of Darlington Motor Speedway. Chris rolled out the red carpet and made Cheryl and I feel like a million bucks. John and Carol Bickford put us up in their really cool cabin in North Carolina. We traveled to Asheville, North Carolina, and I showed Cheryl where I lived while in high school. We went to Pennsylvania, where we visited Bob Weikert's old shop where I raced and saw the battlefields at Gettysburg and lots of other sites.

On one of the Pennsylvania trips we capped off things with a visit to Williams Grove Speedway for a Friday night World of Outlaws show. We visited lots of longtime friends in the pit area and then I took Cheryl out to Beer Hill, where I explained that the fans will probably yell all kinds of disgusting things at the Outlaws. I am happy to report that the fans did not disappoint.

After a little over three years of dating Cheryl and I got married. It's been a great ride so far, no kidding. At this point Cheryl is probably a bigger race fan than I am. She has some races she absolutely will not miss: Calistoga with the Hall of Fame dinner; Trophy Cup; and the Chili Bowl.

Cheryl married a person who was single for more than 20 years, a guy who made all of his own decisions all the way down to which direction the toilet paper rolls off the holder. I wore what I wanted, ate where I wanted, and watched the TV shows I wanted. Obviously getting married required me to adjust some things in order to accommodate a partner.

Cheryl feels that I am a work in progress but she was ready for the challenge. We've been married for eight years now and it's been quite a change. Definitely a good change, for sure. And I'm still in training, believe me. It's a never-ending education and I'll bet I'm not the only guy who is in that situation.

We travel together a lot, and that's nice. We have found all sorts of things we enjoy together and we try to live life to the max. We still have an RV but we don't use it much. We've been to Tulare a few times and that's about it. We are hoping to take the RV to the Midwest for some races but we haven't made that happen yet.

Cheryl's daughter Ronee and her husband Brian have twin boys, Jack and Aidan. They aren't identical; in fact, they don't look anything alike. But they are a kick in the ass. They are six now and of course cute as hell.

Cheryl's son Michael and his wife Gillian have a wonderful six-year-old daughter Shelby, and a really cool four-year-old son, Nixon.

And of course there is my daughter Stephanie and her husband Carlos and eight-year-old Sophia. Sophia continues to cultivate her acting career and it's so fun to watch her develop her skills.

It's a hectic scene sometimes but I love it. I couldn't love all those kids more.

Sometimes I'm amazed to be surrounded by family. There were many times in life that I wondered if I might be all alone in my later years, because that's how it seemed to be shaping up. But it didn't end like that and I'm glad.

My life is great and I wouldn't trade in one tiny piece of it.

Cheryl retired from her job in 2015, and about that time I pretty much stopped the remaining racing-related things I was doing. I guess you could say we're both retired although my deal didn't have a specific retirement date.

We ended up living in my longtime house in Elverta, but we basically rebuilt it from the ground up. We transformed it from a rustic bachelor pad to a much nicer home that is a lot more accommodating for civilized people.

A few years ago we bought a small cabin in Truckee, up in the Sierra Nevada mountains west of Reno. It's a wonderful escape from the summer heat of northern California, and in the winter it's fun to enjoy the snow. I have my dirt bike and my mountain bike up there, as well as my Harley, and I still love to ride. I don't think I'll ever get riding out of my system.

Truckee is a great town, with wonderful restaurants and bars. We probably spend one week a month up there in the summer, a little less in the winter. Winter is still fun but I tend to get cabin fever after a few days of being inside.

As I've grown older I have become more conservative politically, which isn't easy in California. My family is all liberal, so that leads to some stress. We try to stay away from that subject when we're together. And there are actually more conservatives in California than you might think. The strong pockets of liberals are in the cities—San Francisco and Los Angeles, primarily—but in the rural areas it's fairly conservative. We conservatives are still outnumbered out here, however, and we've had to learn to accept that reality.

The closing of my school ended my official involvement in racing. Gee, it sounds awfully final when I put it like that. After a lifetime of racing it seems strange to say it out loud. But I have to confess that I was ready to step away. It's been a welcome transition.

I lived my entire life racing, and now I enjoy doing other things. It wasn't much of an adjustment, really. Everything gradually tapered off, and now I'm only attending maybe 10 races a year.

When racing is consuming almost all of your life, the prospect of quitting scares you. What else would I do? But over time other things came into my life and helped me transition away from the sport. I would much prefer a fun trip traveling somewhere with Cheryl to just another weekend at the race track. I'm not sad or ashamed of admitting that.

There are things I miss—mostly the people. However, I've discovered that I can still stay connected with many of my racing friends, and in fact many of them aren't at the races all that much anymore either. But I still love going to the Chili Bowl, Calistoga, Tulare, and I try to get to Knoxville when I can. I also like to get to some traditional non-wing sprint car races in Indiana. I'm a huge Justin Grant fan and I like to watch him race.

As far as me driving a race car, I'm all done. That was something I did a long time ago.

I suppose if they had a legends race at the Chili Bowl or something like that, it could be fun to try. But I don't have any illusions. My days in a race car are behind me and I'm a hundred percent good with that. There was a time when I don't think I could have honestly said that, but I can say it now.

I guess the thing I'm trying to say is that my life is awfully good right now, even without a race car in the picture. Nothing wrong with that.

I've heard people say that writing a book is therapeutic, and it absolutely has been. It has helped me remember things and has given me a chance to reflect. Absolutely!

It's a funny process. You remember one episode, one story, and that leads to another story you had completely forgotten. Then you talk to somebody and they remind you of other things. There are so many things that were lost in my memory but once I got going they came back to the surface.

I had some good times, oh yes. Very good times. But that was only part of the story.

There were bad things, terrible things, things I couldn't think about until years later and I was done racing. When you start to think about the people who were hurt or aren't here anymore, and you realize that, wow…I was really lucky to live beyond all that. There were guys who had life-changing injuries, and I was able to get through fairly unscathed.

As far as physically, I'm all here and I'm in pretty good shape. There were times, however, when it came very close to a different outcome. You forget those moments very quickly when you're in the middle of it, and you travel on down the road.

Somehow a racer has a place where they store all those bad thoughts and bad experiences, a place where they disappear from your mind.

But they don't really disappear. They're there, but buried.

The years pass and at some point you discover that the bad memories are not as hidden as before. Slowly, they start to come out, and you deal with them. Luckily, by that stage you've quit racing and you can process the bad things a little better.

I'm proud of my career. Sure, there are some races that eluded me, and of course everybody wishes they would have won more. But on the whole I can't complain about the success I enjoyed.

I'm especially proud that my career was diverse. My success came in two different worlds, maybe three. I won in winged and non-wing sprint cars, and I also had success in USAC Silver Crown racing. Plus, I ran pretty decent in midgets as well. You can also throw in the pavement supermodified racing I did at different stages of my career. In the course of telling my story here I hope people become aware of the different types of race cars I had a chance to drive.

If there is one important lesson I could share with a younger racer, it's this: when I turned the dial back a couple of clicks and started having fun racing, I performed better. That's the truth. When I was locked into running a sprint car multiple times every week, the grind caused me to lose some effectiveness as a driver. After 1988, when I decided to approach racing differently and not be as blood-and-guts as before, I was a better racer. That shows in my results.

So if you're a young guy contemplating a career in racing, think about that lesson.

In 2006 I got the call of a lifetime, when I was informed that I would be inducted into the National Sprint Car Hall of Fame. It was a fantastic moment, something I will cherish forever.

Here's a funny story on how I got the news. I was racing in New Zealand, and on a day off I was motorcycle riding with a guy who had helped re-work the track at Western Springs. We were sitting in downtown Auckland eating Chinese food when the guy's phone rang. He answered it, and then handed the phone to me. It was Tom Schmeh of the National Sprint Car Hall of Fame back in Iowa.

"Tom, I have two questions," I said with amazement. "How in the hell did you find me, and why are you calling me?" Tom laughed and explained that he had gone through a great ordeal to track me down, including getting the guy's phone number I was riding with. And the second part of my question was answered when he explained that I was to be inducted into the Hall of Fame the following June. It was wonderful.

Somebody used the word "validating" to describe going into the Hall of Fame. That is absolutely the right word, validating. It describes the feeling perfectly.

Every racer has doubts about themselves, and their accomplishments. You're proud of what you did, but you wonder if anybody else thinks you were any good. Being inducted in the Hall of Fame, being recognized and honored by your peers and people you respect, that's a defining moment.

When you finally realize that people respected you, it's a feeling more meaningful than I can describe.

In 2018 I was honored once again with induction into the USAC Hall of Fame. That was also very special because many of my most respected heroes were USAC racers. A.J. Foyt, Gary Bettenhausen, Pancho Carter, man, those guys were special. To join them in the USAC Hall of Fame was a great honor, and I have a hard time explaining just how much it meant to me.

As we started to wrap up this project the inevitable question came around: How would I want to be remembered?

Number one, I want to be remembered as an accomplished racer. Not just a driver, but a *racer*. Those of us in racing know the difference. A racer is good at reading the race track, getting his car set up, working on his car and doing maintenance, and taking part in everything it takes to get to the race track. So I definitely would like to be remembered as a racer and not just a driver.

Secondly, I'd like to be remembered as a guy who had fun doing whatever it was he was doing. I've enjoyed the people around me, enjoyed the camaraderie, always. And the travel, I've been privileged to see just about every part of America at one time or another. Wow! I've seen a lot, really.

In my life there were some tears, sure. But the moments of fun and happiness have way, way outnumbered the tears. Not even close. So on the whole I've sure been a lucky guy.

At this point we've ran out of pages. If you've enjoyed reading about my story as much as I enjoyed living it, that's great.

I'll say a word of goodbye for Luke Warmwater, too. Somehow Luke always gets the last word, doesn't he?

Thanks for tagging along and I'll see you somewhere down the line. How about we share a cold beer? Let's count on it.

Index

4-Crown Nationals 9, 160, 178, 186, 197, 199
24 Hours of Daytona 241

Ace Lines 100
Acosta, Sal 191
Adelaide Intl. Speedway 255, 266
Adelaide, South Australia 253, 254, 255, 256, 266, 271
Aden, Fred 77
Agajanian, J.C. 27
Air New Zealand 267
Alexander, Fred "The Ace" 241, 242, 243
Allison, Bobby 30
Allison, Donnie 30
All-Star Circuit of Champions 3, 109, 132, 133, 135, 138, 140
All Weld company 88
Alvernez, Gary 156
Anacortes, Washington 234
Anderson, Billy 49
Anderson, Bob 49
Anderson, Dick 144
Anderson, Johnny 46, 49
Anderson, Wendell "Andy" 48
Anderson, Wendell Jr. 49
Andreetta, Mike 42, 45, 67, 80, 163, 195, 248, 250, 251, 252, 266
Andretti, Mario 155
Archerfield Speedway 147
ARCO Arena 282
Arden, North Carolina 30
Arnold, Eric 3
Ascot Park Speedway 49, 51, 71, 72, 91, 94, 107
ASCS sprint car series 193
Asheville, North Carolina 30, 31, 33, 35, 211, 290
Atlanta Motor Speedway 30
Auburn, California 18
Auckland, New Zealand 267, 274, 277, 279, 293
Auld, Doug 3
Australia 8, 42, 44, 47, 51, 59, 64, 66, 68, 69, 89, 132, 147, 148, 247, 248, 250, 251, 252, 253, 256, 257, 258, 259, 260, 261, 262, 264, 266, 270, 271, 272, 273, 274, 275, 277, 283
Australian Outback 256

Bahr, Butch 69, 259
Bailey, Fred 103, 107
Bailey, Sam 103, 106, 107, 108, 109, 130
Baja, Mexico 118
Baker, Buddy 30
Baker, Mel 47
Bakersfield, California 115, 166, 172, 179
Baker, Wally 18
Baltes, Earl 109
Baretta TV show 271
Barker Ranch 67
Bass, Robert 217
Bateman, Owen 250, 265, 266
Bay Cities Racing Assn. (BCRA) 19, 224, 225
Baylands Raceway 7, 88, 103, 105, 107, 117, 118, 130, 131, 145, 148, 180, 265, 281
Bay Park Raceway Park 248
Bedford, Carl 48
Beiderman, Don 30
Bell, Christopher 226
Belleville, Kansas 60, 62, 169-175, 181, 224, 285
Bell Helmets 218
Bell, Johnny 251
Benson, Pete 275
Benson, Peter 279
Bent Dime Saloon 46
Berry, Don 186, 188, 194, 217, 239
Berry, Janet 186
Bettenhausen, Gary 155, 156, 158, 294
Bickford, Carol 290
Bickford, John 7, 117, 217, 290
Biltmore Mansion 31
Bishop, Sam 35
Black Hills Speedway 122
Blaney, Dave 160
B&L Electric 109
Bliss, Mike 175
Bloomington, Indiana 126
Blue Ridge Mountains 31
Boat, Billy 175
Boldrini, Rendy 40, 93
Boltinghouse, Tommy 50
Bolton, Jay 64
Booth, Dave 253
Bourcier, Bones 3
Bowes Seal Fast 41
Boyd, Betty 40, 48, 289
Boyd, Jimmy 40, 42, 46, 47, 48, 53, 59, 73, 95, 103, 104, 193, 289
Boyd, Johnny 48
Boyd, Lew 3
Boys and Girls Club of America 161
Bradford, Ian "Bonds" 262
Bradford, Noel 264
Brand X engines 116, 118
Brandt, Virgil 127
Brazier, Garry 271
Brazier, Kay 271

Brazier, Steve 54, 266, 271
Brazier, Steven 271
Brickyard 400 10
Briley, Aidan 290
Briley, Brian 290
Briley, Jack 290
Briley, Ronee 290
Brisbane, Australia 147
Brisbane Exhibition Ground 251
Bromme, Bruce 71
Brooks, Mike 77, 261
Brown, Davey Jr. 135, 143
Brown, Davey Sr. 135, 141
Browne, Jackson 71
Brownfield, Debbie 232
Brownfield, Fred 231, 234, 235, 236
Browning, Chris 290
Brown, Larry 170, 171, 172, 217
Brown, Richard 141, 148
Brutto, Bobby 111
Bub Industries 217
Buckeye Speedway 139
Buckley, Bill 278
Budget Motors team 47
Bunbury, Western Australia 262
Burrow, Bobby 149
Burrow, Jim 148
Burton, Barbara 251, 252
Burton, Dianne 252
Burton, Larry 18, 19, 37, 40, 45, 247, 248, 249, 251, 252, 259, 260, 266, 273
Butler, Bob 210
Butler, Steve 154, 159, 165
Butte, Montana 289

Caceres, Lisa 241
Cahill, Ken 122
Cahill, Larry 122
Cain, Scotty 18
Calderwood, Dave 173, 217, 274
CalExpo State Fairgrounds 156, 179, 201
California Racing Assn. 51, 71, 93, 116, 166, 191
California Sprint Week 187
California State Fairgrounds 27
Calistoga Classic 19
Calistoga Speedway 19, 27, 52, 80, 82, 84, 187, 194, 218, 223, 224, 230, 290, 292
Cal Stock racing series 18
Campbell, Marshall 132
Campbell, Matt 156
Capital Speedway 20, 49
Carley, Chris 226
Carmichael, California 43, 289
Carpenter, Ed 224
Carr, Chris 217
Carrera shocks 144, 146, 217

Carson City, Nevada 80
Carson, Shane 61, 77, 97, 98, 100, 112
Carter, Dale 272
Carter, Pancho 294
Casa Grande, Arizona 115
Caves, Terry 241
Cedar Rapids, Iowa 122
Champion Speedway 20
Chandler, Danny "McGoo" 237
Charlotte Motor Speedway 30
Charlotte, North Carolina 35, 220
Chattanooga, Tennessee 29
Chicago Bears 161
Chicago, Illinois 127, 247
Chico, California 21, 43, 71, 87, 95, 118, 133, 139, 148, 152, 193, 194, 219, 224, 237, 268, 288
Chili Bowl 182, 226, 228, 231, 246, 290, 292
Christensen, Phil 266
Chula Vista, California 51, 93
Clark, Sherman 18
Clauson, Bryan 172, 224
Clauson, Tim 224, 225
Clovis, California 47, 54
Coastal 181 3
Coeur d'Alene, Idaho 58
Columbia, Missouri 73
Columbus, Ohio 142
Connery, Laura Lee 240
Consani, Bob 158, 161, 163, 164, 166, 167
Consani, Jona 167
Consani, Mike 158, 161, 163
Cook, Duke 116
Copper Classic 158
Cordelia Junction 265
Corder, Charlene 150, 151, 288
Corona, California 49
Cortland, Ohio 108
Coster, Gary 50
Cottage Grove, Oregon 232, 245
Cotter, Dan 161
Cotton Classic 186
Countryman, Tex 91, 156, 158
Cox, Justyn 193
Craft, Cyndi 140
Crockett, Roger 233
Cullen, Keith 119
Cullen, Kevin 240
Cull, Mike 238
Cycleland Speedway 219

Darland, Dave 279
Darlington Motor Speedway 30, 290
Darlington, South Carolina 29
Davis, Bob 46, 49, 51, 53, 55, 57, 193, 248, 251, 252, 259, 268
Davis, Bobby Jr. 49, 131

Davis, Donna 55
Davis, Marcy 55
Dawley, Darryl 82
Day, Jerry 58, 248
Daytona Intl. Speedway 30, 162, 206
Dayton, Ohio 179
Dean, James 50
Delano, California 119
Del Mar, California 185, 202
Delu, Chuck 107, 180
Denver, Colorado 63, 285
DESIGN 500 Racewear 144, 146, 218
Des Moines, Iowa 70, 87, 98, 100, 125
Devil's Bowl Speedway 73, 92, 93, 99, 100, 107, 120
Dewey, Oklahoma 63
Dirt Cup 12, 41, 52, 89, 94, 95, 103, 118, 130, 194, 222, 234, 285
Dirt Road to a Silver Crown 3
Dolacki, Robert 171
Dollansky, Craig 278
Dosher, Thad 83
Doty, Brad 104, 109, 129, 141, 142, 143, 172, 283
Doty, Brandy 283
Doty, Kevin 178
Doty, Laurie 141
Douglas, Rick 81
Doyle's On The Bay 264
Drake, Jay 279
Drake, Mike 279
Duggins, Shauna 240
Dumesny, Malinda 263
Dumesny, Max 262, 263
Dunkle, Gary 59
DuQuoin, Illinois 157, 160, 162, 176, 178, 180, 184, 190, 199, 201
Durst, Ryan 227

Eagle Creek Airport 170
Eagle, Nebraska 285
Eagle Raceway 81
Earnhardt, Dale 161
East Bay Raceway Park 99, 133
Easter, Dick 98, 100
Eckert, Kevin 3
Ede, Fred 200
Edgbert, Chris 237
Edmunds chassis 248
Edmunds, Don 115
Edwards, Jon 3
Ekins, Warrenne 277, 278, 280
Elam, Jack 217
El Centro, California 116, 261
Elder, Ray 18
Eldora Speedway 9, 60, 73, 74, 83, 107, 110, 112, 137, 139, 140, 142, 160, 161, 178, 179, 181, 186, 189, 197, 199, 225

Eldora Sprint Nationals 110
Elliott, Tony 279
Ellis chassis 181
Elma, Washington 42, 52, 231, 232, 235, 236, 245, 248
Elverta, California 17, 208, 288, 291
Elwood, Indiana 154
Emick, Bert 140
Emory, Mike 209
Erickson, Murray 226, 228
Erie, Colorado 54, 78, 130
ESPN 188, 190, 217
Everett, Washington 234

Faas, Leonard 27
Fargo, North Dakota 123
Farmer, Richard 217
Fauver, Rod 194, 220, 224, 246
Ferkel, Rick 51, 63, 75, 97, 98, 112
Figliomeni, Michael 277
Findlay, Ohio 108
Firestone Diamond tires 74
Fischer, Kevin 254, 256, 258
Flammer, Jan 80, 81, 83
Flanders, Bruce 49
Flock, Robby 170, 277
Florida Speed Weeks 261
Fonda, New York 30
Fontaine, Dave 177
Fontaine, Gene 177
Fontes, Ross 42
Forsberg, Andy 230
Forsberg, Candace 230
Fort Dodge, Iowa 100
Foxco engines 178
Fox, Galen 178
Foyt, A.J. 155, 156, 157, 197, 268, 294
Foyt Group 164, 169, 176
Franklin, Johnny 19
Frank, Randy 217, 243
Fred Grenoble 135
Free Form Art Studio 47
Fremont, California 103
Fresno, California 47, 88, 117, 130, 137
Funnel Web spider 256
Furr, Brad 195, 229

Gadda, Bill 80
Gaerte, Joe 140
Galedrige, Al 224
Galedrige, Alfred 172, 224
Galedrige, Bradley 172, 224
Galedrige, Molly 224
Gambler chassis 120
Gamester, Russ 200
Ganassi, Chip 241

Garcia, Ken 105
Garlick, Phil 265
Garrett, Milan 117, 118, 281
Gasoline Alley 47
Gates, Bob 3
Gazaway, Bill 31
George, Elmer 224
George, Tony 224
Gerould, Bobby 3, 223
Gerould, Gary 3, 223
Gerster, Brian 172
Gettysburg, Pennsylvania 142, 290
Gilbert, Terry 139
Gilley's Bar 93
Giving, Alissa 21
Giving, LeRoy 21
Glass, Cheryl 84
God Speed: The Story of Page Jones 182
Gold Cup Race of Champions 20, 21, 40, 42, 46, 49, 55, 68, 86, 87, 107, 186, 219, 237, 281
Golobic, John 215
Golobic, Shane 216
Goodyear tires 63, 175, 273
Gordon, Eric 158, 160, 161
Gordon, Jack 26, 27, 85, 119
Gordon, Jeff 3, 7-10, 117, 159, 160, 163, 164, 270
Gordon, Jimmy 26, 27, 28, 45, 84
Grand Annual Classic 12, 256, 258
Grand Island, Nebraska 69
Granite City, Illinois 100
Grant, Ashley 225
Grant, Justin 224, 225, 226, 292
Grass Valley, California 147, 148, 217
Gravino, Joey 137
Gray, Henley 30
Grays Harbor, Washington 231
Green, Nick 207
Green, Tim 87, 88, 89, 93, 95, 108, 109, 119, 130, 131, 132, 148, 189, 207, 219
Greenville, South Carolina 35
Grenoble, Fred 136, 137
Griffin, Richard 186
Grover City, California 118
Grubbs, Terry 85, 116
Guiducci, Darryl 200
Gunn, Jack 53
Gurney, Chuck 156, 157, 159, 160, 175, 178-179, 180
Guthrie, Bob 48

Hadlock, Jim 21
Hagerstown, Maryland 53
Haka war dance 275
Halibrand speedway wheel 255
Hall, Keith 106
Hall, Scott 245
Hamilton, Davey 166

Hand, Joey 241
Hanford, California 7, 117, 118, 224
Hanson Machine 57
Harley, Selwyn 253
Harrison, Ron 208
Haudenschild, Jac 104, 113, 129, 143, 261, 262, 282
Haudenschild, Patty 129
Hayden, Nicky 275
Hearn, Brett 199
Helmling, Rollie 9
Helms, Greg 59
Helton, Mike 161
Henning, Troy 223
Hernandez, Willie 242
Hery, Travis 225
Hewitt, Jack 10, 25, 153, 157, 158, 160, 161, 179, 189, 200, 202, 230, 231
Hicks, Don 39
Hicks, James 228
Hieber, Gary 160
Highspire, Pennsylvania 53
Hillenburg, Andy 160
Hinchman racewear 242
Hipshire, Rudy 34
Hirst, Kyle 193
Hirst, Rick 46, 89, 115, 219, 246
Hodges, Rocky 140, 270
Hoerner, Bob 200
Hoffman, Garry 265
Holder, Bill 3
Hoosier Hundred 12, 156, 157, 160, 164, 175, 176, 199
Hoosier Tire 175, 176, 185
Hot Springs, Arkansas 12, 148, 149
House, Tray 161, 178
Houston, Texas 197
Howard, Gary 69
Howard, Larry 180
Hughes, Pat "Porky" 218, 227, 230, 232, 233, 234, 235, 236
Hulman Hundred 154, 158, 164, 168
Humphries, Larry "Flash" 157
Hunter, Jack 38
Hunt, Randy 62
Hunt, Tommy 71, 156
Hylton, James 30

I-70 Speedway 111, 112, 113
IMCA 62
Indiana Midget Week 224
Indianapolis 500 154, 155, 224
Indianapolis, Indiana 74, 128, 154, 158, 160, 164, 179, 181, 225
Indianapolis Motor Speedway 10, 17, 159, 224
Indianapolis Raceway Park 159, 165, 169, 170, 188, 189

Indiana Sprintweek 224
Indiana State Fairgrounds 128, 154, 155, 156, 158, 162, 164, 168, 175, 185, 202
Ione, California 224
Irwindale, California 192
Irwin, Kenny Jr. 179, 185
Isaac, Bobby 30
Islip, New York 30

Jack Gordon Ford 26
Jackson, Minnesota 129, 130
Jackson, Rebel 42, 248
Jacksonville, Florida 133
Jacobs, Kenny 10, 143
Jacobson, Gene 217
Jarrett, Kenny 154
Jarrett, Ned 29
Jayhawk Nationals 83, 110, 115
Jeffreys, Frank 138
Jensen Construction 87
Jenson, Lonnie 59
Jerry Smith 76
Jimmy Gordon Memorial 84
Jimmy Sills School of Open Wheel Racing 12, 214, 223, 246
J&J chassis 217
Johns, Bobby 30
Johnson, Dennis 194, 195
Johnson, Dick 20, 23, 24, 25, 26, 29, 31, 206
Johnson, Gary 82
Johnson, Steve 210, 212
Johnson, Ted 73, 237
Johnson, Warren 132
Jones, Alan 255
Jones, Judy 181
Jones, Page 170, 171, 178, 179, 181, 182, 200
Jones, Parnelli 181
Jones, P.J. 170, 181
Jones, Skip 43
Jordan, Dick 3
Judd, Walter 78

Kaeding, Brent 89, 118, 148, 162, 194, 219
Kaeding, Bud 200
Kahne, Kasey 193, 218
Kahne, Kelly 218
Kansas City, Missouri 73
Kaplan, Ryan 224
KARS racing series 53
Kauffman, Keith 53
Kaye, Willie 248, 274
Kear, Shirley 112
Kelly, Earl 98
Kelly, John 147
Kelly Kahne Logging 218
Kelly's Pub 181

Kendrick, Jeff 270
Kent, Steve 88, 132
Kenyon, Mel 268
Keperling, Dave 168
Keperling, Ruth 168
Kepler, Jamie 129
Kepler, Les 117, 118, 119, 120, 121, 129, 145
Kepler, Susie 118, 119
Kerchner, Mike 3
Kings Royal 140
Kinser, Karl 74, 120, 121, 126, 193
Kinser, Mark 131
Kinser, Steve 10, 73, 74, 78, 104, 106, 108, 109, 120, 126, 128, 131, 145, 259, 260
Kirkpatrick, Larry 52
Kline, Mike 264
Knoxville, Iowa 52, 59, 60, 61, 62, 69, 70, 73, 75, 76, 77, 78, 82, 83, 87, 96, 101, 104, 105, 107, 110, 111, 112, 122, 124, 125, 130, 141, 142, 188, 198, 263, 271, 285, 292
Knoxville Nationals book 3
Kokomo, Indiana 224
Kratzer, Janet 139
Kratzer, Sonny 135, 137, 138, 139, 140
Kruseman, Cory 239
KSE Steering 217
Kurtz, Junior 160, 180
KXOA Radio 26

Lake of the Ozarks Speedway 96
Lake Okoboji (Iowa) 129
Lakeside Speedway 73, 77, 100, 109, 110
Lamar, Clyde 55, 133, 193
Lane, Sherry 211
Larson, Janet 219
Larson, Katelyn 220
Larson, Kyle 219
Larson, Mike 219
Larson, Roger 52, 82
Laski, Art 180
Lasoski, Danny 270
Lasoski, George 270
Las Vegas, Nevada 224
Leavitt, Eddie 77
Lebanon, Oregon 232
Lee, Gary 199
Lemley, Brock 221
Lemley, Dave 221
Lewis, Steve 217, 219
Lima, Ohio 110
Lincoln, Nebraska 58, 73, 171, 172
Linder, Fred 74
Lindich, Danny 278
Liverpool Speedway 249, 250, 253
Lloyd, Charlie 40
Lloyd, Mike 40, 53

Long Beach, California 283
Long Beach Grand Prix 162
Lorman, John 47
Los Angeles, California 181
Lovell Brothers 87
Lovell, Richard 115, 118
Lovell, Ronnie 115
Lowe, Bosco 208
Lowery, Tim 71
Lund, Tiny 30
Lynn, Clyde 30
Lysalt, Chuck 52

Madera, California 130
Madera Speedway 87
Mahoney, John 3
Mansfield, Ohio 108
Manson, Charles 67
Mantz, Johnny 18
Manzanita Speedway 51, 71, 84, 93, 105, 107, 224
Maori native tribe 275
Marion County (Iowa) Campground 285
Marion County (Iowa) Fairgrounds 104
Marks, Bobbie 118, 119
Marks, Fred 117, 118, 119, 121, 129, 145
Mars, Charley 246
Marshall, Bobby 63
Marshall, Missouri 77
Martin, Mark 161
Martin, Norman 92
Marvel, Bill 189
Marysville, California 47, 216, 217, 225, 226, 238, 243, 286
Marysville, Washington 245
Mason City, Iowa 60, 70, 96
Mather Air Force Base 69
MAV TV 240
Maxwell chassis 69, 80
Maxwell, Don 59, 62, 69
May, Dub 69
McCarl chassis 76
McCarl, Lenard 59, 87, 122-132
McCarl, Terry 122
McCloud, Don 42
McCormick, Carl 165
McCown, Larry 73
McCoy, Jack 18
McCray, Joel 91, 94, 95
McCreary, Mike 68
McCreary tires 158
McCutcheonville, Ohio 108
McDonald, Shawn 237
McElreath, Jim 155
McGinnis, Deanna 234
McKenzie, Warwick 275
McMahon, Bobby 242

McMahon, Carol 242
McMahon, Paul 242
McMillen, Carol 58
McMillen, Duke 40, 41, 42, 48, 57, 61, 62, 64, 66, 79, 80, 81, 87, 91, 92, 114, 115, 116, 259, 265, 268
McMillen, Jason 57, 116
McMillen, Samantha 58
McMillen, Scott 57, 93, 115, 116
McNish, Russell 81, 111, 112
McSpadden, Lealand 94, 105, 106, 107, 165
McTernan, Joe 237, 241
Medford, Oregon 232, 233
Medina, Johnny "Chewy" 116, 230, 232
Medina, Sarah 233
Medlock, Bill 48
Memphis, Tennessee 131, 200
Mesa Marin Raceway 179
Mesquite, Texas 99
Meyers, Jason 187, 188
Migro, Con 261
Mildred the Love Doll 127
Miller, Bob 111, 112, 191, 192
Miller, Jack 228
Miller, Jerry 45
Millstream Speedway 108, 139
Milwaukee Mile 160, 163, 166
Mini Gold Cup 133, 193
Missouri Nationals 81, 89, 95
Missouri State Fairgrounds 76
M&L Plumbing 163, 200
Moffett, Mike 33
Moller Brothers 180
Montgomery, Jimmy 18
Moore, Kaye 15
Moore, Sid 249, 250, 263
Mopar engine 183
Morales Bros. Tamale Wagon 166, 192
Morris, Dick 59, 77
Morris, Trevor 267
Motor Sports Press Assn. 18
Mount Gambier, South Australia 262
Moyes, Dave 217
Murphy, Jeff 262
Murray, Richie 3

Naify, Jim 156
Naify, John 156
Nance, Carroll 132
Nance chassis 74, 76
Nance, LaVern 82, 132
Nance, Marvell 133
NASCAR 18, 29, 30, 31, 49, 161, 164, 219, 220
National Car Rental 35
National Speed Sport News 3, 41, 106, 107, 112, 180, 181, 223

National Sprint Car Annual 3
National Sprint Car Hall of Fame 11, 39, 293
Nazareth, Pennsylvania 197
New Smyrna, Florida 146
New Zealand 64, 152, 181, 189, 247, 248, 267, 268, 274, 275, 276, 278, 279, 283, 293
Nichols, Don 110, 111, 113
Nichols, Harold 110, 111, 112, 113
Nicholson, Leroy 40
Noblesville, Indiana 189
Noffsinger, Brad 164, 166
North Central Kansas Free Fair 170
Northern Auto Racing Club (NARC) 39, 40, 43, 46, 52, 57, 64, 80, 103, 148, 194
Northern Sprint Tour 232
North Star Speedway 61

Oakland, California 18, 253
Oakland Exposition Building 19
Odessa, Texas 225, 226
Ohio Sprint Speedweek 12, 108, 109, 138, 140
Oildale, California 181
Oji, Artie 156
Oklahoma City, Oklahoma 107, 133
Oliveri, Frank 249
Olson, Kevin 231
Olympia Beer 75
Omaha, Nebraska 130
Oolitic, Indiana 126
OPEN WHEEL Magazine 3, 64
Opperman, Jan 58
Orcas Island, Washington 234
Orlando, Florida 197
Orrville, Ohio 139
Osborne, Lee 130
Osborne, Todd 270
Oskaloosa, Iowa 59
Oskie, Jimmy 51
Oval Nationals 71, 186
Owen, Anne 87, 88, 130
Owen, Virgil 87, 88, 130, 131
Oxford, Maine 30

P-51 Mustang 241
Pacheco Speedway 18, 19
Pacific Coast Championship 49
Padjen, John 148, 156, 217, 268
Panch, Marvin 18
Paniagua, Jim 242
Pankratz, Wally 160
Paragon, Indiana 74, 154
Parakai, New Zealand 277
Parramatta Speedway 259
Parsons, Johnny 155, 160
Pasadena, Texas 93

Patterson, Gary 27, 40, 42, 45, 50, 52, 54, 55, 61, 63, 70, 80, 82, 85, 95, 145, 248, 250, 252, 253, 254, 264-269, 271
Patterson, Jimmy 42
Paulson, Hans 63
Paxton, Lynn 53
Payton, Walter 161
Pearson, David 30, 35
Penn National Speedway 53
Pennsylvania Posse 108, 135
Pennsylvania Speed Week 53
Performance Racing Industry show 217, 289
Perris Auto Speedway 71, 186, 191
Perth, Western Australia 8, 261, 262, 264, 270
Petaluma, California 102, 103, 187
Phoenix, Arizona 104, 105
Phoenix Intl. Raceway 158, 197
Pinkney, Mike 96
Piper Cub airplane 284
Pismo Beach 118, 119
Pittman, Daryn 226
Placerville, California 43, 129, 130, 132, 149
Plastic Express car 160
Playle, Dave 218, 275, 279
Pombo, Al 20
Pombo-Sargent Classic 118
Ponzo, Jerry 148, 237
Poor, Phil 154
Port Royal Speedway 120, 134
Presley, Elvis 71
Prickett, Clyde 87
Prince Leonard 264
Pryor, Kelly 129
Purssell, Ernie 27
Pusateri, Dave 145

Quad City Speedway 108
Queensland State Championship 147

Racing Wheels newspaper 42, 223
Ram chassis 248
Ram Race Cars 58
Rankin, Max 41, 43
Raper, Jim 104
Rapid City, South Dakota 129, 130
Rapp, Norm 40
Raymond, Mike 249, 252, 253
Redding, California 47, 48
Red Line Oil 217
Reeves, Stevie 171, 181
Reiff, Walt 27, 252, 253
Reno, Nevada 291
Republic County Hospital 171
Rice, Larry 155, 217, 251, 264, 266, 267
Richardson, Bruce 64
Richardson, Jim 151

Richmond Intl. Raceway 183, 184, 185
Riego Inn 22
Rio Linda, California 18, 29, 192, 208
Rio Linda Junior High 24
Riverside, California 29
Roberts, Kenny 212
Robinson, Bill 59
Rosamond, California 18
Roseville, California 20, 26, 42, 45
Roseville Speedway 20
Ross, Walt 42, 61, 70
Rotorua, New Zealand 279
Round Tree clown 276
Rowley Park Speedway 253, 255
RPM Engines 217
Rule, Greg 129
Rush, Garry 52, 258, 266

Sacramento Bee 48
Sacramento, California 9, 17, 19, 26, 27, 37, 42, 49, 51, 55, 69, 79, 85, 97, 98, 111, 119, 156, 158, 159, 163, 166, 179, 184, 185, 192, 197, 200, 201, 202, 203, 217, 219, 223, 261, 268, 282
Salter, Ron 278
Sander Engineering 229
Sander, Glen 229
Sanders, Tommy 73
San Diego, California 185
Sanford, Fred G. 216
Sanford, Lamont 216
San Francisco, California 248, 249
San Jose, California 133, 187, 193, 224
Santa Clara, California 51
Santa Maria, California 194
Santa Rosa, California 19, 158, 167
Sargent, Bob 174
Sargent, Marshall 20, 273
Satui Winery 187
Saucier, Daryl 133, 217
Sayer, Leo 274
Schatz, Donny 217
Schmeh, Tom 293
Scott, Gary 77
Sears, John 30
Seattle, Washington 289
Sedalia, Missouri 63, 73, 76, 81, 95, 112
Sedro Woolley, Washington 234
Selinsgrove Speedway 53
Seymour, Bobby 189
Shadle, Bill 42, 57, 66, 253, 254, 255, 256, 258, 265, 273
Sharon, Ohio 108
Shaver Racing Engines 217
Shaver, Ron 217
Shoppe, Phil 208
Shores, Lloyd 74

Shultz, Steve 76
Shuman, Ron 106, 116, 164, 165, 169, 176, 186, 191
Sidney, John 262
Sidney, Ohio 138
Siefert, Bill 30
Sierra Nevada mountains 291
Sills, Carleen 17, 30, 68, 203, 204, 205
Sills, Cheryl 224, 225, 240, 244, 246, 285, 288–295
Sills, Jimmy Sr. 17, 284
Sills, Karen 50, 70, 77, 78, 85, 88, 89, 98, 100, 101, 119, 125, 130, 132, 138, 142, 144, 146, 261, 283, 288
Sills, Marcy 69, 87, 88, 93, 119, 207
Sills, Marilyn 17, 20, 26, 248, 251, 284–287
Sills, Peggy 17, 19, 68, 211
Sills, Raleigh 17, 24, 25, 26, 205
Sills Zavala, Stephanie 50, 64, 107, 114, 119, 126, 130, 132, 138, 139, 142, 146, 153, 272, 281-284, 289, 291
Sills, Valerie 17, 208, 211
Silsby, Tom 80
Silver Dollar Speedway 21, 87, 268
Simmons, Gillian 290
Simmons, Michael 290
Simmons, Nixon 291
Simmons, Ron 47, 48, 52, 288
Simmons, Shelby 291
Simpson, Archie 73, 75, 76
Simpson, Bill 218
Simpson Race Products 218
Singer, John 77
Sinnott, Richard 217
Sioux Falls, South Dakota 52, 122
Skagit Speedway 41, 42, 89, 94, 103, 104, 118, 130, 149, 189, 194, 218, 221, 222, 234, 285
Sky Valley Speedway 41, 42, 58
Slack, Eric 270
Smith, Danny 74, 109, 129, 178
Smith, Jerry 73, 74
Smith, Randy 77, 122, 270
Snellbaker, Smokey 53
Snider, George 20, 156, 160, 169, 175, 179, 197-199, 200
Snow, Don 49
Southard, Duke 146
Spartanburg, South Carolina 35
Speed Sport Magazine 3
Speedway Motors 73, 97, 259
Spencer, J.C. 30
Spirit Lake, Iowa 129
Springfield, Illinois 160, 162, 174, 180, 184, 197, 199, 201
SprintCar & Midget Magazine 3
Square Bush clown 276
Standley, James 144, 218

Standley, Katie 218
Standridge, Joyce 3
Stanton chassis 107
Stanton, Gary 78, 107, 116, 141, 167–173, 175, 176, 177, 180, 183, 186, 188, 189, 190, 197, 199, 202, 261
Stapp chassis 76
Starr, Dwayne 45, 64
Steele, Dave 198
Stevenson, Chuck 18
Stevenson, John 77
Stewart, Tony 179, 183, 226
St. Louis, Missouri 177
Stockton, California 91
Stoneking, Dick 82
Stoops Express 154
Stovall, Chuck 218
St. Paul, Minnesota 61
STP Oil Treatment 62
Stratton, Cary 3
Stribling, Carla 259
Stribling, Steve 259
Stricklin, Dave Jr. 227
Stroppini, Gil 47
Sturgis, South Dakota 217
Sue, Beverly 67
Sue, Wayne 42, 67, 264
Sullivan, John Boy 58, 62, 63, 64, 69, 70, 156
Sullivan, Pat 3
SuperTrapp mufflers 103
Swartz, Charlie 78, 260
Swindell, Jeff 106, 109, 131, 160, 162, 165, 282
Swindell, Sammy 104, 105, 128
Sydney Harbor 264
Sydney Herald 266
Sydney, New South Wales, Australia 248, 249, 250, 252, 253, 256, 259, 265, 268, 271
Sydney Showground 249, 253, 259, 265, 266
Syracuse, New York 146

Tampa, Florida 99
Taylor, Bill 3
Taylor, Cotton 35
Taylor, Ernest 35
TCR chassis 170, 217
T.C. Roberson High School 31
Team 6R Racing 178, 200
Terre Haute, Indiana 225
Tervitt, George 267
Texas Highway Patrol 92
Texas Tavern 249, 253, 259, 264, 265, 268
The Motorhead Traveler TV show 240
Theodore Racing 255
Thompson, Dean 71
Thorpe, Jim 119
Thurston, Dave 225

Thurston, Wendy 225
Tiner, Johnny 193
Tiner, Mack 193
Tiner, Randy 193, 195
Tiner, Richard 193
Tiner, Rod 193, 216, 229
Tiner, Rod Jr. 193
Tiner, Steven 193
Tobin, Bob 81, 85
Tognotti, Don 45, 156, 163, 248
Tognotti Speed Shop 64, 69, 98
Tolsma, Randy 169, 175, 178, 179
Tomlinson, Crockett 109
Tony Bettenhausen 100 160, 174
Topeka, Kansas 83
Torque Multiplier Transmission 45
Travolta, John 93
Trenton, New Jersey 30
Trickle, Dick 158
Tri C Special 193
Tri-Holiday Championship 84
Tripp, Erin 276
Tripp, Ron "Sleepy" 260, 275, 276, 278
Tripp, Shay 276
Trophy Cup 290
Trostle, Bob 52, 70, 77, 82, 87, 89, 95, 96, 261, 262
Trostle chassis 96
Trostle, Dorotha 96
Truckee, California 291
True Value Hardware 161
Tucker, Peter 254
Tulare, California 195, 290, 292
Tulsa, Oklahoma 133, 228, 231
Tunks, Bob 266
Turkey Night Grand Prix 286
Turrill, Deuce 78, 79
Tuttle, Bob 89, 96, 97, 98, 99, 100
Tuttle-Easter Ace Lines car 96
Tuttle, Janan 97, 99
Tuttle, Rob 89, 97, 98, 99, 104
Twin Cities Speedway 216

Ultra Shield 176, 217
Ulyate, Ed 191
United States Auto Club (USAC) 3, 9, 12, 43, 153, 154, 156, 161, 162, 163, 165, 168, 169, 174, 181, 183, 184, 185, 188, 189, 191, 192, 195, 197, 198, 201, 224, 225, 226, 268, 293, 294
University of Missouri 75
Unser, Al Jr. 78, 261
Urban Cowboy movie 93
USAC Hall of Fame 12, 294
USAC Media Guide 3
Utz, Bill 77
Vacaville, California 43
Vallejo, California 103, 107

Vallejo Speedway 38
Van Conett, LeRoy 252, 253
Vancouver, British Columbia 240
Van Patton, Dave 52, 70, 71
Ventura, California 217, 239
Ventura Speedway 240
Verona, California 25
Vertullo, Dave 219
Vodden, David 88, 145
Vogler, Rich 157, 159, 262
Volusia Raceway Park 133, 146
Vucannon, Leo 39
Vukovich, Bill Jr. 20
Vukovich, Billy III 166, 167

Walker, Bob 195
Walker, Jeff 189, 279
Walker, Tyler 188
Walt Disney World Speedway 197
Wanless, Ron 251, 259, 261
Warmwater, Luke 12, 144, 148, 149, 190, 295
Warren, Joe 31
Warrnambool, Victoria, Australia 255, 256, 258, 262
Waterman, Sid 217
Watertown, South Dakota 123
Watson, A.J. 159
Watson, Ed 3, 20, 29, 37, 41, 43, 45, 69, 71, 248
Watson, Shirley 44
Wayne County Speedway 139
Weikert, Bob 134, 135, 139, 140, 142, 143, 290
Welch, Gene 264
Weld, Kenny 82
Weld, Rick 77
Wellington, Jim 148
Wenatchee, Washington 232, 234
West Capital Raceway 7, 19, 38, 41, 42, 46, 47, 48, 49, 50, 79, 80, 81, 84, 86, 87, 180, 193, 223, 268
West Des Moines, Iowa 96, 101
Western Springs Speedway 248, 268, 274, 275, 276, 278, 293
Western World Championship 84, 105
West Memphis, Arkansas 53, 97
White Pigeon, Michigan 137
Wichita, Kansas 132
Wilbur, Ed 264
Wilhite, Roy 47
Wilke team 159
Williams Grove Speedway 53, 54, 139, 290
Williamson, Kramer 53, 95, 270
Willow Springs Intl. Speedway 18
Willsky, Shawna 234
Wilmot, Wisconsin 135
Wilskey, Dick 42
Wilson, Bob 3

Winchester, Indiana 198
Winterbottom, Garry 266
Witness Productions 3
Wolff, Thomas 31
Wolfgang, Cori 260
Wolfgang, Doug 61, 70, 73, 77, 82, 84, 100, 104, 130, 134, 135, 145, 162, 259, 260, 282
Wolfgang, Jeri 260
Wolfgang, Niki 260
Wood, Dennis 164
Woodruff, Kenny 52, 59, 73, 74, 87, 113, 248
Woodside, Jay 76
World of Outlaws 49, 73, 74, 78, 87, 91, 99, 100, 105, 107, 108, 111, 112, 115, 116, 118, 119, 120, 122, 126, 128, 129, 130, 132, 133, 135, 137, 142, 145, 153, 188, 192, 193, 229, 235, 236, 237, 260, 278, 281, 290
Wright, Garry 251
Wright, John 41
Wrinkle, Tom 139
Wristen, Jimmy 246

Yarborough, Cale 30, 35
Yarbrough, Lee Roy 30
Yeager, Chuck 34
Yeley, J.J. 200
Yip, Teddy 255
Yolo Club 50

Zarounian, Gary 9
Zavala, Carlos 283, 291
Zavala, Sophia 284
Zine, Mike 289
Zine, Sherry 289

Dave Argabright has covered auto racing since 1980 for *NATIONAL SPEED SPORT NEWS*, *SprintCar and Midget Magazine*, *OPEN WHEEL Magazine*, *PRI Magazine*, *Car and Driver*, and *Road & Track*. His broadcast experience includes work as a pit reporter for MAV TV, TNN, CBS Sports, Speed TV, and the Indianapolis 500 Radio Network.

Dave is a 2014 inductee in the National Sprint Car Hall of Fame. His professional honors include the "Outstanding Contribution to the Sport" award from the National Sprint Car Poll, and the "Frank Blunk Award for Journalism" from the Eastern Motorsports Press Assn. Dave is a six-time recipient of the "Media Member of the Year" award from the National Sprint Car Poll.

OTHER BOOKS BY DAVE ARGABRIGHT

STILL WIDE OPEN - with Brad Doty

AMERICAN SCENE - A COLLECTION

HEWITT'S LAW - with Jack Hewitt

EARL! - with Earl Baltes

LET 'EM ALL GO! - with Chris Economaki

LONE WOLF - with Doug Wolfgang

FAST COMPANY - with Speedy Bill Smith

LET'S GO RACING! - with Rex Robbins

ON TOP OF THE WORLD - with Larry Moore

MODERN THUNDER - with
John Mahoney and Pat Sullivan

The Jimmy Wilson Collection
SPRINT CAR SALVATION
FAST AND FEARLESS
SPRINT CAR SHOWDOWN
SPRINT CAR CHALLENGE
SPRINT CAR LEGEND

Book reorder information:

American Scene Press LLC
P.O. Box 34
Noblesville, IN 46061
(317) 598-1263
orders@daveargabright.com

www.daveargabright.com